SUMMER
FISHING
IN
LAPLAND

Juhani Karila

Translated from the Finnish
by Lola Rogers

PUSHKIN PRESS

Pushkin Press
Somerset House, Strand
London WC2R 1LA

Original text © Juhani Karila 2019
English translation © Lola Rogers 2023

Published by agreement with Helsinki Literary Agency.

Summer Fishing in Lapland was first published in Finnish as
Pienen hauen pyydystys by Siltala Publishing in Helsinki, 2019

First published by Pushkin Press in 2023

FINNISH
LITERATURE
EXCHANGE

This work has been published with the financial assistance of FILI –
Finnish Literature Exchange

1 3 5 7 9 8 6 4 2

ISBN 13: 978-1-78227-893-1

Designed and typeset by Tetragon, London
Printed and bound by Clays Ltd, Elcograf S.p.A.

www.pushkinpress.com

SUMMER
FISHING
IN
LAPLAND

AN INTRODUCTORY TOUR

We approach the pond from the stratosphere.

First we see Lapland. It has three parts: (1) Exciting Western Lapland. Big ski resorts, *meänkieli* dialect, great artists like Timo Mukka, Kalervo Palsa, and Reidar Särestöniemi. (2) Exotic Northern Lapland. The Saami people, tundra, migrating reindeer, Lake Inari, Arctic char. (3) Stupid Eastern Lapland. Swampland and mosquitoes. Of no interest to anyone.

Except us.

We're rushing toward it, even against a headwind. That can't be true. The earth itself wants us to go west.

But I make up my own rules of nature.

We're approaching from above so that you'll understand. Lapland is big. Even as far north as Sodankylä and driving at top speed, it would still take you almost five hours to reach the Arctic Ocean. Forget that—driving is a poor measure. There aren't many roads. Or buildings. Or people. There's wilderness. Nondescript stretches of boggy grassland that look leftover, like the debris brushed away and tossed up north by God when he finished putting in the moors and meadows and rain forests everywhere else in the world. God is such a shit! I shouldn't exaggerate. The highlands are beautiful. But the rest of it! Not that I'm complaining. At least there's nobody here, so there's plenty of space. The idea of Lapland is a combination of size and emptiness. A horizon pierced by scruffy spruce, appalling desolation that keeps the people mute and the myths strong. Myths. They feed on fear. They condense into monsters that wander the bogs like machines set in motion long ago that no one knows how to turn off. They swim in dark waters. They crouch in the crawlspaces under attics with round, burning eyes like owls. And far outside the villages, beyond the woods and lakes and fens, are nameless creatures who watch over their kingdom, looking out at the wan lights of the houses from atop the distant fells.

Adjust your focus on that side channel of the Kemijoki River. That's the Kitinen River. At the village of Vuopio there are two inlets that break off from the Kitinen. They're called Iso-Uopaja and Pikku-Uopaja—Big Inlet and Little Inlet. Our target is Big Inlet. It's round and deep. At its stagnant bottom are pikes the size of fallen logs… In the middle of Big Inlet is Manolaissaari, Dead Man's Island. That's where Slabber Olli does his business. But we're not going there. We're aiming at a spot a little to the left of it. There is a little creek that feeds into the inlet and I thought we might land next to it, prettily, like butterflies. Or crash into it. *Splat!* The swamp is nice and soft to crash into in June. Here, let me pull you out of the mud. *Shmloooomp.* And a good smack right in the ear. *Thwack!*

Welcome to the world! Don't look at me—look around you. Perfect. A song thrush is cooing in the pines, and just ahead a black cloud of mosquitoes is rising from the swamp.

eeeeeeeeeeeeeeeeeeeeee

Annoying, is it not? You'll get used to it. Don't wipe the mud off, buddy. It's good protection.

eeeeeeeeeeeeeeeeeeee

Let's follow this creek trickling through the grass. Pesky water bugs... Try to stay on the tussocks as you go. They roll under your boots, I know, but they hold, unlike the spaces between, which can suck your leg under right up to the thigh. Then the bog bogeys come swarming and pull off your boots and take a nibble at the soles of your feet. A nasty feeling. One time in Saukkoaapa... Now the mosquitoes have found us, and they're crawling all over us. Look at the bloodsuckers, poking at us with their snouts. Do not waver! They can't get through. The mud's hardened. It's like wearing a coat.

Thank your good luck there aren't any stripefoots around. They're as big as helicopters. Those vermin can lift a grown person into the air, shove a stinger into their eye, and suck out their insides. Then they drop the dry husk into a willow thicket and it hangs there on the branches, fluttering like laundry.

The house you see on the right bank is the Ylijaakos' place. Nobody lives there anymore, but there will soon be people coming and going.

Would you believe that a month ago this whole area was under a meter and a half of water? The spring meltwater forms a large lake. That place where we landed was an excellent spot for whitefish just a week ago.

See that narrow indentation, almost like a path? That was made by the hero of our story. And there's our creek again. Let's follow it like a rainbow and see what treasure is at the end. But first, more willow thicket. It's bent over as if someone had made a passageway through it, and something like that is exactly what happened.

In the middle of the thicket is the Back Pond. A shallow puddle saturated with fertilizers, where the fish have a strong taste of silt. Perch as big as oven mitts.

We'd better get a move on! Did you think we had arrived? No, no, no. After this willow thicket there's still more swamp and sludge. And puddles. Then a hundred meters of flood plain.

It's just the tussocks squelching...

Sometimes I feel like the world isn't going to sink into the sea or turn into a desert, it's just going to become one big swamp. The fields will sink into the swamp. The little villages will sink into the swamp. Road signs, roundabouts, skyscrapers... they'll all sink into the swamp. Even the ridges and mountains will sink. And the swamp will spread over lakes and oceans like some horrible disease that dims the sun and leaves the fish in darkness, so thick you can walk from Africa to America on a continuous, quaking bog filled with cottongrass, the whole planet one big trickling, chirping, sloshing bog fit only for whining mosquitoes and a new, intelligent being that moves over the damp on long, mechanical legs.

But that won't happen for some time, and now we have happy news. We're nearing our destination. Yes, that pond peeping out in front of us has been our goal all along.

Welcome to Pike Pond.

If you think the Back Pond is shallow, you should see this one. Thirty centimeters at its deepest. Though that's a subjective judgment. The water's as thick as pea soup, and somewhere in the broth there's a black pike.

This is the stage for our story, and there on the bottom is the slimy main character. Or one of them.

This is what we came for.

But hey! How did the pike end up living in this wetland? As I said, in May this is a lake. When May turns to June, the water starts to drain away. The water level starts falling right before your eyes, and the fish, slowed down by the freezing conditions, don't realize that they should start flapping their fins and head to the river. Some of them hang around like dopes, as many of us so often do at life's turning points, and soon they find themselves trapped in a flood pond. Then a game of attrition begins as the fish start eating one another. There are usually a few pike, a school of perch, and a few roach left stranded in this pond. The roach are eaten first, then the smaller perch. And so on.

In the end, the only fish left is one lone pike. Left in horrible circumstances. There's no food at all, so the pike has to trawl the surface for scurrying dung beetles, and if all goes well some foolish vole might decide to take a swim now and then... All the pike can do is float, and grow thin, and wait for death.

Did you hear that? A car door slamming. Our hero has arrived. That means we're ready to begin. She has three days. I don't have even a second—I'm starting to sink. No thanks, I don't need any help. The sinking is to be expected. I just came to visit, to guide you a little. To show you. And don't forget...

THE FIRST DAY

I

Due to a string of regrettable occurrences, Elina Ylijaako had to catch a pike from a certain pond by June 18th every year.

Her life depended on it.

She set out in her car on June 14th, when the floods up north were sure to have receded, so she would be able to reach the pond if she wore rubber boots. She left early and drove all day. The farther she drove, the fewer the towns, service stations, and villages along the road became. The trees got shorter. Eventually, even the villages ran out. Nothing but forest.

Now and then an oncoming car would come around a bend in the road and she would slow down. The drivers in the cars motioned for her to turn back immediately.

A sign along the road said: TELECOMMUNICATIONS LINKS END IN FORTY KILOMETERS.

Elina came to a strip of clear-cut about fifty meters wide. In the middle of the cut stood a white guard booth. A boom barrier blocked the road. Elina pulled up to the booth.

A bored-looking guard in a gray uniform leaned out of the open window. He had dark perspiration stains under his arms. A table fan hummed in the booth. Elina rolled down her car window and said hello. The guard went straight into his litany. He told her that the nation of Finland did not recommend that she go any farther. If she nevertheless chose to continue, all insurance would cease to be valid and Elina would be held solely responsible for whatever befell her.

"I'm from here," Elina said.

The guard stretched out his hand. Elina handed over her identification and the guard looked at it. He glanced at Elina, then back at the card. He handed the card back and said, "Haven't I seen you before?"

"Yeah," Elina said.

"It's hot as hell," he said. He turned to look at the thermometer on the booth wall. "Twenty-eight degrees in the shade," he almost shouted.

"Whew."

"Never take a government job," the guard said.

"OK."

"Well, you have a safe trip now."

The guard lifted the boom. Elina raised a hand and drove on. After the clear-cut, the forest returned on both sides. The road was empty. Elina stepped on the gas.

There was a stab of pain in the big toe on her right foot, broken in a fight.

When she'd crossed the Arctic Circle, Elina started glancing in the rearview mirror and scanning the sides of the road. If she saw a dark, low form, she slowed down until she was sure it was just a stump or a root. She turned on the radio. Every station was forecasting heat waves, wildfires, and floods.

Now and then she pulled over at a turnout, faced the woods, and stood silently with her eyes shut. She imagined a bar graph in front of her, two rectangles rising and falling as she breathed. Rising. Falling.

With each stop, the number of mosquitoes increased.

She drove past Loon Spit and didn't even glance toward the houses on the riverbank. The town appeared from the forest like a dream. Disappeared like a dream. She reached her home village of Vuopio at ten in the evening. The sun was still high in the sky, turning the world the color of an old newspaper, yellowed and used. Elina turned right toward the bridge and drove slowly across. The wide river glistened below. When she reached the other side, she turned left and drove along the bank toward the house where she grew up.

On the left, just before the last curve in the road, was Asko and Efraim's house, then Hoot's cabin. The windows were dark. Elina drove the last straight stretch. At the end was a sign: ROAD ENDS. She turned into the yard. There were four buildings surrounding it. The old sauna, her father's childhood house—which they called "the old house"—the main house, and the barn. The driveway was lined with tall aspen trees. Elina parked in front of the barn and got out of the car. She could hear the drunken melody of mosquitoes and redwing thrushes. The flat, jaded sulk of a brambling. Near the rise between the barn and the old sauna, a pine tree stood like a sentry on the boundary of two worlds, dry land and the swamp, and leaned toward the swamp, which lay at the bottom of the bank, damp and patient.

Elina awoke the next morning to a loud noise. She got out of bed, looked out the window, and saw a cuckoo. It was sitting in an aspen, calling out the time to anything alive. She had never seen a cuckoo so close before. When she went to the window, the bird fell silent and flew away.

She looked at the empty aspen and thought about her task for the day: to catch the pike.

She had slept in her old room. It had a bed, a bookshelf, and a table and chair. Nothing else. She'd given everything else in the house to Hoot.

Elina sat down on the edge of the bed. She ran her hand over her head, her hair buzz-cut to a three-millimeter stubble.

The haircut was part of the ritual.

She straightened her right leg and examined her toe, black and swollen. It looked worse than it felt. She ought to do something about it.

Elina limped into the hallway. On the left was the living room, with maps of bird habitats and charts of migration routes and drawings of ducks' feet that Hoot had put on the walls. She turned right, into the kitchen. She found a week-old issue of *Lapin Kansa* on top of the freezer, tore a strip from a page, and wrapped it around her toe. She found some scissors in the cupboard, cut a length of duct tape, pulled the paper tight, and wrapped it with the tape. A sturdy package.

She put the scissors back in the cabinet. Fixed to the cupboard door was a map with Hoot's penciled marks on every place where he had encountered raskels.

Elina started the coffee dripping, opened the narrow ventilation window, and looked outside. She hadn't had anything to eat the night before, but that was normal. Her appetite was always the first thing to go. There were the same birds making a racket as there had been fifteen years ago. Thrushes, wagtails, swallows. Or they looked like the same birds, but they were different birds. They covered the yard, trees, and buildings.

. . .

If you looked out and thought just about birds, you saw them everywhere. Swallows zoomed like jet planes in and out of the barn's loft windows. Thrushes hopped evenly along the ground. Now and then one would freeze in place and you had to really squint to tell if it was a bird or a lump of mud.

Elina drank her coffee and felt like a brittle husk. One time, when her father was sitting in this same spot, doing a crossword puzzle, he heard a scratching of claws on the floor. He looked down and saw a weasel. It looked him right in the eye, as if it were the real owner of the house.

"How does such a creature even know where my eyes are?" he wondered.

At her mother's funeral, Elina asked her father why they had built the house at the edge of a swamp. He said his family had always lived there, and it was a spot her mother found particularly to her liking.

Her mother had looked the whole place over thoroughly before they were married. She'd made a map of the area and drawn their future house on it, this house, on an east–west axis, so that it would lie across Lapland like a builder's level. She explained that this way the building would complement the pattern of what was already there in the landscape. The river, the forest, the hills.

He had stared at his wife. A small woman with short, coal-black hair and small, coal-black eyes that reflected no light.

"I see," he said. "I guess that's what we'll do then."

They'd built the house together. It was a long, one-story

house. Quite different from the other houses in the village, which all had a large central room with a wood oven in the middle. This house had no central room at all. The small kitchen, where Elina sat at the table, was off a long passageway that stretched through the house from end to end, with a living room at one end and a mud room at the other.

"Like the engine and the bridge," her father had told her when she was a child. "We built you a spaceship."

At night Elina would lie awake in bed and listen to the pounding noise that came from the walls and ceiling. She imagined that it was the sound of the spaceship's engines propelling the ship through the darkness. But she thought that it was probably the sound of mice running through the hollow walls. Just ten years after the house was built, the mice had already eaten nearly all the insulation, and in the winters her father had to cart load after load of firewood into the mud room from morning to night.

In the summers they killed the mice with poison and caught them in traps. One time, her father set a trap by digging a hole in the ground along one of the mouse trails. He put an old pickle jar in the hole and filled it up halfway with water, so the mice running past would fall into the jar. In the mornings her mother would collect the dead mice from the jars and mousetraps and throw them up onto the mounded shoulders of the root cellar, among the fireweed and the raspberry bushes.

Then, when dusk fell, Elina and her mother and father would sit in the sauna and watch out the window as owls came flying in over the forage field to land on the rounded roof of the cellar.

.   .   .

Everything Elina had done came rushing back.

The birds fell silent.

The clock finished striking.

Guilt squeezed the air out of Elina's lungs in a familiar, continuous pressure. Fffffffpt.

She laid her head on the table. Banged her head against it. "Shit," she said. "Shit. Shit. Shit."

She sat up straight again.

"Right. Don't even start."

She got up and paced back and forth across the kitchen. She spread her fingers and shook her hands in front of her, as if she'd received an electric shock.

She sat down on the floor. Leaned sideways and fell over. Curled up in a fetal position. It didn't help. She got up. Walked into the living room. Looked out through every window, then went back to the kitchen. Shook her head.

"Shit. God-damn shit."

She picked up a pencil from the table and wondered whether she could break it in two. She put the pencil down again. She had promised Hoot she wouldn't break things anymore. She leaned a shoulder against the refrigerator. Its cool, smooth door. Then she lifted her head and rammed it so hard against the refrigerator door that the jars on the shelf inside jingled.

"Ow! Hell," she said, holding her head. "Hell, hell, hell."

She laughed, went to the mirror, and said:

"You just need you some grub. Eat something."

She made some oatmeal and spooned it slowly into her mouth, like coal into a furnace. Then she went back to her room and put on a sturdy pair of cargo pants. She sniffed at yesterday's shirt. Still smelled like smoke. She tossed it into the laundry basket, found an old, loose, gray shirt in the wardrobe, and put it on. She went to the utility room for some bug repellent and rubbed it on her face, neck, and arms.

She found her rubber boots in the mud room, put them on, took a baseball cap from the rack and put that on, opened the door, and stepped outside.

It was nine o'clock in the morning but the bees and horseflies were already buzzing slowly around the yard, numbed and directionless in the heat. They were chased by dragonflies, which were chased by swallows. Ranks of gleaming, metallic carrion flies sunbathed on the walls of the barn.

Elina went in to look for fishing rods.

It was cool in the barn. There were mosquitoes inside, delighted to be served breakfast in bed. They swarmed excitedly around her and she swatted them dead on her arms and neck. She tried to keep in constant motion. It helped, with the mosquitoes and with the thoughts waiting in her head for any idle moment.

She had decided to get the pike out of the pond first thing. She looked among the skis in the corner but there were no fishing poles there, then she rummaged through the hay poles and bird feeders and mopeds. The whole place was crammed with stuff. When the elk dressing room was moved to another spot, her father had started using the barn to store anything they didn't need on a daily basis—which was quite a lot of things, because in his later days he didn't do much except sit on the veranda and drink beer and look out at the swamp.

There were barn swallows' nests up in the ridge beam. Baby swallows peered out of the holes and chirped at her.

She went to the cow stall and the mosquitoes followed her. There was an old hot-water heater there that had floated in on a spring flood. Her father had cleaned it up and made it into a fish smoker. In the old days, people in the village used to drag their junk onto the ice in the spring and let the river carry it downstream where it could be a nuisance for somebody else. There were tons of stuff at the bottom of that river. Toilet seats, fridges, freezers, cars.

She found a rod with a baitcaster reel under a wad of garden row cover. There was a tackle box, too, no doubt left there by Hoot.

She didn't see a rod with a spincaster reel. She would have preferred a spincaster, because then she could cast with one hand, and she could use lighter tackle, like ten-gram Doppler spinners and Rapala ultralight crankbait. The baitcaster had a cork handgrip that was crumbling in places. There was a spot in the middle where it had been broken, wrapped in duct tape.

Elina tried bending it. The tape held.

It would do.

There was already a steel leader on the line, bent from pike bites. Elina opened the tackle box, took out a nine-centimeter popper wobbler, and attached it to the leader. She put a few spoons and spinners and another small lure in an old eyeglass case and shoved it in the side of her boot. Then she walked out into the yard and looked up at the white clouds. They moved unhurriedly across the sky like mutant angels. Elina thought: This just might be a very good day.

She was absolutely wrong about that, though.

There were nettles and willowherb growing behind the barn. Hoot had mowed a narrow path through the weeds, and Elina took it. The air lay over the yard thick as oatmeal. Elina whistled an old tune and a song thrush answered her.

Young rosebay mingled with the nettles, pushing their way up out of the ground, pale, straight, and eager. In just two months they would be taller than her, bent over with their red-blossomed heads hanging, surrendered to August. They would gradually turn color from the stem outward, dry up, and die where they stood, and snow would cover them, cover the whole landscape, and nothing would make any sound, just drifts of snow everywhere, and above it all, the moon.

There was a farm road behind the barn that bordered the woods and led from there down the bank and through the fields and bogs and willow thickets between Big Inlet and Little Inlet. Elina followed it down the bank, then turned off the road and trudged across the swamp. She passed the Back Pond where large perch hunted. The Back Pond was edged with thick stands of willow that scratched red and white streaks into her bare arms. It felt good.

She kept walking. Now and then a mosquito caught her scent and made a careful approach and she smacked it. The swamp stank. The ground looked dry but her feet sank several inches with every step and water trickled among the weeds. Each time she picked up her foot there was a sharp smacking sound, as if her feet were sweet lollipops and the swamp was reluctant to surrender them. She was careful of her right foot, but the wrapping seemed to be holding. She walked over sphagnum moss, marsh tea, and cottongrass. She trampled shoots with tough stems that twined over and under one another like electrical cords. The cranberries were blooming. Their pale-pink blossoms hung from the tips of their stems like pearls. Too beautiful for this mire. There were thick mounds of them in places, and she aimed for those; the ground was firmer there. She kept moving. The bog bogeys started moving faster when the weather warmed, but thankfully they were still pretty slow. Everyone knew that moose and reindeer which tried to cross the wide fen islands sometimes stumbled into bog holes and were sucked under and the bog bogeys burrowed into their juicy carcasses.

It was such a lot of work to be alive and perform the senseless tasks of living, like the one she was performing now. It would be so much easier to sleep under the cold bog.

Now the horseflies had smelled her, too, and were flying loop the loops around her. Clouds played and shifted over the woods and it occurred to her that she wasn't moving. Only time was moving—she and the bog bogeys and even the clouds were just a series of still images. Then she was at the edge of the pond.

It was the same as always—a smelly gap in the bog grass. In the middle grew a dozen sickly looking reeds. The water was filled with brown debris that loomed like towers, stretching toward the surface of the water.

It was late morning and, strictly speaking, very bad weather for fishing. Elina set the brake loose on her reel, pulled the rod back, and swung it in a wide arc. The popper flew and landed with a splash in the middle of the pond a meter from the stand of reeds.

She let the bait just float there. If the pike was alive—and it always was—it had turned toward the sound now, stiff as an old submarine.

The solitary fish's systems were slow to get going. It hadn't eaten in many days, just lain half asleep on the muddy bottom, waiting to die, but now its hope was renewed, its senses straining to their utmost. It was analyzing the swirl of water and sludge with fins trembling and eyes wide, wondering whether some food had arrived.

Elina jerked the rod. The popper dashed forward ten centimeters, splashed across the surface, and landed with a plop.

A trail appeared in the water, coming from behind the reeds, and Elina did nothing, because the pike knew where the popper was now. The water churned and the bait sank. Elina jerked the rod. The pike was hooked.

It weighed about a kilo and it did what pikes do—it started to pull. First it pulled left, then it pulled right. Elina turned the rod, keeping it at a ninety-degree angle to the line. She tightened the brake. The pike had to work to fight the full strength of the rod.

The water splashed. The fish grew tired.

Elina held the rod in one hand. With the other she took off her cap and slapped it against her leg. An assortment of insects fell dead into the bog. She put the cap back on and started reeling in.

When the pike was a meter from her, she raised the rod and lifted the fish out of the water. Then her fishing line broke.

Snap.

Clouds slid over the pond.

She grabbed the end of the broken line and examined it. It was transparent and uneven. She let out more line, grabbed a length with both hands, and tugged.

Snap.

She tried to remember the last time she replaced the line on this rod. She couldn't recall ever doing it.

This was the first real setback she'd had in five years. She'd always caught the pike on the first cast.

Elina felt a little excitement now.

She tied a sixteen-gram Krocodile spoon straight to the line. She slipped the end of the line through the loop of the lure twice and stared at the resulting twists of line, at a loss. How did you tie a lure on again? She started to wrap the line around itself. Her fingers remembered.

She needed both hands now, which gave the horseflies an opening. One tried its blades on Elina's wrist. Nipped. Elina wet the knot with spit and pulled it tight a with a smooth, gentle tug.

Then she flicked the fly away.

She bit off the excess line, reeled the spoon in to the tip of the pole, lifted the rod back, and cast. The pike immediately bit.

"Haven't you learned anything?" she said.

She intended to tire the fish out properly this time. To be careful and only give it a little resistance, gentle enough to keep the line from breaking again, but active enough to keep the fish working. She intended to sap all the pike's remaining strength, guts, and will to live, until it was driven ashore by the sheer force of apathy. Then she could just squat down and pick it up as easily as a dropped grocery receipt.

She loosened the brake. The pike started to pull. It pulled toward the center of the pond and the brake whirred as the line payed out.

Two things worried her. If the pike had swallowed the lure it might bite through the line. And secondly, if it circled the middle of the pond it would wrap the line around the stand of reeds, and then the line would tighten and she would lose contact with the fish. If that happened, one sharp tug could break it again.

That she could do something about.

She kept the line straight between her and the fish and walked around the pond in the direction the fish was swimming so that the clump of reeds was never between them. The pike was swimming clockwise. Elina walked, coaxing the fish like a good idea you can feel coming. She talked to herself to help keep herself patient. Described every step she took, every jerk of the pike on the line.

She didn't have a second's peace from the bugs now. Her neck and hands were wet with sweat that had washed off the insect repellent, and mosquitoes were biting. They sat down and felt around for a good spot with their flexible snouts. A mosquito's snout is a fantastical, six-part instrument. It has two outer piercing tools and next to them two spreaders to keep the puncture open. Between those is a pipe the mosquito uses to pump its saliva into the blood to keep it from coagulating. And then there's the straw. The mosquito sucks up blood and excretes the water from it in droplets from its rear end.

These cleverly assembled blood-pumping and reproduction devices were assaulting Elina by the hundreds.

Mixed in with the mosquitoes were the flies. Deerflies with startlingly green eyes, swift, nimble, and silent, and swarming around the deerflies were horseflies. Black turds with wings. They made test landings all over her, probing her shirt and trousers and cap. Searching for skin. They burrowed into her hair at the edges of the cap, snipped her scalp open, and ate. They fought for space on her arms and wrists. They had chitin knives in their mouths and sawed at her with them, and when the blood came spurting out they buried their faces in the wound. Horseflies were living Swiss Army knives built by Satan himself, because they had spoons in their mouths, too, for ladling up the blood. Their dark, hairy rear ends pulsed and filled with blood until they were plump and turgid with it, and when they finished they flew heavily off to find a place to lay their eggs, any patch of grass next to the water, never far away in terrain like this.

And around the horseflies sputtered hawker dragonflies, blue and glittering. They snapped up the horseflies, dropping on them from above and wrapping their strong legs around them like iron bands. Dragonflies kill horseflies by biting their heads off, then landing on a branch to eat. The largest dragonflies never land at all. They whir in place, majestic and horrifying, beating their wings and scanning their environment with all-seeing eyes. They eat all of the horsefly except for the wings.

Elina killed mosquitoes and flies with her free hand. She slapped them on her arms, shirt, and trousers. Her left hand turned dark with guts and exoskeletons. She wiped the remains on her trousers, which had become an insect graveyard. She walked undeterred around the pond, intent on the circus of the hunt and of death. Her toe throbbed. She staggered. Every so often she had to put her free hand on the ground for support, and when she did the bugs had free rein to bite and slice and feast and ladle her up.

And all around her in the grass and twigs and branches crawled bugs and beetles of every kind, each one seeking the success prescribed to its own species. They wrestled and some of them fell in the pond and floundered there, at the mercy of an unfamiliar element. Then the water skippers skated onto the scene. They thrust their snouts into their victims and secreted enzymes that dissolved the other insects' internal organs, then they sucked up their liquefied remains. They were like knick-knacks made of thin sticks glued together and brought to life by a malevolent curse, and they all stuck their straws into their prey and sucked them up, leaving empty shells behind. If a really big bug like a horsefly happened to fall in the water, as many as ten water skippers would come in for the attack, surrounding it and feasting like hyenas.

The large spruce trees on a fen island waved their branches back and forth in the faint breeze, as if they too were trying to lure prey.

Once in a while a bird flew into the trees and was never seen again.

Under the water skippers, the pike moved. It was like a cudgel, its head wide like a crocodile's, its body tapering toward its tail, long and dark as it made its way through its own murky world, bending its flexible body, then snapping straight again with an impassive flick as it glided onward. How gracefully it swam with just those small movements. And how awkwardly Elina went trudging after it.

She was wet with sweat and blood. Bugs that had wriggled under the edge of her cap crawled through her hair. They had sucked themselves so full of blood that they couldn't get back out again, so they just droned and buzzed in their overcrowded prison. Bugs had crawled into her ears only to find no future there. They felt trapped and struggled and whined, an unbearable noise coming from inside her own head. Something was constantly pinching or biting her, the pain spread evenly over her entire body. Her feet hurt, too, and being punished this way was satisfying to her.

How wonderfully, how slowly and painfully, the time passed here at the pond. She and the fish were both using up their strength. She slogged over the bog, its dispiriting yieldingness. The pike swam around the pond, its dogged resistance like a cross it bore. The question was whose strength would give out first. Elina focused on just one thing: putting one foot in front of the other.

She realized too late that her line was hanging slack. The pike had stopped circling. It floated motionless in the middle of the pond, which meant that it might be ready to give up.

She didn't give it a rest break. She jerked the line, forcing the fish into motion. It drifted reluctantly near the shore, just two meters away. Elina walked with exaggerated stealth toward it in three wary strides. The last stride was on her right foot. Her toe gave such a throb of pain that she almost yelled. The pike opened its mouth, its gills spread wide, like wings. The line and leader swished from its lower lip. Elina crouched down, hoping that the pike was ready. That the shadow of her outstretched hand wouldn't frighten it, would on the contrary feel like salvation.

Elina looked into its eye, a murky pearl with the world falling into it in a fog of movement and color. It didn't register defiance, or desperation. The fish just did what it could, because it could.

It propelled itself to the middle of the pond.

And they started all over again. And again.

Then Elina had an accident. Her right foot, numb and aching, stumbled into an unexpected low spot. She lost her balance and fell on her backside with a splash, into the cold, wet bog. She scrambled upright and yanked her foot out of the muck. Roared in pain. The foot came out, but not the boot. She stood there with nothing but a woolen sock on her right foot. The swamp sucked on the boot, gurgling with pleasure.

The brake on her fishing rod gave a shout and the line started to pay out.

The pike was circling the reeds again.

Elina made a leap. The fish was half a revolution ahead of her. The line was nestled against the reeds, threatening to tangle. The fish tugged. Elina lifted the rod as high in the air as she could. The line cleared the two outermost reeds, and then another, but the plants in the center were taller; they just bent in the middle, then not at all, and the line cinched the whole godforsaken bunch of them into one tight green tuft. Elina lunged. The swamp squelched. The lunge was a mistake. The pike sensed the hurried movement and darted forward, making a complete circle around the ragged reeds. It was all over. Wrapped around the snag, the line wouldn't give, and the fish couldn't move. It started to strain against the line. Elina yanked and twitched at the rod. The reeds just waved at her. The pike curled back on itself and sprang, and the line didn't hold. It broke.

Elina immediately turned her back on the pond. She didn't even stop to get her boot. She deserved this. All of it. She headed back home in a laborious, lopsided trudge, her right foot on fire, her sock letting out a sickening splat with every step, the constant cloud of insects around her making a nightmarish racket.

When she reached the house she took off her wet clothes, hung them on a nail in the mud room to dry, and threw her sock in the trash. She carefully unwrapped her toe, which was pulsating, black, and numb. She threw the tape in the trash and got in the shower. The water fell rather than showered, the pressure minimal. She looked at her mangled toe and the water swirling around it. Blood, dirt, and dead mosquitoes.

She dried herself and looked in the mirror. Her face was covered in angry red bumps. They would get redder and angrier once the insects' proteins had done their work.

She spoke to the mirror:

"I'm bent, but not broken."

Then she let out a loud laugh, because she always hated those old sayings and she was horrified that there was still so much of the day left and she was already dead tired.

This was just the sort of misery she needed. She tried to be grateful for it.

She limped into the kitchen and turned on the radio. It said that the extraordinary heat would continue in Lapland, and that severe storms were expected. Elina taped up her toe again. She searched the cupboards, took out the jars and the bags of flour, and found some cinnamon rusks. Their best-before date was last year. She tested one with her teeth. It was as hard as a rock. She put it in her mouth like a pacifier, to moisten it, sucking the sugar off, and sat down in the same chair where she had sat in the morning and listened to the radio, which recited a catalog of dire weather events in various countries, manifest signs of the end of the world. She thought she should go shopping.

She should go to the bait shop to buy some new fishing line and to the co-op to get some food.

2

Elina drove into Vuopio, past the old houses along the river. They were built after the war, on the same foundations as the older houses, which had been burnt to the ground. In every yard there was a pen with a yapping dog in it. In every yard there was a garage, shed, or sauna with a contraption made of chain-link fencing on the roof for drying elk.

Dazzling early-afternoon light sparkled on the river. She drove over the bridge and turned onto the main road of the village. There was a co-op and a fishing-gear shop. She pulled up in front of the latter. It was called Vuopion Viehe—The Vuopio Lure—and was run by a man named Keijo. One time a man from Somero had come to town and started a competing fishing-supply business, but it was the sort of thing that would never fly because everybody did their shopping at The Lure.

Elina sat in her car and gathered her strength. In one corner of her windshield sat a horsefly with its front legs held imploringly against the glass, ready to surrender. She imagined that her car was on the moon. Surrounded by gray desolation, airlessness.

There was a knock on the side window. Elina jumped.

Simo the Shit was peering into the car. He was holding a wooden mask of an old man. He'd made it by gluing evergreen cones, rocks, and bits of wood and lichen to a disk of wood. She read his lips: Buy. Elina got out of the car, put her hand on the old man's shoulder, and asked him how he was. "Father Shit," Simo the Shit said, holding out his woodwork. Elina shook her head and said, "See you later," before going into the shop.

Keijo was sitting on a stool behind the counter trying to twist a crankbait lip with a pair of pliers and cursing to himself.

Mounted pike and salmon heads decorated the walls and an old fishing net hung from the ceiling. There were tables of reindeer skulls, on one table a stuffed fox stood heavily draped with lures, and on the floor next to it was a shell casing as long as your arm with plastic sunflowers poking out of it.

Elina went to the shop once a year, and every time she went it was crammed with more odds and ends and fewer fishing supplies. It was hot inside. Electric fans were set up on various surfaces, humming full blast. They rotated slowly from side to side like radar devices and made the dangling fishing lures flutter with a tinkling sound.

"Afternoon," Elina said.

Keijo let his eyes fall on his customer.

"Look who's here."

"What's up."

"Not much. Not much at all."

Elina looked at the rotating rack next to the counter. Jigs, hooks, lure rings, and swivels. She spun the rack around. On the other side were shiny forty-centimeter steel leaders and black fifteen-centimeter titanium leaders, three to a box. The titanium ones were more expensive.

She grabbed a box of them and put it on the counter. Keijo glanced at the box, then back at his work. "Anything else?"

"New line."

"Uh-huh."

"Got any that's braided?"

Keijo gave the crankbait lip a twist. "We sell monofilament."

"I'll take that."

"What weight?"

"I guess I'll do a zero-point-fifteener."

Keijo set the lure down in his lap and looked at her. "What you fishing for?"

"Pike."

"Are you insane?"

Elina laughed, but Keijo was serious. The fans hummed.

"Make it twenty, then."

Keijo went back to twisting the lip. "Tell me something," he muttered, lifting the lure and staring into its painted eyes, as if he were asking the lure a question and not Elina. "When you take a shit, do you shove your head in the toilet?"

"I can't remember what all the numbers are. I'm in kind of a hurry."

Keijo fiddled with the lure a bit as if to say that it wasn't his problem.

"Make it a thirty," Elina said.

"When you go after this pike…" Keijo said. Elina groaned. "Are you going to hold onto the hook and throw the rod in the river?"

"Does the weight of the line really matter all that much?"

"A fisherman knows. Or woman."

"Why don't you just give me a —"

"And are you sure about those leaders?"

"Why?"

"Just wondering."

"Yes, I'm sure. That line —"

"I got forties, too."

"What?"

"Just that those short leaders are more for something like a perch, don't you think? And I was under the impression you were after pike."

"I don't like the long ones. They influence the motion."

Keijo held up the pliers. "These," he said, "influence the motion."

"Listen, am I going to have to go to Sodankylä to get some line?"

Keijo stood up and yelled:

"There's no call to go to that reindeer heap to get you some line! You can get your line right here!"

He took a two-hundred-meter spool of Abu 0.30-millimeter monofilament line from the shelf behind him and put it on the counter. He punched the price into the register and muttered:

"Sodankylä. Pfft. No telling what kind of crap they'll sell you there. Stren or something…"

"But Stren's good line."

"Pfft. No telling what kind of crap a spool of Stren will be."

"I think the line that just broke on me was the Abu. I bought it here."

"When I was a kid we didn't have line."

"Is that so."

"Or a rod and reel."

"You don't say!"

Keijo's index finger paused over the cash register. "Way we did it back then was to tie a piece of wire on the end of a stick."

Elina stared at Keijo's raised finger, wishing it to move. And it did move, away from the cash register, and a low moan escaped from Elina's throat, and Keijo came out from behind the counter and lifted up his hand as if he were holding an invisible stick. Then he started tiptoeing around the shop.

"We'd find ourselves a shallow bay," he whispered, hunching over and moving in a circle around her. "Search out where there were pike stewing in the shallows... There!" Keijo pointed at the jig rack. "We'd creep up close..." He made his way toward the rack and stretched out his invisible stick. "And we'd slip a loop of wire around the pike's snout and give it a yank. Like this!" He swung his arm upward. "Sometimes it'd cut the pike right in half. My brothers and me would pull pike out all summer, throw 'em in a hot pan, and eat 'em before they were cooked. We couldn't wait."

He leaned against the counter and smiled, sunk in memory. "Then we'd shit out a tapeworm."

Elina dug out her wallet, counted out the correct amount in bills and coins, and stacked them on the counter. She crammed the spool of line and the box of leaders into her cargo pockets and headed for the door. "Thank you!"

"Tell me something," Keijo called when she was halfway out the door. She turned reluctantly and looked back into the shop. It looked small and dark. Keijo was standing at the counter like a troll who's forbidden to leave his cave.

"Why do you come here?"

"Huh?"

"To this village. You don't have anything here anymore."

"I have my house."

"Isn't it Hoot's house?"

"No, it's mine."

"And always at the same time. Is that how your vacation works?"

"I've come at other times. You just haven't seen me. Thank you and goodbye!"

Elina stepped through the doorway.

"I'm sure I would've known. Hey, listen!"

Elina stood on the front steps. The sun shone hot on her sore neck. She held the door open a crack, refusing to open it any wider. A person outside the shop might have thought she was in the middle of a tricky hostage situation trying to negotiate with a barricaded criminal.

"Buy something else," Keijo said.

"What?"

"New Rapalas."

"Don't need any."

"We got fluorescent colors…"

Elina slammed the door shut, went to her car, and drove to the grocery store.

The Vuopio co-op was a two-story building in the middle of the village, a hundred meters from The Lure, on the same side of the road.

Elina climbed the red steps, running her hand over the familiar railing, and went inside. A bell jingled.

"Hello," Heta said. Then she recognized the customer. "Is that Elina?"

"Hello," Elina said, forcing herself to smile. "Me again."

"It's always such a surprise to see what a grown-up you've become."

"Have been for many years now."

"But you used to be so little."

"Yep."

"More than once or twice I was your babysitter."

"Yep."

"You'd sit on my lap and we'd do puzzles and I'd feed you your gruel. Remember that?"

"Yeah. You got anything to put on the bread?"

"Nothing to speak of."

Elina looked at the full shelves. Then at Heta, who was smiling and gazing at her with her one good eye and a certain look, as if Elina were three years old again and asking to play with a hunting knife.

Elina scratched her neck. "Nothing at all? That looks like ham over there."

"We've got bologna and sliced meats, but no southern deli things."

"Don't need 'em. I'll take two hundred grams of the bologna."

"Our own meat's good enough."

"Always has been."

"Your type usually wants stuff cut paper thin, with a honey marinade."

"What do you mean my type?"

"Southerners."

"But I'm not… Listen now…"

"I'm just teasing you. So what would you like?"

"Two hundred grams of bologna and a packet of crisp-bread. And some coffee filters, since I'm probably out."

Heta grabbed the items from the shelf behind her and put them on the counter. She got a plastic bag from under the counter and put everything in it and started talking about the time Elina ran away when she was five years old and Heta had to go running after her. Chasing each other across a hayfield, like a fox after a rabbit. Elina was running her legs right off and Heta almost had a heart attack but finally caught her and gave her a good hiding. Heta said that Elina had always been a strong-headed, moody, peculiar child, just as her mother was a strong-headed, moody, peculiar adult. Maybe that's why Heta had always liked Elina so much.

"I was in a hard place when your mom died," Heta said. She looked for a moment like she might burst into tears, but she pulled herself together and scrunched her face into a smile.

As a child, Elina had once asked Heta what had happened to her eye. Heta told her that she had hidden it somewhere around the house, in a secret spot where it could watch over Elina whenever she, Heta, wasn't there. After that, Elina had dreams about waking up in the night to find Heta's eye resting on the blankets in front of her, as big as a football, staring at her.

"It's nice that you still come home to visit," Heta said. "To check in on the house, check on Hoot. He doesn't have too many friends. Everybody thinks he's raving mad, but I've always thought he was a nice fellow."

"Mm-hmm."

Heta picked up the plastic bag and handed it to Elina. "You're not planning on going to Pike Pond, though, are you?"

Elina took hold of the bag straps. "Why?"

"It's not a good idea."

Elina tried to take the bag, but Heta held onto it. "Bad things'll happen to you there," she said. "It's a dangerous place."

"Can't be all that much more dangerous than any other place," Elina said, trying again to lay claim to her groceries. But Heta didn't relent. She flashed an apologetic, creepy smile.

"But you won't go there, will you?" she said.

Elina shrugged.

"No offense, now, but you look pretty terrible," Heta said. "Face eaten up. Did you go to that pond?"

"What is this, an interrogation?"

"That pike is not normal."

Elina wanted out of this store, immediately. She was tugging at the bag, trying to wrest it from Heta's clutches, when the bell rang, the door opened, and Esko walked in, shouting hello.

Esko was a turnip-farmer from across the road. His blue overalls were covered in sawdust. He stopped on the doorstep. Looked at Heta, then at Elina. At the bag on the counter between them, which they were holding onto like a long-awaited, shared gift. Heta let go of the bag. Elina took it. Heta wiped her hands on her apron and said hello.

"Oh…" Esko said.

"Hi," Elina said.

"Didn't mean to interrupt anything."

Heta dismissed the idea with a wave of her hand.

"What can I get you, Esko?"

"Sea salt," Esko said, still not taking a step any farther into the shop.

"I'll be going," Elina said.

"Stay right where you are," Heta said. She took a packet of salt from the shelf and slapped it on the counter with unnecessary force. "Here you go."

Esko stood in the doorway like a wary mink at the mouth of a trap.

"Didn't mean to interrupt anything," he said again.

Heta shook her head.

"You're not interrupting anything. Here's your sea salt."

"Right," Esko said, approaching the counter.

"How's that fence project you got going, Esko?" Heta said.

"Home stretch. But I gotta start wrapping it up, 'cause there's a storm on the way."

Heta tried to nail Elina to the spot with a stare, but she was already at the door. Esko handed his change to Heta, who didn't even look at him. She came out from behind the counter and shouted, "That pike is not normal. Do you hear me?"

Elina opened the door and walked down the steps to her car. Heta followed her out.

"Stop!" Heta shouted.

Elina tossed the shopping bag onto the back seat of the car. She looked southwest. Thick, dark clouds like the burnt bottom of a rice pudding were gathering there.

Elina got into her car, closed the door, and started the engine. Heta was still standing on the steps, her mouth moving.

Esko peeped out from behind her. Elina stepped on the gas. Even through the crunch of the gravel and the roar of the engine she could hear Heta shouting, "Don't ever go to that place again!"

Elina sat on the front steps in a cloud of insects, winding the new line onto her reel. A dense, gray row of thunderheads was rising from beyond the swamp.

She had less than an hour.

3

Elina strode across the swamp in Hoot's old, oversized rubber boots, her feet shoved into two pairs of woolen socks.

There was a soggy rut through the muck where she'd tramped through before. She wondered how the pike was doing, whether it still had an appetite, or if it had died, and what she would do if it had.

A buzzard hovered overhead. Maybe it could see a misfortune about to happen.

Elina got to the pond before the clouds did. She unhooked the black nine-centimeter Rapala lure from the rod line guide, pressed the reel release, and swung the rod back, ready to cast.

Then, on the other side of the pond, the knacky surfaced.

It rose up out of the water slowly, like an ancient statue uncovered by a receding tide. It was as beautiful as a Greek god. Elina knew that it could look like a man or a woman or an androgyne, depending on the person it was trying to entice. Anyone who made the mistake of looking into its eyes would get lost in them. Some people fell in love with the knacky, and some were so love-struck that they walked straight into the water and drowned.

She lowered her rod and looked at the knacky. Tried to see its structure, woven from lies.

"What are you doing here?" she said. "This isn't a proper body of water for you."

The knacky wiped the slime from his cheeks. "I see you are well informed about my preferences."

His voice was deep and resonant, the voice of a singer.

"And what is your errand here?" the knacky asked.

"What does it look like?"

Elina cast her lure. It plopped into the water a meter from the knacky, like a pool toy. The knacky watched with interest as she reeled it in. There was no indication from the surface of the water that anything lived there in the goop.

The knacky floated with just his head and shoulders above the water. It was a complete mystery how the rest of his body fit in the shallow pool.

"A rather unusual time to go fishing," he said.

He peered at the sky, gray with thickening clouds, threatening a rain that people would be talking about for a long time.

Elina didn't say anything; she just cast again.

Then the pike struck. It swam out of the stand of reeds, bit hard, and pulled. It had a new strength, but Elina had a new fishing line. She started to reel it in. The pike kicked, but its protests made no difference.

The knacky's words did, though.

"Don't give up," the knacky said.

The pike started to eat Elina's tackle. It opened its gaping maw and snapped up half the lure, then all of it. Elina reeled harder. She tried to keep the line pulled taut, but the pike was insatiable. It surged again and swallowed the leader. Now the whole rig was inside the fish, hooks and all. All she could see was the line. The pike bit, the line snapped, and for the third time that day the fish got away and disappeared into the rusty layers of pond water.

Elina stood on the shore, stupefied. The knacky laughed and clapped excitedly, like an opera buff on opening night. Then he started raking his hands through the water as if he were looking for soap dropped in the bathtub. He found something and picked it up. It was the pike, her pike, held in his slender hands.

"Give it to me," Elina said.

The knacky paid no attention. He blew on the pike, which was on the brink, ready to shuffle off this mortal coil. The hooks on the lure had punctured the fish's organs. Blood was flowing out of its mouth and gills. There were red slashes on its sides like skid marks. Its eyes gleamed like oily, strangely human machines. The knacky lazily unhooked the popper and the Krocodile from the fish's jaw and laid them on the shore.

Then he reached a long, thin finger into the pike's mouth.

"What do you think you're doing?"

The fish trembled. Elina was sure it was giving up the ghost, but the knacky was still patiently poking around inside it. Then he fished out the slimy lure. No guts came out with it.

Elina stretched out a hand.

"I'll take that," she said. "The pike, I mean."

The knacky laid the lure on the ground next to the other tackle. He chattered quietly to the fish, stroked it, rinsed its mouth and sides with water. Held it like a clammy, watery Christ. And lo and behold, the bleeding stopped. The pike breathed and lived. The knacky lowered the fish into the water with both hands.

"Would you listen to what I'm telling you?" Elina said.

The knacky let go of the fish. It floated. Then waved its tail and disappeared.

"Damn you!"

The knacky grinned. Opened his mouth and laughed. The wind started to blow. It brought fat gray clouds with it from beyond the forest. They darkened the sun. In the dimness, the pond and the knacky began to blend into one, and Elina turned and walked away, knowing without looking that the place where the pond had been was now a dark opening, a portal to somewhere.

4

Elina unplugged all the electrical cords except for the one connecting the freezer. She sat in the dark kitchen. Enormous gusts of wind swept over the yard. She watched a dogged thrush searching the ground for food. A blast of wind grabbed the bird and tossed it down the hillside.

In weather like this, energy, beings, and thoughts moved between worlds. This knowledge was older than the village, older than log construction or the recipe for gunpowder.

It started to rain. Rain fell in a downpour and the wind bent it horizontal and dashed the drops on the roof, walls, and windows like buckshot.

Her mother was born in the middle of a storm like this.

Elina stared out at the rain for ten minutes. Then a dark form appeared in the yard. It materialized from the barn doorway. It was cone-shaped, flapping like a ghost and making its way quickly across the open space, toward the house. Every hair on Elina's body stood up. She craned her neck and watched the figure moving toward her. It disappeared around the end of the house. Toward the door. There was a thumping sound on the steps. What should she do? What move would make a difference? The door opened and closed. A clatter at the back entryway. Elina was halfway to her feet when the door from the mud room opened and before her stood Hoot, draped in a rain poncho.

"Evening."

"Evening."

They stared at each other.

"Is anything wrong?" Hoot asked.

"No. Why do you ask?"

"You look like you're ready to jump out of your boots."

Elina sat back down. Her heart was pounding. "Nah. Just a little startled."

"Well, I can tell you there's not a thing out there but a hell of a lot of water and wet."

Hoot carried his backpack and rain gear into the mud room. He came back to the kitchen, sat down across from Elina, and asked her how she was.

"No pike today."

"I see. How'd that happen?"

Elina opened her mouth but couldn't think where to begin. She shook her head.

Hoot was wearing a rough red flannel shirt, cargo pants, and a belt with a hunting knife in a sheath attached to it. He and Elina looked out the window. The storm was trying to tear the aspens and birches out of the ground.

"You don't have any lights on at all in here," Hoot said.

"No."

Hoot got up and fetched a candle from the cupboard and carried it to the table. Lit it with a match. They sat on either side of the light and stared out into the darkness, where their own flame was repeated in a line of other yellow lights that stretched into the distance.

"Feel like some supper?" Hoot asked.

Elina drew circles on an empty envelope with a pen. "Why not."

Hoot took a cleaned pike out of the refrigerator and turned on the gas range. He got out a frying pan and cut the fish into pieces. There was a flash outside. He cut a thick slice of butter into the pan and set it on the burner. A clap of thunder. He broke two eggs into a bowl and beat them with a fork. He poured breadcrumbs into another bowl and added salt. Then he dipped the chunks of pike in the egg and rolled them in the breadcrumbs. The butter was sizzling in the pan. He scooped the fish out of the bowl with a spatula and put them on to fry.

Elina smelled the aroma of butter and fish.

"I bet you haven't eaten today," Hoot said.

He turned the chunks of fish over and lowered the flame. Put a lid on the pan. He got out some plates, forks, and knives from the cupboard and carried them attentively to the table, like a waiter in a fancy restaurant. He gave Elina the tail pieces, because they were her favorite. Took the middle pieces for himself.

They sat at the table and ate earnestly in the candlelight. The storm rolled over the house and did its best to pry loose whatever it could. It tore away blossoms and branches and pieces of Styrofoam and a watering can that whirled across the yard. Hoot watched the watering can go with displeasure and made a mental note of where it went.

"I couldn't find the spincaster," Elina said.

Hoot picked a fishbone from between his teeth and set it on the edge of the plate. "The bees started a hive in the porch roof. I smacked at it with the spincaster and broke the thing."

"There wasn't some other stick you could use?"

"It was the closest thing."

"So that's what happened to it."

"It was kind of a stupid thing to do. But you found the baitcaster?"

"Yeah."

Elina started telling Hoot about her experiences at the pond. Hoot listened. Every so often he laughed; the story was so ridiculous.

When she told him about the knacky, he was amazed.

"What in the world was it doing there?"

"I don't know."

It was generally understood that the knacky disdained the muddy eye of a swamp. It liked clear water. People had seen the knacky rise up out of a lake, miserable, coughing up pondweed and catgrass and cursing the farmers whose fertilizers were making the home of the water spirit go to weeds.

The knacky was an unforgiving creature. If a farmer left a tractor out all night too close to the shore, the knacky would come out of the water after dark, climb into the cab, and drive the tractor into the river.

The knacky tickled swimmers' feet. It stole worms from fishhooks and pulled the hooks straight, too. It filled fish traps with rocks so they couldn't be pulled up without a winch. Net fishers met the worst fate. The knacky knocked them out of their boats and wrapped them up in their own nets, a catch to make the lake-draggers shudder.

Sometimes one of the villagers would get so mad they'd try to shoot the knacky with a rifle—and miss, of course—and when the rest of the village heard of it they would take off their caps with sad looks, knowing that the shooter wouldn't see another Christmas.

Hoot kept setting the forks and knives in different positions on his plate and rearranging words in his head.

"That pike sure is important to you."

"It is."

"All I can say is that if the knacky has marked that pond for itself, this thing could get dangerous."

"I've got tricks."

"I don't doubt it."

They looked out at the storm. The sky behind the barn was broken in two, like a Prussian-blue canvas divided by an artist's glowing white brushstroke from top to bottom. The yard lit up in freeze-frame. Then went dark again. The house was shaken by a crash, as if a train had come rushing under it. The knives and forks clattered against the plates, the windowpanes tinkled, and Elina and Hoot held onto the edge of the table as though they feared the rapture.

"Good God," Hoot said.

Hail started to fall from the sky. The hailstones were as big as swallows' eggs and they flattened the rose starts and the rhubarb and anything else that the rain had left standing. Great white chunks of hail bounced over the grass and piled up in the hollows. Then the downpour stopped. They looked at the yard and wondered what else was about to hit them. It started to rain again.

"Can't you tell me?" Hoot said. "What's wrong?"

Elina didn't answer.

"Maybe it would help."

"Maybe it would."

"Well, out with it then."

Elina continued drawing circles.

"Have you been over to see Asko and Efraim?" Hoot asked.

"Haven't had time."

"Maybe that's best. That you haven't had time."

"Yeah."

"Asko's memory has gotten pretty bad."

"Yeah," Elina said. "Been away for long?"

"Just one night. I went up behind Jurmusjärvi to see if the goshawks had built their nests."

"See any?"

"There was one."

"I saw Simo the Shit at the fishing shop."

"What's he up to?"

"Selling his Father Shits."

Hoot laughed.

"I'd've thought he'd be dead by now," Elina said.

"Nothing can kill him. You know where his name comes from?"

"No."

Hoot told her the story. Simo the Shit's real name was Jussi. How it got switched from Jussi to Simo, Hoot didn't know, but the shit part came from the fact that Jussi used to clean out the village's septic pits. He would use a tractor to tow his tank into the yard, stick a pipe in the septic pit, and suck up the waste, and then spread it over his fields as fertilizer. One time it happened that the pipe got stuck and he couldn't get it to come out. Jussi moved the hatch to the side and tried to get a better look down into the septic pit, but he tripped or something and fell head first into the hole. And he found out what the trouble was among all the shit down there. At the bottom of the hole there was an old man holding onto the end of the pipe with both hands. When the old man saw Jussi, he let go of the pipe and grabbed onto Jussi and started to pull his hair and ask him why people weren't worshiping Father Shit, the god of feces. Jussi was so shaken that his eyes rolled back in his head. He told the old man that nobody in the village knew that shit had a god. Father Shit got mad then, and started to really wrestle with him. For three days and nights they tugged and wrestled down there in the sludge. Finally, Jussi got Father Shit in a chokehold and made him promise to let him go back to the land of the living. And Jussi got out of the hole. He smelled so bad that birds a hundred meters off fell down dead from the tree branches. Jussi gave up his sanitation job after that and started drinking and making Father Shit masks. He's been called Simo the Shit ever since, and that was at least forty years ago.

"That can't be true," Elina said.

"Stranger things have happened."

Elina said she had a couple of stories, too.

The first one went like this: Thirty years ago Elina's father, Kauko Ylijaako, got tired of cows, their stupid faces, and he called Asko right then to come over and get them that same evening and take them to the slaughterhouse.

Then her father converted the barn into a dressing shed for the elk-hunting club. As soon as the snow melted, workmen came from town to tear up the floor planks and pour a new cement floor so the blood could drain off more easily. They hung rails and hooks from the ceiling and used them the next fall to hang the elk.

Elina would peek from the doorway when the old guys were scraping the hides off the elk with their knives. Sometimes they just grabbed hold of the hide with both hands and pulled. It made the same sound as pulling a rag rug off a snowdrift after it's been left out in a freeze.

Then, one fall morning, a frakus came out of the woods, tore the doors off the barn, tossed some elks over its shoulder, and started lugging them away.

Elina's mother happened to be looking out the window when the barn doors went flying into the air. She went out into the yard and walked up to the frakus and said it couldn't have any more elk. The frakus asked her what she intended to do about it. And she told him he could take the elks if he could beat her at finger-wrestling.

The frakus turned around and looked at her in amazement. Then he held up his finger, which was as thick as she was, and looked at her fingers, and started to laugh. The frakus laughed so hard that the elks fell off its shoulder, and then the frakus himself fell on the ground and rolled from side to side, laughing, and then its stomach tore open.

But there was nothing surprising about that, since most everyone knew that the way to fight a frakus is to make him laugh himself to death.

When they'd carried the barn doors back up from the riverbank and pulled the frakus behind the tractor into the woods for the stripefoots to carry off, Elina asked her mother, "Weren't you scared of such a big frakus?" And her mother asked her how a frakus kills a person. "With his fist," Elina answered. "That's right," her mother said. "He smashes you so hard you're flattened like a pancake. There's no time to suffer much."

The second story was about the first time Elina went into the woods alone, a thing she was specifically forbidden to do. The woods were peaceful and banal, quite a disappointment, actually, and she went back to her own yard. It was only then that she noticed that a raskel had followed her. She ran inside the house and watched from the kitchen window as the raskel trudged curiously back and forth across the yard, teetering like it was drunk. It picked up a pine branch and started scratching the side of the barn with it.

Elina went to tell her father, who was cleaning blueberries, that there was a raskel in the yard, and asked him if she could keep it. Her father ran to the window. Then he rushed outside and let out a terrible roar, picking up rocks and throwing them at the raskel, which put its hairy hands over its face to protect itself, screeching and running back toward the forest.

Elina, crying, asked him, "Why did you do that?"

"Raskels and people don't belong together," he said.

Her father told her about Elviira, whose only son fell in a well and died. Elviira took in a pet raskel. She dressed it up in her son's trousers and put it in a bed with a blanket at night and took it for walks in the village in the daytime. She tried to teach the raskel to say good day to people they met, and it did eventually learn to say something like "ggdeh." Elviira was proud when the raskel gave this greeting to Auvo Pasma, the old police chief, but he was not at all impressed. On the contrary, he was deeply shocked and told Elviira that she ought to let the dogs loose on the thing, or shoot it, and that dressing a forest creature up and treating it like a human child was a godless thing to do. Elviira took this hard and she stopped going out. Nobody saw her or the raskel for a whole week, until one day the raskel showed up, alone, at the co-op, wearing Elviira's dress, and pointed at a stick of sausage. Heta, horrified, gave the sausage to the raskel, who put a markka and two spruce cones on the counter. Then it tottered serenely out of the shop, tripping over the hem of Elviira's dress. Heta called Esko across the street and he got his rifle and shot the raskel in front of the store. Elviira was found at home, strangled in her own bed.

Hoot smiled, because he knew these stories well.

"Nothing like that has happened in a long time," he said. "Haven't seen a frakus in ten years. Even longer since I saw a stripefoot, and there are fewer raskels, too. That's what happens when every spring's hotter than the one before."

Hoot wasn't originally from Vuopio. He moved there from the south before Elina was even born. He first got a job helping at the sawmill, then he delivered the mail for a while. Eventually he ended up as the custodian at the health center, a job he'd been retired from for six years. Hoot was considered cracked because he talked about birds in warm tones and wasn't even a member of the hunting club. Elina guessed he was about seventy years old, but it was impossible to tell. Life had worked hard on Hoot's face. There wasn't an untouched spot on it. His body was strangely mismatched with his ancient head.

He was as thin as a weasel and his movements were quick and precise. Elina had never seen him wear glasses. He could point out a minuscule speck at the top of a distant pine tree and see that it was a redstart, or see a reindeer grazing a hundred meters away and name the owner by its earmarks—and woe be unto anyone who claimed otherwise, unless they had their binoculars with them.

Hoot talked like a native and seemed to know how to do everything—which only showed that he was from someplace else. Locals only knew their own territory. Reindeer-keepers knew about reindeer, elk-hunters knew about elk, and it was a rare villager who'd ever heard of a redstart. Only people who came in on the train learned to do everything, because they couldn't be certain if they could call the place their own, and that uncertainty followed them till the day they died.

The thunder and rain relented. Hoot carried the dishes to the sink. He said he was going to watch movies. That was his way of saying that he was going to sleep.

"Going out early for some bird stuff, but I'll be back in the evening. Take care of yourself."

"Yeah."

"'N' don't forget to eat."

"Yeah, yeah."

"Gooood night."

"Hey."

"What?"

"Could I have your wristwatch?"

Hoot glanced at his watch, then at Elina. "What for?"

"I need to be able to see the time. It's important."

"I see."

Hoot took off his watch and handed it to her. "Don't lose it."

The watch had a frayed, brown-leather band. Elina fastened it on her wrist.

"I won't. Thanks. Night."

Hoot went into Elina's parents' old room, which he had made his bedroom, and closed the door.

Elina decided to take care of one more thing. She went to the mud room and got her dad's old frame backpack. She packed it with fire-starting gear, a small hatchet, a lean-to tarp, rain clothes, and clean underwear. She packed enough canned food for three days. She took the pack to the entryway and set it in the corner. Just in case.

Then she sat at the kitchen table for a long time and looked out at the storm-beaten yard. She thought, Today was nothing.

Tomorrow she would get to work.

THE SECOND DAY

5

Janatuinen used Gunnarsson's belt to make a tourniquet for his leg, then she drove him to the hospital entrance, waited for the nurses to get him and his suitcase out of the back seat, asked them to close the car door, and drove off without a glance in the rearview mirror.

It was a two-hour drive from Oulu to the border. One hour in, Janatuinen sat in a service-station café, eating breakfast and looking out the window. The wind was dying down. Birch branches tapped wearily against the glass, as if knocking to get in.

The border came into view at nine a.m. The guard booth had a broken window. The window frame had been taken out and leaned against the wall of the booth. The barricade boom was broken, too, and had been carried behind the booth in two pieces. In its place was a green Suzuki jeep, parked in the middle of the road. A boy in a billed cap sat in the driver's seat asleep, his head resting on the steering wheel.

Janatuinen rolled down the driver's-side window. The guard in the booth looked like he'd been up all night. He said that travel in Lapland was not recommended. He was just about to reel off all the reasons for this when Janatuinen cut him short by showing him her police identification and handing it to him.

"So they've sent you to this godforsaken place, too, eh?" the guard said, handing the card back.

"Yeah."

The guard looked at Janatuinen's car, a twenty-year-old red Toyota Corolla, then leaned out of the booth and spit on the ground.

"That the piece of shit they gave you?"

Janatuinen smiled.

"Can that thing even pass inspection?"

Janatuinen made no reply.

"Government jobs sure are shit jobs, aren't they?"

"If you say so."

"Yeah. You have a safe trip now."

He twirled a hand to signal to the boy in the jeep to move. The boy didn't respond. The guard picked up a broom from a corner of the booth, reached out the window with it, and smacked the brush end against the top of the jeep. The boy woke up. The guard pointed the broom at Janatuinen's car. The boy put the Suzuki in reverse and backed into the ditch.

Janatuinen arrived in Vuopio around noon and drove through the village. A storm had tossed pine and birch boughs into the road. Janatuinen swerved and maneuvered around them as carefully as a student at a driver's test, then continued past toppled mailboxes and road signs. There was a man sitting at the bus stop with a stack of wooden slabs covered in glued-on buttons and moss and different colored plastic tiles. He held one out to Janatuinen, apparently trying to sell it. Janatuinen drove on. A reindeer with matted fur crossed the road, pulling an empty children's sled. There were log houses that looked like they had been standing for at least a hundred years, with large porches and neatly ochered walls and white window frames, and some houses with roofs fallen in and yards that looked like garbage dumps. Those houses, too, had curtains in the windows and a car parked in front. In one yard was an enormous plastic cloudberry, as big as a sauna. It had a door, left open. It was a sauna.

Janatuinen came to the end of the village, pulled in at the meeting house to turn around, and drove back.

A shop called The Lure looked like it was open.

"Hello," Janatuinen said, entering the shop.

"Hello!" Keijo yelled, and fell off his seat.

Janatuinen went to the counter and looked over it. Keijo was lying on his back on the floor.

"Did you hurt yourself?"

Keijo jumped to his feet and got back on his stool.

"No, no… I'm a professional, heh-heh. Who are you? I mean, how may I help you?"

"I'm Police Detective Janatuinen."

Keijo turned pale.

"But you're a girl. I mean a woman."

Janatuinen made no reply. Keijo stared at her with his head tilted.

"What's your name?" she asked.

"Ollila."

"First name?"

"Keijo."

"I'm looking for Elina Ylijaako."

Keijo nodded.

"I know her."

"Have you seen her lately?"

"Ain't seen her," Keijo said, taking a spoon lure from the rack and wiping it with a rag. "May I ask why you're looking for Miss Ylijaako?" he asked.

"I can't tell you that."

Janatuinen looked around the shop. She took a yellow box from a shelf. It had a rubbery yellow fish inside. She had no idea what you were supposed to do with it. The box was covered with a gray layer of grime. She put it back on the shelf.

"How's business?"

Keijo nodded. "Good! Good! There are lots of fishermen around here. You're lucky if there's room to get your boat out on the river, heh-heh! Our specialty is hatchery trout. Boy, are they stupid fish."

"And you definitely haven't seen Elina Ylijaako?"

"Noooo…"

"You sound uncertain."

"Well…"

"Well?"

"You're really police?"

Janatuinen scowled.

"Yes. I thought I made that clear."

"So you know how to evaluate… situations?"

Janatuinen gave Keijo a long look.

"Listen here. Tell me right now whether or not you've seen Elina Ylijaako, and anything else you know about her activities and her location."

"Take it easy, now, Mrs. Policeman!"

"Miss."

"Oh yeah?" Keijo licked his palm and smoothed back his dirty black hair.

"Listen, sir."

"We had a policeman once."

"I'm going to have to —"

"He's dead now."

"Pardon me?"

"Had a little mishap."

"Is that a threat?"

"No, no! What I mean is… um… His name was Onkamo. Died on an elk hunt. Friend shot him through the lung."

"I'm just about ready to arrest you," Janatuinen said.

"No, don't! It was an accident! I mean… Could you come to my house?"

"Whatever for?"

"I have a sorta situation there. Ongoing. Maybe you could take care of it? Then I'll tell you what I know about Elina. I wasn't threatening you. Just tryin' to tell you some village history… Thought it'd make you feel more at home… I'm not what you'd call a big talker…"

Keijo wrung his hands and looked at her.

"I'm sure you're aware that you can't make deals with a government employee."

"I'm not making deals. This is an emergency."

"And yet you're here manning the shop?"

"Gotta earn a living… I'm telling you, I have a real problem. It's hard to explain. I need a cop. Can you help me?"

Janatuinen let out a long sigh.

"Tell me what the problem is," she said.

"A break-in at my house."

"When?"

"Right now. I mean, the break-in was yesterday, but they're still there."

"Who is?"

"It is."

"It?"

"I don't know its name."

"And it's occupying your house?"

"Exactly! Occupying. It's practically taken over the place." Janatuinen nodded.

"I see."

"Will you help me, Miss Officer?"

"Just give me a moment," Janatuinen said, turning toward the door.

"Of course. Take your time, Officer…"

Janatuinen went out onto the porch and lit a cigarette. Looked around at the village. An old woman walked past the guy selling the masks, said something to him. He yelled back at her. The woman stopped and went back to where he sat. They started talking.

Janatuinen remembered the advice Commissioner Kyyhky had given her.

"Whatever happens, just go along with it. Say yes to everything."

Kyyhky had been to Lapland twenty years before to solve a tax-evasion case connected with a dam project. He'd left on a two-day trip and ended up staying for two months. He lost one leg, his hair turned gray, and, according to his colleagues, he was never the same after that.

And besides, the whole thing was a wash, he'd said. He never solved the case.

He also said that the locals wore long johns right up until midsummer, but Janatuinen couldn't believe that, because she was roasting in nothing but jeans and a T-shirt.

She smoked. She watched a pine weevil climb up the porch railing. It was comically slow, but resolute, taking one step, then another, steady as a machine. As if it knew exactly how much time it had. It climbed to the roof, then steadily forward until it was above her. Then it stopped. She tilted her head back and looked at it. If she hadn't seen it moving, she would have thought it was a knot in the wood. The pine weevil loosened its hold and dropped inside her T-shirt.

"What the hell?!" Janatuinen shouted. She stuck her hand in her neck, found the bug, and threw it down in front of her. The bug bounced once and lay on its round back. It kicked its feet helplessly. Janatuinen crushed it with the toe of her shoe. A white paste squirted out from under the bug's black shell.

"Shit," she said, scraping the gunk off her shoe onto the edge of the porch. She stubbed out her cigarette in an old beetroot can and went back inside.

"Show me the way," she said.

"Will do. It's over there, by the river."

Keijo leaned the porch broom against the door of the shop. Janatuinen got her pack out of the back seat of the car and put it on. Spruce cones, boards, and storm-tossed trash were scattered in front of the shop. Keijo walked over to a pine cone and kicked it.

"It's nasty when the wind blows trash around like that," Janatuinen said.

"This is nothing compared to what's coming."

Keijo waved Janatuinen toward a path behind the shop. They walked between blackcurrant and raspberry bushes. Their leaves had a pungent smell. Keijo was wearing flip-flops, what people used to call thongs years ago. Raggedy trousers with a hole in the rear end and nothing underneath to cover him. His shirt was gray in a way that gave no hint as to what color it had been originally. The ensemble as a whole was topped by a swaying head of tangled hair with who knows what living in it.

This ragamuffin padded sedately along, like a gnome leading prey to his lair.

The plant life around them was a tart green. The sky filled with high-flying swallows again. Lower in the air were wagtails, their white bellies skimming the shrubbery.

The quantity of light stung Janatuinen's eyes. Commissioner Kyyhky had absolutely forbidden her to wear sunglasses.

There was a buzzing sound to her left. It was a longhorn beetle flying toward her, its antennae spread. She swatted it with the palm of her hand and it spun out into the raspberries.

"Why don't Laplanders have addresses?" Janatuinen asked.

"Things change. One day a stripefoot comes along and picks up your cabin and carries it three hundred meters, and you got yourself a new address. And then there's magic."

"What magic?"

"Curses. If you don't mind my asking a question—we don't get much police around here—Why'd you come here?"

"Somebody had to do it."

"Uh-huh."

Janatuinen explained that she'd had a partner, but he'd had second thoughts when they got to Oulu.

"I understand," Keijo said.

They reached a lot where a typical, small postwar veteran's tract house stood. In the yard was a cage with a doghouse inside and on top of the doghouse was a dog, barking.

"Quiet, Rowdy," Keijo said.

The dog wagged its tail and tilted its head. Then it continued barking.

"Is the intruder dangerous?" Janatuinen asked.

"Don't know if I'd say that."

Keijo opened the front door and went inside. Janatuinen followed. They passed through a mud room into a house where knotty woodwork prevailed. There were tables, wall clocks, chairs, all carved from knotty, burled wood. There was a knotty shelf chock full of knotty mugs and ladles.

Keijo walked into the living room, sat down on the sofa, and picked up an evening paper from the coffee table. He told Janatuinen she could find the intruder in the kitchen.

"Everything here seems to be all right," Janatuinen said.

From somewhere else in the house there was a crash, like things being dropped on the floor. Keijo turned his head and shouted,

"Calm down, now! I brought you a fishing buddy."

"What do you mean, a fishing buddy?" Janatuinen said.

75

Keijo waved a hand. "Go on in."

"What do you mean, a fishing buddy?"

Keijo waved his hand again. There was a large red-brick stove with a door next to it. That was where the sound was coming from. Janatuinen walked over to the door.

"Hello? Police here."

A noise like something going down a drain. Like sucking or lapping or slurping something up.

"What is in there?" Janatuinen asked Keijo.

"Go see for yourself."

Janatuinen unzipped her pack and took out a pistol.

"Hold on, now," Keijo said, and started to stand up, but Janatuinen had already grabbed the door handle. She tugged the door open with her left hand, then raised it to support her right arm, held straight in front of her, clutching the pistol as she took one step backward. In that pose, she met the thing that was in the kitchen, and her world was changed forever. Janatuinen let out a shout. She backed up, taking aim at the creature crouched on the kitchen table.

It was holding a large soup pot in both hands, drinking from it. Janatuinen retreated until her back was against the far wall of the living room, her gun pointed at a monster with fur as black as if night itself had taken the form of curly, flowing tresses. Keijo came up to stand beside her, holding up both hands and repeating, "Don't shoot! Don't shoot!" The monster climbed down to the floor and looked straight at Janatuinen. Its eyes were hard and hot and glistening like marbles rolling in an open flame. It didn't flinch at the sight of the pistol. Maybe it was a thing that bullets couldn't stop. It opened its wine-red mouth, wet and meaty, a flash of teeth inside. Then it picked the pot up in its long hands again.

"For Pete's sake, put that gun away," Keijo said.

"What is it?" Janatuinen asked, her pistol still raised.

"A raskel."

"A what?"

"The king of Sweden. Is the varmint eating my soup?"

The raskel dropped the empty pot on the table and it rolled onto the floor. Then it calmly looked at each of them in turn. It took a deep, deep breath, like the buddha, or a very large pug. A stream of air blew in and out of its enormous nostrils.

"He wants to go fishing," Keijo said. "And I can't go."

"Fishing?"

"Put your gun away now."

Janatuinen lowered the pistol. The raskel sat down and stared.

"The fishing rods are on the back steps. Take them. The boat's on the bank. The black river boat. No need to hurry."

Keijo walked into the kitchen, just as if a specter concocted from fairy tales and scary stories had not walked into his house, as if they weren't both in mortal danger.

"You ought to say something to him."

Janatuinen went to stand beside Keijo. The raskel didn't seem nervous about their approach. It looked at them contentedly. There were leaves and mud and forest litter in its fur. There was also trash all over the kitchen floor, where the creature had obviously been having a good long romp. All the cupboard doors were open. Pots and pans and dry goods had been pulled out and scattered. The sink was filled to the brim with macaroni.

"This is Miss Police Officer," Keijo said. "She's going to take you fishing."

The raskel seemed to snap to attention.

"Let's not get ahead of ourselves now," Janatuinen said.

Keijo nodded his head at the raskel.

"So get packing!"

He made a little jerking motion like tugging on a fishing line. The raskel let out a howl, leaped to the floor with startling speed, and rushed toward them. Janatuinen gave a yell and jumped out of his way. Keijo just leaned back a little. The raskel sprinted right up to them, big and black and full of forest bluster. Then it ran out of the kitchen and out of the house.

Keijo picked up the pot and cursed and started cleaning.

"He just has an urge to go fishing... Can't you just do it? Damn it, the critter ate my frankfurter soup... Made it yesterday. Hey, if he puts an arm around your neck, like this, just tickle his armpit. And talk to him. He likes that."

Janatuinen shoved her pistol in her waistband. "You know that isn't my job."

"Just fish with him for a little bit. I can't."

"Shouldn't it be in the woods?"

"He don't want to. Don't you know that raskels want to be people?"

"I don't know anything about them."

"I see."

"Should I neutralize it?"

"Don't talk crazy."

"It is a nuisance animal."

"Hogwash."

Janatuinen made a sweeping gesture that took in the kitchen. Keijo, who was sweeping food and leaves up off the floor, straightened up and leaned on his broom.

"Have the Tervos over to play pinochle and the house'll look just like this in the morning."

"But I don't know how to fish."

Keijo looked at her like she was crazy.

"The raskel'll teach you."

6

That night Elina lived through it all over again.

She dreamed that she woke up to the tinkle of shattered glass in her home in the south.

She got up and went into the living room. In the middle of the room stood an enormous crane that had flown in through the window. Under its wings it had a man's arms, and it was using them to pick up the flat-screen TV.

This is really bad timing, Elina thought.

She told the crane to put the television down. The crane took a step back and turned its bird's head. It had red, fiery eyes. Elina took a step toward it and grabbed hold of the television. The crane slammed her on the shoulder with its bill. Elina backed away. Her shoulder was throbbing. She picked up a broomstick she kept by the bookshelf to help with her stretches, and approached the crane again. She waved the stick, trying to hit the crane's legs. The bird jumped nimbly out of the way. It lunged at her with its beak again, aiming for her head. Elina dodged it. When she came at it a second time, the crane threw the television at her. Elina instinctively raised her right foot. The television came smashing down on her toe and clattered to the floor. The crane spread its wings, beat them two times, and rose into the air. It was above her now, hitting her with its beak again. Elina whacked the side of the beak with the broomstick. The crane struck again. Elina got hold of its beak with her left hand, dropped the stick, held on with both hands, and slammed the crane to the floor. Then she got on top of the bird and pinned its arms to the floor with her knees. She held onto the bird's beak as it thrashed and kicked at her back with its legs. It had terribly sharp claws. Elina held the bird's beak down against the floor. The crane's unblinking red eyes stared at her. She let go of the beak with her right hand and felt the bird's abdomen. She was searching for a place where it had been cut open and sewn back together. She found it, dug a finger in between the stitches, and tugged them loose, widening the opening. She eventually fit her whole hand inside the crane. She felt around in the fluffy sawdust. Her fingers touched something hard. It was the bird's heart, and she pulled it out. The flame in the bird's eyes went out, and it went limp. Elina got up off the crane, panting. She opened her fist. In her palm lay a little piece of dark rye bread.

Elina sat up in bed and swallowed. She slowly assured herself that she was in Vuopio.

She got up and walked into the kitchen in short, old-lady steps. Her internal organs felt watery.

Elina knew that this was another warning.

In the kitchen, she took a painkiller, rinsed it down with water, and sat at the table, waiting for the pain to relent.

It didn't relent. She looked out the window into the yard, which was still beaten down, like she was. Branches strewn across the grass. Tattered leaves and broken flower stems. Birds everywhere, yelling with surprise at surviving the night.

"I'll give up when I've lost both my arms and legs," she said out loud. "And not even then."

She got up. The water in her stomach sloshed.

"Damn it. It's now or never."

Elina got a kettle out of the cupboard. She filled it with water, set it on the stove, and lit the burner. She checked the clock to see if Hoot's watch was telling the right time. She got her mother's diaries from the bedside table, four leather-bound notebooks, and sat down at the kitchen table to study them. There wasn't much about the knacky in them. It mostly just said that it isn't wise to have anything to do with the knacky.

She looked out the window and thought about it. She remembered an old story about the knacky sitting on a dock, shaking a pair of dice in its fist and shouting to passersby to come and play with it.

Elina got up to look for a deck of cards. She searched all the kitchen cupboards and finally found a pack in a drawer under some candles. She spread the cards out on the table and started reassembling the deck so that every other card was either an ace or a king, with all the cards in between either a two or a three. When the aces, kings, twos, and threes were used up, she arranged the next batch of cards in the same way with queens and jacks, fours and fives. She checked to make sure she'd done it all right. She finished by switching a couple of kings with twos.

The water was boiling. Elina poured some hot water over some instant oatmeal. She took a rubber band from the pencil holder on the table and wrapped it twice around the deck of cards. Stirred her thin, oversoft oatmeal and ate about half of it. Then she got dressed and put the deck of cards in her pocket, where it felt hard and flat, like a rifle clip.

She pocketed some bug repellent and her baseball cap, tucked the hunting knife in her boot, and was on her way.

Elina walked the same path from tussock to tussock, to the same stand of willows. At the spots where her boots had rubbed the bark away, the layer beneath shone like bone. She braced herself on the same branches. They bent a little lower every time she did. One branch finally gave way, and she didn't have the strength to adjust her footing.

Elina fell slowly, like a drunk, sliding down the bent branch into the thicket.

She clambered up again, heavy and panting, cursing. Most of all she cursed the fact that she'd not known how weak she was. She patted her pocket. The deck of cards was still there. She kept walking. Her clothes were wet again. She was starting to wonder whether she'd been in the swamp since yesterday. Whether she might have slept in the willow thicket and only dreamed about Hoot and her bed.

When she'd passed through the stand of willows, she stopped. A doe elk was standing in the swamp. They stared at each other. The elk looked like as if it might want to ask for directions. As if the storm had scrambled its compass and left it completely befuddled. As if it had forgotten what it was.

The elk tramped onward—as good a direction as any—and Elina stood and breathed and let it pass her in peace. She waited until the elk was gone and she couldn't hear it anymore, then continued walking.

She saw the knacky from a long way off. He had dragged an old fish trap from somewhere and bent it into a throne to sit on. The knacky was lounging in this chair on the other side of the pond, idly waiting.

Elina stopped on the opposite shore. The fish trap was ancient and rusted, but the knacky managed to grace it like an aristocrat. He gazed at her with a bored expression in his blue eyes and he was totally naked, as smooth and gray as a dolphin. He was beautiful and horrible, like a toy from the future.

The knacky was completely bald. The shape of his skull made you want to rest your hand on it. There was a story of a glassblower who wanted to make a work of glass in the shape of the knacky's head. The glassblower requested an audience with the knacky. The knacky wished the glassblower welcome, and that same evening the knacky was tilting back the scoured skull of the glassblower and drinking from it.

"You forgot your fishing rod," the knacky said.

"You know as well as I do that it isn't any use to me."

"No. No, it isn't."

"I need that fish."

"I believe you."

"I've got a suggestion."

"So have I."

"Oh yeah?"

"Yes. You will apologize to me and the pike."

"I see."

"And then you will turn around and walk away and never return."

"That's your suggestion."

"Yes."

Elina took off her cap, wiped the sweat from her brow, and put the cap back on again.

"Can't do that."

"I guessed as much. But at least I have offered you a means of escape. I fear that won't be possible going forward."

"I don't have that option."

"Then tell me what you had in mind."

"First I want to see it."

"See what?"

"The pike. See if it's even alive."

"So little trust," the knacky said, and jerked its chin up.

The pike slowly rose to the surface of the water. The first thing visible was its dark nose. Then its back and tail. The fish swam in a clockwise circle, like a trained pet. Elina's stomach twisted. So close.

The pike slipped out of sight.

"Satisfied?"

Elina nodded. She took the deck of cards out of her pocket.

"We could play for it."

The knacky sat up straighter.

"You're suggesting a card game?"

"Yeah. For that pike."

"And what if I win?"

"You can have my car."

The knacky pressed his fingertips together.

"Let me bring you up to date on my needs."

"I've got money, too. Cash."

The knacky stroked his bald head.

"I like games, I must admit—so you have in that sense tugged the right thread, so to speak. I like games very much. But the stakes are questionable. They don't seem commensurate. A car or some cash in exchange for an entire life…"

"Well, what do you want, then?"

"I want you to stake your own life."

Elina cleared her throat. Shifted her weight from one foot to the other.

"And what if I do?"

"If I win, I get your soul. If you win, you get the pike."

Elina turned the cards over in her hand.

"Agreed."

"How fun!" the knacky said, closing his eyes and rubbing his hands together with a chuckle.

"On one condition," Elina said.

The knacky opened his eyes, like two frozen wells.

"If I win, I get the pike. And you never come back to this pond."

The knacky stared at her. "Those are the stakes?"

"Yeah."

The knacky waved a hand.

"Whatever. The much more important question is what game we will be playing."

"How about katko?"

The knacky grimaced, as if his throne were suddenly red-hot.

"What a conventional choice! Can't we play canasta? You need four people for that, but I could invite some friends. The sea beast would be delighted to join us… I know! We can organize a tournament!"

Elina shook her head.

"I don't know how to play canasta. I know katko. We've gotta play a game that we both know. First hand wins. One and done."

"What a bore! All right."

The knacky rose from his throne and walked toward Elina with a back as straight as a ballet dancer's. Elina wondered how it happened that creatures from another world were either terribly beautiful and intelligent or unbelievably ugly and stupid. Mosquitoes flew around the knacky, but never touched him. They had some sort of arrangement.

There wasn't anything in the swamp to use as a table. Elina squatted where she was, ready to deal the cards onto the damp ground, which was undulating. The bog bogeys had found her.

The knacky came and squatted across from her. The bog bogeys immediately dispersed.

The knacky was very close to her now. He smelled like expensive hand cream.

Elina felt a pain like a worm digging in under her breastbone. She closed her eyes and took a deep breath. When the pain had what it wanted—her full attention—it withdrew into its den.

Elina opened her eyes. The knacky was looking at her in apparent delight. She started to deal the cards.

"Hold on," the knacky said.

"What now?"

"You have to shuffle first."

Elina forced herself to look directly into the knacky's eyes, which were a mixture of ice and intelligence. Attempting to keep her voice nonchalant, she said:

"I already shuffled them."

The knacky studied her.

"It isn't fair. You might be trying to cheat me. I insist that you shuffle them again."

Elina stared at the cards. She had to react quickly.

"Whatever you like."

She picked the cards up off the ground and slipped them into the middle of the deck. She grabbed a few more from the bottom and dropped those into the middle of the cut, and then a few more.

The knacky clicked his tongue.

"You're shuffling wrong."

"What?"

"You're putting them all in the same place."

"I'm shuffling in the normal way."

"Give me the deck."

"I can handle it, thanks."

"Are you trying to cheat me?"

"Don't be silly."

"I want those cards to be properly shuffled. Give me the deck."

Elina shook her head and continued. The knacky sighed. He shot out a hand, so quickly that the movement was invisible to the naked eye, and the cards went scattering across the soggy ground. Elina let out a yell. The knacky started gathering up the cards and said that he would be in charge of dealing.

"Certainly not," Elina said, and started picking up cards herself. For a moment, they were in a race to pick up the cards. When they each had their own deck, Elina held out her hand.

"OK, you've made your point," she said. "I'll shuffle them better."

"As long as you do it thoroughly this time."

"OK."

The knacky gave Elina his cards.

She gathered up the deck with trembling hands. She dealt the cards out into six piles. The knacky asked with feigned sincerity if she was all right. Elina nodded. She gathered the piles up, laid the pack in her palm, and held it out to the knacky.

"You want to cut?"

The knacky reached out with a long finger and pushed the top part of the deck a couple of centimeters toward her. Elina moved the cards the knacky had chosen to the bottom of the deck and dealt, pondering how fast she could run in a swamp. Not fast enough. Not in this condition, with this toe. She glanced around. Looked to see if there was anything she could use as a club. Stunted willow bushes. Nothing. Absolutely nothing. She had the hunting knife. A negligible advantage against the knacky.

She should strike quickly. She shouldn't even attempt anything else. She would do it the moment the last card was played.

She had no intention of dying here.

She picked up her hand. All hearts. The ace, queen, six, four, and three.

She was not going to die here, damn it.

The knacky stroked his fine, slender chin with one hand and laid down a card.

It was the five of hearts. Elina took the trick with the six of hearts.

"You've been coming to this pond for five years now," the knacky said. "That's a long time to come asking for trouble. Isn't it nice when wishes finally come true?"

Elina thought about her strategy options. There was really only one.

"That's none of your business," she said, and laid down the ace.

The knacky tilted his head. Smiled.

"It hardly matters. You'll soon be telling me everything."

The knacky played the four of clubs. He didn't follow suit, which meant he had no hearts, let alone a high one—which meant that Elina had won.

She laid the rest of her cards down on the damp, undulating ground.

She lifted her hands to her face and took two deep breaths in the darkness beneath her palms.

What unbelievable luck.

The knacky laid down his cards. Jack of diamonds, king of clubs, ace of clubs. The small muscles of the knacky's chin were moving. He nodded faintly, as if he had made a decision.

"You broke the rules," the knacky said.

"I did not."

The knacky stood up and walked back to his throne.

"You stacked the deck ahead of time to give yourself the advantage. This game is null and void."

"You have to keep your promise."

The knacky sat down on the throne.

"You cheated."

"You can't back out now."

"You may go."

Elina thought. She had the hunting knife. The knacky was unarmed. He stared at her with eyes like dark gashes.

He could flay her as easily as skinning a fish.

"Go now," said the knacky. "I shall not let you live a second time."

Elina looked at the pond. No options. She turned and walked away.

When she'd gone, a magpie flew from the edge of the woods to where the cards were, picked up the jack of diamonds in its beak, gave it a shake, dropped it on the ground again, and flew away. The cards lay scattered in the swamp, white, as incongruous there as the knacky was, sitting on his throne with his chin in his hand. Perfectly still.

7

Elina walked from the swamp straight to the barn. She picked up a Finnish dartboard lying on the workbench, carried it out to the yard, and hung it on the barn wall, on a nail used only for hanging dartboards for the past thirty years. She pried five rusty red darts from the wall and walked five meters away. She turned and looked at the dartboard. Walked back to the wall, nudged the dartboard three centimeters to the left, went back to her throwing spot, and put her left heel against the marker stone and her right heel thirty centimeters behind it. She raised the dart in her hand. Lowered it and brushed a mosquito off her cheek with the side of her elbow. Started throwing.

Miss… Two… Seven… Seven… Eight.

She used to have matches with her father when she was a child. The loser had to carry the wood to the sauna. Every Saturday and Wednesday.

She retrieved the darts and threw again.

Six… Seven… Eight… Seven… Nine.

She fetched the darts.

Elina's body swayed forward, back. She didn't really aim so much as she searched for the right rhythm, like a burglar feeling for the tumblers when picking a lock. She believed that the right rhythm would reveal the invisible route from her throwing hand to the bull's-eye.

Six... Seven... Seven... Nine... Eight.

The knacky knew what a fix she was in with the pike. The knacky wasn't going to let her near the pond again.

Nine... Nine... Three... Eight... Nine.

She couldn't shoot the knacky.

Eight... Six... Four... Nine... Nine.

She would have to coax it away from the pond.

Nine... Miss... Four... Eight... Nine.

She had only one option. She'd known it the whole time.

Nine... Eight... Nine... Seven... Ten.

She looked at the dartboard and counted. Forty-three. Enough to not have to carry the firewood. Ordinarily.

She walked to her car and drove toward town.

Elina turned onto the bridge and only then realized how dirty she was. What bad shape she was in.

She glanced at her watch. Almost one. She didn't have time to make herself presentable. She had to bake a rhubarb pie. A gift for an ally she had never met. She had read about it in her mother's diary. She knew the instructions by heart. She knew the place, and the right words.

And besides, she was desperate.

She drove on, going through a mental shopping list. Wheat flour, eggs, buttermilk. She was going to town because she couldn't go to the co-op. Heta knew something. Elina didn't want to find out what.

It was twenty-eight kilometers from the house to town. Halfway there, Elina pulled off at a bus stop, ran across the ditch into the woods, and threw up everything she'd eaten that morning. She leaned against an aspen tree and closed her eyes. She heard the creak of a bicycle on the road. She turned to look. Salme was riding past, wearing a green-frame backpack, with plastic bags hanging from both handlebars. Salme rode from town to Sodankylä and back once a week, picking up bottles and cans from the ditch. That was how she earned her bread.

Elina raised a hand. Salme nodded and rode on. Salme's earnings had fallen because people didn't throw as much trash into the ditch as they used to.

Elina waited for her to ride out of sight, then walked back to her car.

The next thing she passed was four reindeer lumbering along in single file on the left side of the road. They were a dreadful sight. Their eyes were big and black, as if they'd been crying all night long. Their fur was ragged and blotchy. They were pestered by mosquitoes and horseflies, a walking dinner. They were tormented by maggots growing under the skin on their backs and hatching now, leaving them with painful, seeping wounds.

Elina slowed down; the reindeer might jump into the road at any moment. The tortured creatures didn't even glance at her car. They walked on with their heads down, like a funeral procession, as if they had just learned of the death of their savior and were on their way to the burial.

Elina reached the town. It was like Vuopio, only bigger. In addition to an ice-cream stand, a church, and an inn, there was also a cluster of other businesses—a hair salon, a bank, a bar.

The first people to build houses there had arrived four hundred years ago. The frakuses, raskels, and elves came down from the hills and razed their cabins right down to the foundations. The inhabitants escaped the attack in boats. The frakuses laughed and hurled the stone foundations of their former homes at the boats. When the monsters had crept back into the hinterlands, the people returned. They rebuilt their village, and the frakuses howled with rage and put a curse on the village so that their cows wouldn't give any milk, nor their fields any crops. So the people had to leave again. But as the curse faded, they came back again. Every time they were thrown out, they came back, in slightly larger numbers, and slightly tougher, perennial as ants or mosquitoes, and Lapland learned that occupation was inevitable.

There was a grocery store next to the shopping center. Elina pulled up in front of it.

A hawk owl was perched on a short post in front of the store, looking around at the town as if the place itself were a direct challenge.

Everything in the store was as Elina remembered it. The arrangement of the place never changed. It was as if the spot for each item, the brand, the position on the shelf, had been decreed in holy scripture. Elina walked past the fruits and veg, took some eggs from a shelf on her left, turned right and walked to the dry-goods section and picked up flour and leavening, then returned to the main aisle and optimistically grabbed a packet of meatballs for lunch. She took a right turn into the milk section. Elina knew exactly where the buttermilk was, and she walked as if asleep, thinking about what she had to do and what was going to happen, and only raised her eyes once she had reached the refrigerator case.

Inside the case, half bent over, was Jousia.

ELINA AND JOUSIA'S FIRST ENCOUNTER,
OR HOW ELINA GOT HER HAT BACK

At the beginning of August, the middle-school children in town and those from the surrounding villages were all tossed into the same schoolyard, with no choice but to work out a hierarchy among themselves. The town kids had the home advantage. They worked their way through every newcomer and then through one another, sparing no one from being sized up and assigned a precise rank.

At recess, Elina stood next to the door, mute and aloof, which made her an ideal target. The girls surrounded her, pointing at her clothes and declaring one by one that she was ugly. Elina didn't react. The girls said her face looked like the backside of a frakus and she was fat and she smelled like a raskel. Elina still didn't react. One of the girls pushed her, and she swayed and remained silent. The girls laughed.

That same day, rumors started about her—about her sexuality, the health of her skin, her parents. The following week, everything that could be stolen from her was stolen, from her shoes to her pencil case. One day in November, Janna Keippana took her knit hat off her head at recess and threw it in a rowan tree.

Everyone waited to see what she would do.

Nothing.

Jousia Mäkitalo walked toward the rowan tree.

"Don't go get it," Janna Keippana warned him.

Jousia fetched the hat and took it to Elina without saying a word. It was their first encounter, and they didn't even look at each other. Elina was staring at the ground, and suddenly her hat came into her field of vision and remained there, in her hand.

They were both punished for this. Janna Keippana took the matter straight to the top—to her brother Joni. Joni was in ninth grade and taller than most of the other students, and he was as no-good as he was tall.

Joni brought two of his minions with him. They grabbed Elina and rolled her in the snow like rolling fish fingers in breadcrumbs, turning her and twirling her, changing directions every so often. When Elina was completely worn out and covered in white, they left her buried in the snow and made their way toward Jousia, who was defiantly awaiting them. Joni led the pack, as big as Goliath. Jousia made a lunge for him. He tried to push Joni over, but Joni didn't budge an inch. Joni grabbed Jousia and smashed him into a snowdrift. Then the threesome spent a good while rubbing their victim down with icy snow. They shoved snow down his coat collar and the waistband of his trousers, and filled the trouser legs up, too. Throughout this operation, Jousia yelled, cursed, and hit. The bullies laughed. It's more fun if the punching bag fights back.

This episode did not change Elina's behavior one bit. She fetched her shoes and socks from the nettle patch where a classmate had thrown them, and when someone smashed bubblegum in her hair, she cut it out with scissors. She made bullying her so easy that after a while it did nothing to increase her attackers' reputations. On the contrary, if someone took it into their head to dump pea soup in Elina's lap at lunchtime, the other kids snorted in embarrassment.

And so she was left in peace before the end of the first school term.

The boys came to school on mopeds, quad bikes, tractors, and riding lawn mowers, and on snowmobiles in winter. During recess, they would gather around the snowmobiles, leaning against them and comparing one to another. Joni led these discussions. They built ramps for doing jumps with them. They would sit on them and rev the engines, competing to see whose machine made the most noise.

Jousia got a knife and cut the tracks on Joni's snowmobile. When Joni was riding home along the bottom of the ditch, the track broke and Joni flew head first over the handlebars. The next day, Joni came to school on a tractor. Jousia poured sugar in the tank, and on the way home the motor ground to a halt at the first crossroads.

Jousia was given a thrashing weekly. He vowed revenge every time. The principal summoned the parties concerned to a crisis meeting. At the meeting, Jousia stared down the teachers, the bullies, and the bullies' parents. He told them all that he was opposed to any sort of wrong, whether in the schoolyard or in the classroom, and he didn't need anyone explaining anything to him. Jousia's parents said they thought their son was just suffering from loneliness. "Be quiet," Jousia commanded, and when his parents said that he sometimes wrote letters to invisible friends, he got up and walked out. The fights continued.

Jousia was a poor fighter, but bottomlessly tenacious. He fought back until he was tied to a tree or so exhausted he couldn't lift his arms.

He took revenge on others' behalf, too, though nobody asked him to. He would protest if he felt that he or someone else got the wrong grade, whether the victim of the injustice was the best student in the class or his sworn enemy. The teachers listened to his tirades with a crooked grin, mortified, because his argument was watertight, every time.

At recess, when the boys grabbed Jousia, the teachers looked the other way.

The school terms passed. A couple of weeks before the end of middle school, Jousia and Elina's class had an assignment in religion class called "Me and the World."

The class was supposed to divide into pairs, interview each other, and then tell the rest of the group about their interviewee's view of the world. Someone raised a hand and asked if they were supposed to talk about their hobbies. The teacher said that the assignment was about what they thought about the world and what events in the world looked like to them. The students sitting near the windows started looking outside. One boy said that his father told him the social democrats were society's enemy number one. Another child announced that she planned to make a list of everything she saw on one day and nothing more.

The pairs were chosen by lot. Jousia drew a name from the basket, glanced at it, then at Elina, and dragged his chair up to her desk. Jousia informed Elina that the subject was important to him and he wanted to do it right. Elina nodded and stared at her desk. Jousia said that he thought Elina should come over to his house so they could interview each other thoroughly. Elina nodded.

"Hey," Jousia said.

Elina raised her head. Jousia stared fixedly into her eyes and asked her, slowly, "Is that OK?" Elina straightened up, opened her mouth, and said:

"Yes, that's fine."

"Next Saturday?"

"OK."

It was May. There were still patches of snow in the ditches and great heaps at the ends of buildings where it had been piled all winter. The ground around the piles of snow trickled and gurgled incessantly. Chaffinches shouted in the pines, curlews in the fields. Great glistening drops of water were free-falling from the eaves, and Elina didn't yet know that from this spring onward the sounds of water and birds would always remind her of these happy days.

Jousia's house was on Loon Spit, two kilometers from town. It was thirty kilometers from her house in Ylijaako. She got there by bicycle. She rode on twisting forest roads, which added five kilometers to the trip. She didn't want to take the risk of having someone from town see her.

Jousia's place was a pale-blue two-story house on the riverbank. He was sitting on the porch steps in sweatpants and a T-shirt, reading a book. When Elina rode into the yard, he put the book away and shaded his eyes with his hand.

"I baked some rolls," he said.

He sat Elina down at the kitchen table, set down a platter of enormous hot rolls, and urged her to take one before they got cold. Elina took half of one. The roll was steaming. She spread butter on it and took a bite. It was frightfully good. Elina started to laugh. She put her hands over her mouth.

"Is it bad?" Jousia asked.

Elina emphatically shook her head. Jousia thought she might be choking, and leaped to his feet. Elina swallowed and said that the roll was extremely good, thank you.

"That's good," Jousia said, and sat down again.

Elina would have liked to take some more, but she didn't dare.

Jousia had a blue lined-paper notebook and a pen. He tapped the tip of his pen against his upper lip and said that no one in school knew anything about Elina. This was such welcome news to Elina that she whinnied.

"Sorry."

"Why don't you ever defend yourself?"

Elina shrugged. She picked up a crumb from her plate. Then it occurred to her that she wasn't going to get through this meeting without speaking.

"It doesn't feel like I should," she said.

Jousia wrote her answer down in his notebook.

"Don't you have any self-respect?"

Elina started to sweat.

"Don't know what I would do with it."

"Everyone oughta have respect for themself. Otherwise people will walk all over you."

"That's OK."

"All right then. What do you think about the world?"

Elina pondered this.

"I like to go fishing and to look at birds."

Jousia looked fed up.

"We're not supposed to just list our hobbies."

"Right," Elina said, staring at her lap in shame.

"Sorry, but that just sounds so boring."

"It's better than brawling."

Jousia's eyebrows rose.

"Is that what you think I do?"

"I didn't say that."

"But you meant it."

Elina scratched at the edge of the table with a fingernail.

"I don't want to fight or anything."

"But I do. That's what you think."

"Well. I need to think about that."

Jousia leaned back.

"OK."

Elina poked at the table.

"Well," Elina said.

Jousia sat up and picked up his pen. Waited.

"Maybe it's more that I think you shouldn't let the world win."

"Oh? In what way?"

Elina scratched her head. Maybe she should say it.

"Remember when you got my hat out of the tree?"

"Course."

"I knew there was no way to win. Not by those rules. So I decided that I wouldn't play by those rules. That they have no right to decide how I feel."

She thought for a moment.

"I mean, I wasn't going to let them get under my skin. So, yeah, I could say for sure that I have self-respect."

Jousia wrote.

"Are you a follower of Gandhi?"

"No. I just don't want any attention."

"But you can't just let things be."

"Why can't I?"

"Because then things will always stay the same."

"Uh-huh."

"A Stoic," Jousia decided, and wrote it down. "But you must let it out somewhere," he said.

"Let what out?"

"Well," Jousia said, and waved the hand holding his pen. "You know what I mean. Your feelings."

Elina shrugged again. She realized she shrugged a lot, and decided not to do it anymore.

"Well, I like to look at bird books."

Jousia covered his face with his hands.

"You are fucking weird."

"Yeah."

"When they start fucking with me, I do art."

"Huh?"

"Artworks. But ask about everything else first," Jousia said, tearing out a couple of sheets of paper and handing them to her. He gave her his pen, too, then crossed his arms and waited.

"OK," Elina said. She glanced at the rolls, but Jousia paid no attention.

Elina asked, "What is your view of the world?"

Jousia said he was "an individualistic utilitarian." He said he supported the freedom of the individual and he thought that the individual could do whatever he wanted to do, but the individual also had a moral responsibility to those around him and, ultimately, to the world. The individual should try his best to make the world a better place to live in, both for himself and for others, and this responsibility was both local and global.

"Talk a little slower," Elina said.

"OK," Jousia said. He talked about the categorical imperative and anthropocentric ethics. He talked about biocentric ethics and racial discrimination in the United States and genocide in Africa and Asia. He talked about sustainable development and free markets and the dangers associated with them. Every now and then he stood up and parroted famous speeches, right down to the little gestures. He quoted books. Elina didn't catch half of what he said, but she kept writing and wondering how a person could keeping droning on for such a long time, so sure of his subject and his own charisma. Then he talked about the music he listened to and the movies he watched, linking them, however tenuously, to his own personal struggle, on all fronts and at every possible level. He finished by saying that he had considered the matter for a good while and come to the conclusion that he could help society best by becoming an artist.

Elina laid the pen on the table. She had filled a whole page. "OK. I think I got it all down."

"Good. Wanna go look at what I made?"

"Oh, you mean the art?"

"Yeah."

"I guess so."

They went across the yard to the horse stable. Jousia turned his head and looked at the river and Elina examined his profile. His chiseled chin and resolute expression.

Jousia opened the stable door and said he was making sculptures. They walked past the stalls. Three dark horses snorted and watched them pass. They came to a large room at the end of the stable that Jousia said was used as a garage, and sometimes a workshop.

There was a Honda Monkey moped in the corner, with goose's wings attached to its sides with wire. It looked like the contraption could take off into the air.

They stood and looked at it.

"How's it look?" Jousia asked.

"What are the wings for?"

"What do you think?"

Elina walked around the moped.

"It's OK if you don't like it," Jousia said. "I've accepted that I won't be understood in my own time."

"OK. That's a good attitude, I'm sure."

"That was a joke."

"OK."

Jousia scratched his chin.

"So, with this piece, I'm examining freedom. What's that look for?"

"What look?"

"What are you thinking? Be direct."

"It's nothing."

"Is it too obvious?"

"I don't know if I'd say that."

"It is obvious."

"It's quite good."

"I didn't expect to make a masterpiece right off the bat," Jousia said, sounding like he did expect it.

Elina sneezed.

"Your eyes are watering," Jousia said. "Are you all right?"

"Yeah."

Elina wiped her eyes. She sneezed again.

"I think I'm allergic to horses."

They left the stable. Jousia apologized for not asking beforehand. Elina assured him it was fine. She should go home now, though.

"You should come over again." Before Elina could answer, Jousia said he thought their project wasn't finished.

"We still have time before we've gotta turn it in. Could you come on Monday after school?"

"I guess so."

"Wanna take some rolls with you?"

After their second meeting, Jousia suggested that they show each other the most important places in their lives.

"Because talking can only take you up to a certain point," he said. "There should be something concrete, so the other person can really know you."

Jousia rowed Elina across the river to the opposite shore. Then they climbed up the riverbank and walked across plowed brown fields. The fields were filled with lapwings, like white flowers against the dark-brown earth.

The birds followed them as they strode over the plowed furrows.

They climbed up onto a rise with a half-built log cabin at the top. It had a foundation, walls, and a roof, but through the windows you could see that the rooms were empty and unfinished. The door was fastened with a sturdy padlock. Jousia said it was built by a southerner who had inherited the land. He had started building the cabin years ago, and one day when he was finished working he went to have coffee at a local farmer's place, to get to know his neighbors. The southerner saw a frakus's skull on the man's wall and asked him what the hell it was. And the farmer told him. This was hard for the southerner to take. He assured the farmer that it must be some prehistoric animal. When the farmer corrected him, the southerner just nodded, but he kept looking over at the skull the whole time he was there, and after that evening he was never seen again.

Jousia said he came to the cabin in the summertime to read, because there was a nice breeze on the porch that kept the mosquitoes away.

He went up the steps onto the porch and leaned his back against the cabin wall. From the northwest they heard the sounds of a pack of raskels calling to each other in low growls whose meaning no researcher had ever deciphered.

"To me, this cabin symbolizes the incompleteness of life," Jousia said.

Elina ran her hand along the skin of a stripped log and wondered what she thought the cabin symbolized, but to her it was just a cabin.

"I'm gonna leave this place someday," Jousia said.

"Won't you miss anything from here?"

"No."

"Not even the river?"

"The river?"

"I think it's great here."

Jousia slammed the sole of his shoe against a porch pillar. "There's nothing great about this place."

"Even the trees are special."

"This whole place," Jousia said, drawing a line with his finger across the horizon, "should be fucking covered with buildings and concrete. That would be good."

The next day was Elina's turn. She got up at six a.m. and cleaned her room. She went into the kitchen, got a rag, and started wiping the table. Her father came into the kitchen. Asked if she was all right.

"Is it too much to ask to live like people in this house?" Elina said.

"Is someone coming over?"

"Jousia Mäkitalo."

"For the homework project?"

"Yeah."

"Sure is a long project."

Jousia came over straight from school. He went into every room and told Elina she lived in a really pleasant house. He expressed the same opinion to her parents. Elina's father looked at the young man with eyes wide. Her mother was mute, inscrutable. Elina was ashamed of them from the bottom of her heart. She bustled Jousia into the mud room. They put on rubber boots, Elina grabbed the fishing rod next to the door, and they headed to the swamp.

When they reached the shore of the pond, Jousia scratched the back of his head. "Interesting choice."

Mosquitoes buzzed around them. Elina unhooked the line from the rod loop.

"What do you bet I can catch a fish with one cast?"

"From that mud puddle, you mean?"

"Yeah."

"If you catch one, I'll do your homework."

"Thanks," Elina said, and cast.

The pike Elina tugged ashore was small and thin. It weighed half a kilo at most. The fish lay in the swamp grass, thrashing its tail from side to side like an angry fetus delivered too early. Elina picked it up by the neck and looked into its eyes, into the dark holes at their centers. Shook herself free of what she saw at the bottom. Then she whacked the fish on the top of the head with the handle of her knife. The pike trembled. She hit it again. Scales flew like sparks, and the fish went limp.

Elina cut a length of willow about twenty centimeters long and shaved off all its offshoots except for a couple of centimeters of the lowest shoot on the branch. She stuck the willow stick under the pike's gill flap and twisted and pushed it until it poked out of the fish's mouth. Then she grabbed the end of the stick and pulled and jiggled it until the fish slid down onto the forked shoot. Then she hoisted the pike into the air and turned it from side to side in the deep afternoon glow, like honey, that surrounded them.

Elina said that according to her mother the pike is an ambassador. It has the power to swim freely from one world to another. Even this individual fish might have visited hundreds of different dimensions and experienced realities that would shatter human consciousness.

"And yet here it is, hanging from a stick," Jousia said.

They went back to Elina's house. As they walked behind the barn, Elina threw the pike into a patch of globeflowers at the bottom of the bank.

"That's a good frying fish," Jousia said in surprise.

"You can't eat a pike from Pike Pond."

"How come?"

"I'm not sure. Hey, do you wanna see something cool?"

They went inside. Elina's father was in the kitchen, chopping up pickled whitefish. Her mother was hanging out laundry in the sauna. Elina took Jousia into her parents' bedroom. She made him sit down on the double bed, opened the drawer of the night table, and took out a black, leather-bound notebook.

"What's that?" Jousia asked.

"My mom's diary."

She sat down next to him and started leafing through the pages.

"Are we allowed to look at this?" Jousia asked.

"No."

"Good."

In the book were drawings, numbers, and diagrams. Strange symbols. Some pages had a pressed flower or a spider or a butterfly between them.

"Here it is," Elina said. She showed him two pages densely covered with writing. At the top was the title: Pike Pond.

Elina read out loud:

"'There's a pike in the pond every spring. It always looks the same. Kauko says he caught it ten summers in a row. His dad caught it twenty times. There was one year in between when nobody remembered to ask about it, and then there was a bad harvest. The place is propitious. We're going to do a spell there.'"

"And then there's a spell," Elina said.

"Let me see."

"Wait. It says here that the last time the spell was done was eight years ago."

Jousia stared at Elina.

"Did your mom do some kind of magic at that pond?"

"For sure she did."

"I want to see it," Jousia said, and took the book out of Elina's hands. He started to read:

"Deep within the pike's intestines…"

"Stop."

The voice came from the doorway. Jousia dropped the diary into his lap. Elina's mother slipped over the threshold like a ghost and stood in front of them.

Jousia held out the diary and said:

"Here."

"Children are interested in forbidden things," Elina's mother said in a neutral voice, like a doctor describing symptoms into a Dictaphone. Jousia held out the diary again. When it was clear that Elina's mother wasn't going to take it, he put it down in his lap. After a moment he set it down on the bed.

"Sorry," Elina said.

"I told you to stop," Elina's mother said to Jousia, "because if those words are said in the right place at the right time, they can cause terrible damage. Absolute…"—she paused a moment—"…destruction."

"OK," Jousia said.

Then she turned to Elina.

"The reason I told you that you can't look at my diary is that there are things in it that you don't yet understand. So they're dangerous. In time, all my notes will belong to you. You just have to wait."

Having said this, Elina's mother exited the room as silently as she had entered it.

Elina put the diary back in the drawer. They ran out into the yard and all the way behind the barn, just in case.

"Your mom's really weird," Jousia said.

"Yeah."

They looked at each other, smiled, and burst out laughing.

"I almost shit my pants," Jousia said.

"I thought you weren't scared of anything."

"I'm not. Except your mother."

"I'm scared of her sometimes, too."

"I guess you know what they say about her around here."

"Yeah."

"They say she's a witch."

"Yeah."

"Is she?"

Elina mumbled, "I guess she is, a little."

"Are you?"

"What do you think?"

"Don't look at me like that."

"I don't know. Maybe."

The forest in front of them was like a wall. They listened to the twittering and chirping coming from within it. As if the spruces and birches and pines were singing, instead of the birds that lived in them.

"You've gotta do my homework," Elina said.

Jousia took her hand.

"What?" Elina said.

He didn't say anything.

"Is something wrong?"

Jousia held onto her hand. Whispered something.

"What did you say?"

He let go.

"Just that it sure is a pretty evening."

8

Janatuinen picked up the fishing poles next to the back door and headed down the steep path to the shore. The riverbank stretched in both directions as far as the eye could see. It was covered in globeflowers. There was a boat on the bank—a tar-blackened, long, narrow riverboat pulled halfway ashore. It was held by an orange rope stretched tight from the bow to the hillside, where the anchor lay under a large rock. The river beyond was wide and swift. There were small whirlpools, and in places the current seemed to be moving upstream. Waves of different tempos churned and collided. It made Janatuinen nervous. It felt as if the river were designed to taunt her. She was also nervous about the clouds that filled the sky above the river. They rushed along with the current, as if all of nature were on its way somewhere that only it knew about.

It was a swirling window into a world that was foreign to her. She was reluctant to get mixed up in it. And on top of that there was the raskel, pacing impatiently back and forth next to the boat.

Janatuinen had to make a decision. She could just walk back to her car and drive away.

She thought about her partner, Gunnarsson.

She had been awakened at four in the morning by shots and yells. She had pulled on a hotel bathrobe and run to his door. He was in the room next to hers. Gunnarsson had left a shoe on the threshold to hold the door open. Janatuinen burst in and saw him lying on his back on the floor next to the bed.

He stared at her with wide eyes, his pistol lying beside him. Blood was spurting out of his leg.

"I'm not going to Lapland," he hissed.

The raskel noticed Janatuinen hesitating. He gave a yelp and started waving his shovel-like hands at the boat. The time for deciding was over.

She thought about foisting a fishing pole on the raskel. He might be happy to go out on the water alone. But when she got to where the raskel was and tried to hand the rod to him, he paid no attention whatsoever. He just sighed and laid a hand on Janatuinen's shoulder in a teacherly manner, the way only a local can. As if he knew about her struggle. He had a broad smile on his furry frog face, and when Janatuinen felt his fingers on her, felt their strength, she had an inkling that more than one tough opponent had measured that strength in some serious games. She could guess how that had turned out. She looked into the raskel's eyes—two tunnels with stars twinkling at the bottom, and, beyond the stars, green and purple galaxies turning slowly on their axes. Janatuinen blinked and forced herself to look at the entire canvas of the raskel's face. It, too, was disturbingly strange.

Whatever happens, just go along with it.

"Well, hell," Janatuinen said. "Let's go then."

The raskel scrambled into the boat. He sat on the stern seat and held tight to the sides, gazing at her with a hopeful look, like a child boarding a rollercoaster.

Janatuinen used her foot to shove the rock away from the anchor. The rock rolled over to reveal a brown, cylindrical object. It was unbelievably heavy. Janatuinen lugged it to the boat with both hands, panting and cursing Lapland and her own career choices. The raskel watched her labor with satisfaction. Janatuinen bundled up the rope and threw it in after the anchor. She gave the boat a shove. It moved lightly, slipping into the water. Janatuinen took two quick steps and jumped in, just like she used to do as a child at the lake cabin, in another life.

She grabbed the oars. The raskel started screeching—apparently he wanted to row. Janatuinen lifted her hands in surrender. They got up and switched places as the tippy boat was already moving, carried away from the shore by an undertow. The boat spun sideways, rocking. The raskel tried to get past her. He crowded so close that for a moment they were in each other's arms, she and the monster. He smelled strongly of forest. Janatuinen was sure that they were about to go overboard. She put her hand on his back and shoved. The raskel grunted and eventually squeezed past her. They were both still on board.

The raskel sat down, picked up the oars, and started to row. The boat spun and the frustrated raskel started to roar. He threw the oars into the river, first one splash, then another, and they bobbed away on the current. The raskel turned his back on Janatuinen, got on his knees, and put his long arms in the water on either side of the boat. Then he started to paddle. He paddled in long, powerful strokes, and eventually the boat started to move. The raskel let out a whoop to celebrate his own ingenuity and picked up speed. He paddled them a good way upstream. They were a hundred meters from Keijo's house when the raskel remembered why they had come to the river in the first place. He stopped paddling, picked up the cylindrical thingum that served as the anchor, and pitched it into the river like a bomb. A column of water soaked them, the rope unspooled as the boat continued downstream, then it pulled tight and the boat stopped with a small jerk.

The raskel sat down. He looked like he was waiting for something.

"What?" Janatuinen said. "Oh yeah—the fishing poles." She picked them up and gave one to him. It occurred to her that they had no worms or whatever people put on their hooks here, and she wondered what he would think about that.

The raskel snatched the pole from her hand and either didn't know about bait or didn't care. He flung the bobber into the water in one swift motion. Janatuinen dropped hers in, too.

They fished. The river was smooth and quick. It carried leaves and bits of grass past like commuters on either side of the boat. The sun came into view between the clouds and illuminated them. The raskel's coat gleamed like the fur of a well-brushed German shepherd. He stared fixedly at the bobber. Motionless, eager. The river pulled their lines straight and tugged the bobbers sideways. The water moved onward like time, past the bobbers, past Janatuinen and the raskel, unable to take the boat with it; their fishing idyll, or nightmare, bathed in light.

Janatuinen braced her rod between her knees and got out her cigarettes. "I hope you weren't planning to stay here too long," she said.

The raskel stared at his bobber, but his small black ears, tufted at the top, were twitching. He was listening.

"I still have things to do today," she explained. She had witnessed some shocking things—in everyday places like living rooms, roadsides, and back yards. She had seen what people are capable of doing to each other. Seen the harebrained schemes and well-laid plans they were capable of thinking up to destroy one another. And she had learned what she was capable of doing to people. That might be what astonished her most of all. So why shouldn't a thing like this exist? A raskel.

"Everybody told me not to take this assignment," Janatuinen said. "They seriously advised me against it, over and over."

The raskel stared at his bobber. Janatuinen leaned an elbow on a knee and held her cigarette between her fingers.

"I don't like the countryside," she said. "At all. I don't like dirt, or cows, or gravel roads, or rednecks. But here we are."

She blew out smoke.

"What do you say to that?"

The raskel smiled.

"Do you like listening to me chatter?"

A barn swallow dropped from the sky and perched on the side of the boat between them. It turned its head and looked at the raskel. Then at Janatuinen. It spread its wings, beat them rapidly. A silent launch, and it was in the sky again.

Janatuinen flicked her cigarette butt into the river.

"Don't you have any friends?" she asked. "Family?"

The raskel's eyes were half closed.

"I understand. A tough subject. I myself was supposed to come here with my partner, but he decided to quit in the middle of the game."

Janatuinen shaded her eyes with her hand. She should have brought sunglasses.

A boat was approaching from downstream. She watched it come toward them. Two men, one in the bow, one in the stern. Fishing rods on both sides of the boat. Trolling. A little three-stroke motor putt-putting up the river. They glided past. The raskel waved at the men. The one at the motor lifted his hat. Janatuinen wasn't sure whether he was greeting her or the raskel.

The men in the boat disappeared around a bend.

"Haven't we been at this long enough?" Janatuinen said.

Off to her left was a small, round, black stone in the water near the shore. Had it been there the whole time? Janatuinen squinted and looked again. It was gone.

She pressed her right hand over one eye, then the other, peering across the water. There were spots in front of her eyes. The stone was closer to the boat now. Then it disappeared. It wasn't a stone.

Janatuinen realized they were in danger.

She glanced at the raskel. Every hair on his body was standing on end.

They heard a bang under the boat. Janatuinen stood up. The boat rocked. She looked down. Another bang, against the bottom of the boat. Something knocked on the boat's bottom three times. The raskel was staring in the direction of the sound, too. Janatuinen watched the river on either side of them. On her left, a hand rose out of the water and grabbed the side of the boat. Then another hand.

"There's someone there!" Janatuinen yelled, crouching down. She grabbed the hands and pulled. From out of the water emerged a head, shoulders, an entire naked person. It took her a second to understand that something wasn't right about it. The body was blue and pale. The arms she was holding were cold and slimy. The rescue victim lifted its head. Janatuinen stared at a face that had two muddy white beads for eyes. A dark gash for a mouth.

"What the hell…" she said, and tried to struggle free, but the tables had turned. Now the creature was holding onto her wrists. The grip of its fingers was strong. It was pulling itself into the boat. She could see its pale back now, the bony lumps of its vertebrae. It was as silent as the schools of fish it had come from, and had no mechanism taking in air or breathing it out again. No heart pumping blood to its limbs.

But it was pleading for something. Its mute mouth groping for something. She could see little teeth in its mouth, like wet stones. It wanted meat.

The raskel stood up. He wrapped his hand around the creature's head and lifted. The creature's pale face turned toward the raskel like the accused, ready to accept any possible sentence. The raskel punched it in the face. The skull gave way, collapsed into itself with a dry crunch, like Styrofoam. The grip on Janatuinen's arms loosened and the creature slipped into the water soundlessly, sank with a strange gracefulness, and was carried away by the current. Janatuinen sat in the bottom of the boat and looked at her arms, trying to comprehend. She looked at the raskel, who calmly returned to his seat, like a babysitter who'd just broken up a scuffle. The river behind the raskel was rising. It rose up like a wall, or an arm, and grabbed him, jerking him backward. Three more creatures shot out of the water. Two were hanging on the raskel's body, one on each side, and the third had a stranglehold on his neck. They were pulling him backward into the water. The raskel roared and flailed. The slender creatures tugged tenaciously, as if they were instruments of some greater power. Janatuinen opened her backpack, took out her pistol, and snapped the safety catch off. She lifted the gun, stepped toward the raskel, and reached over him. One by one, she pressed the barrel right between each creature's eyes and fired.

The attackers fell slowly backward, dark holes in their foreheads, mouths opened as if in the throes of a divine vision. They sank into the dark water. Echoes of the gunshots ricocheted over the river from both banks. Janatuinen stood in the middle of the boat with the gun in her hand and looked around, but there didn't seem to be any of the creatures nearby. The raskel jumped to his feet. Janatuinen pointed toward Keijo's house.

"Head for shore."

The raskel immediately started paddling in that direction. The boat started to move, then the anchor resisted. Janatuinen put her pistol in her waistband and pulled up the anchor, and the boat jerked into motion again. They came ashore some distance upriver from Keijo's house. The raskel leaped out of the boat and stood gawking as Janatuinen dragged it onto land. She wrapped the anchor rope three times around a young birch tree.

Then she walked upstream, and the raskel waddled obediently after her.

9

Elina panicked. She made an instant U-turn, swinging around so fast that she knocked her shopping basket against the shelf behind her and a liter of orange juice fell to the floor with a thud. She didn't stay to see if Jousia heard the noise. She walked quickly toward the door she had come in, only to find that it had no handle on the inside. She went back to the dry-goods section, put her basket on the floor, then went to the checkout counter and walked through, past the clerk, Timo Leppänen, who watched her as she went. Finally, she found a door that would open. When she got outside she looked for someplace to hide, but all she saw was the empty road and the cars parked in front of the store. She walked around to the back of the store, where the loading dock and dumpsters were. She couldn't fathom how it hadn't occurred to her that she might run into Jousia. She crouched behind a large cardboard container and waited.

When a minute had passed and nothing happened, no one seemed to have followed her, and she was apparently safe, she sat down on the ground, pulled her knees up against her chest, and closed her eyes.

Twenty minutes passed. She looked at her watch. She didn't have time for this. She should be on her way home by now.

She slapped herself on the cheek.

"Get going."

Elina peeked around the corner of the grocery store and studied the parked cars. She didn't know what kind of car Jousia drove.

She withdrew behind the garbage again. Looked at the place where she had been sitting. Hard-packed grit. There were plants poking out from under the dumpster. Yarrow, ox-eye, plantain weed. When the village was built here, the ground was excavated and graded. Paved with asphalt. But the plants didn't much care. They could grow through anything. They used every crack, every crumbled spot, and they sucked every possible bit of nourishment from the gravel. It was like they had never heard of defeat.

Elina made her way slowly and warily, like a rabbit ready for a surprise. Then she straightened up and walked across the parking area and back into the store. She didn't see anyone but the clerk Timo. He was putting bags of nuts on the shelf. Elina peeped between the shelves. No one. No Jousia. Her shopping basket was still where she'd left it in the dry-goods aisle. She picked it up, went to the checkout, waited for Timo to come back behind the counter, and paid for her groceries.

"Mäkitalo was asking about you," Timo said.

"What?"

"Jousia Mäkitalo. He just left. He said that if I saw you I should tell you you're welcome to come to his house for a visit."

"OK," Elina said.

She drove home.

She went into the kitchen and opened up the package of meatballs and ate one. It didn't taste like food. Good. She ate another one. She got a knife, went out to the hail-pelted rhubarb, and broke off three stems that were reddening up like blood vessels. She cut off their large stalks and brought them into the kitchen, washed and peeled and chopped them. She thought about Jousia. She turned on the radio and beat together eggs and sugar. Ate a meatball. She added the milk and butter. The batter smelled good. For a little while, Elina felt as though she were spending a pleasant day in the kitchen. Then she remembered Jousia again. Come for a visit, indeed. She added flour and baking powder and mixed it in. She poured the batter onto a cooking sheet and pressed chunks of rhubarb into it, carefully and symmetrically, as if they were amulets and each one had to be in the right place or their magic wouldn't work. She placed the sheet in the oven and watched as it baked. The dough rose and darkened. It looked like it would turn out well. She hoped it would be good enough.

She took the pie out of the oven and didn't wait for it to cool. She cut a large corner piece and stuffed it in her mouth. Hot and good. She cut another piece. She sat down and waited for what her stomach would say. It didn't say anything. She sliced the rest of the pie, put a few pieces on a plate for Hoot, and left it on the counter, covered with a napkin. The rest she arranged in an old biscuit tin.

She was ready.

Keijo was on the shore to meet Janatuinen, with his dog. He was standing with his hands in his pockets, on the spot where the boat had been, and the dog was standing next to him, barking. Keijo watched the two of them coming along the shore toward him.

"Where's the boat?"

Janatuinen pointed behind her.

"We pulled it ashore down that way."

"Uh-huh."

The dog came up to Janatuinen with his ears back, sniffed her pant leg, and wagged his tail. Janatuinen thought that if she touched the dog she might catch something.

"The oars are another story," she said.

"How so?"

Janatuinen pointed in front of her.

"They went thataway."

"Uh-huh."

Keijo looked with satisfaction at the river, as if this were proof that Janatuinen had done a thorough job.

"I heard something that sounded like a shot," he said.

Janatuinen described the creatures that had come out of the water and what she and the raskel had done to them.

"Oh, those," Keijo said.

Janatuinen stared at him. The raskel stood next to her like a lackey. The dog snuffed at his furry leg and whimpered. The raskel eyed the dog like a snack.

"What are they?" Janatuinen asked.

"River wretches."

"What?"

"Poor devils who drowned in the river."

"Do you mean they're dead people?"

"Yeah. My cousin mighta been among 'em."

Janatuinen looked at the river. It looked innocent enough. Near the shore, a school of dace was nibbling floating insects from below.

"What else should I know?" she asked.

"About what?"

Janatuinen pointed at the raskel, who was calmly breathing in and out, seeming satisfied with the day's amusements. The dog had returned to Keijo's side and was keeping a sharp eye on the raskel.

"What else is there around here that I should look out for?"

"Well… There might be bears in the woods."

"I'm talking about monsters."

"What monsters?"

Janatuinen pointed at the raskel again.

"You could say the same about the Tervos' boy."

Janatuinen sighed.

"Where is Ylijaako?"

"She's on the other side of the river. Cross the bridge and turn left, then keep going till the road runs out."

Janatuinen thanked him and climbed up the riverbank. Keijo, the dog, and the raskel followed. Janatuinen walked past Keijo's house and through the brush to the fishing-gear shop, where her car was parked. The old man she'd seen at the bus stop was leaning against her car with a round, flat piece of wood in his hand. He looked like he'd been there a while. When he saw the three of them coming, he gave a start, extracted himself from the support the car offered, and stood swaying on his feet. Janatuinen thought the fellow had been startled by the raskel, but he was actually looking at her.

"Buy one?" the old man said, holding out the piece of wood in a mechanical, listless manner.

"Pay no mind to him," Keijo said.

"Hold on," Janatuinen said, and took off her backpack. She got out her wallet. The old man's swaying stopped abruptly. He hardly dared to breathe. Maybe he was afraid that he might somehow, with some innocent gesture, spoil the sudden surge in demand.

"How much?" Janatuinen asked, pointing to the doodad he was holding.

The old man stared at Janatuinen's wallet very ceremoniously, as if it were a holy relic. Janatuinen glanced at Keijo. He didn't say anything.

Janatuinen checked her wallet.

"Will this do?"

The old man stared at the bill she was holding and said, "Coins."

"Pardon me?"

"I take coins."

"This much in coins?"

The old man nodded.

"Yeah."

"All right."

Janatuinen turned the contents of her wallet out in the old man's hand. He put the money in his pocket, gave the piece of wood to her, and left.

"Thanks very much," Janatuinen yelled. The old man didn't respond, just continued walking toward the village.

"Do what you like," Keijo said, watching him go.

"I'll be on my way," Janatuinen said.

"Bon voyage."

Janatuinen got in her car, put her pack in the back seat, and started the engine.

It was stiflingly hot inside. She rolled down her window. The back-seat door opened. Janatuinen looked in the rearview mirror and saw the raskel sitting in the back seat, grinning.

"Could you get out please?" Janatuinen said.

The raskel gave a snort and snickered.

"He's just a big dog," Janatuinen said. Then she let out the clutch and drove off.

I O

Janatuinen drove to the end of the village, turned onto the bridge, drove across it, and turned left. She glanced in the rearview mirror. The raskel was sitting in the back seat, sweetly serene, and if the movement of the car was an unusual experience for him, there was certainly no indication of it.

The car used to belong to Commissioner Kyyhky. It was the same wheels he'd used when he came to Lapland years before. Janatuinen had intended to go in her own three-year-old Audi, but Kyyhky had rejected the idea out of hand. He said that driving a newer model would arouse suspicion and she should take his car.

The Toyota had no third gear and its left-turn indicator worked only sporadically, but it had a steering wheel and a gas pedal and it got her where she was going.

Fields, houses. Janatuinen drove slowly; she wanted to see everything. The atmosphere on this side of the river was even more peculiar than on the village road. Every yard formed its own kingdom. One house had four cars in the yard, stacked in a pile. Another had a rosebush at one end, surrounded by a concrete shot-put ring, and a man spinning around, ready to heave a shot.

"Look at this place," Janatuinen said.

They cruised past handmade mailboxes and gazebos with odd ornamentation. Empty barns like colossal larval insect casings. Some of the barns were still in use; even in the car you could hear the sound of milk machines and cows mooing. There were cows in the fields, too, lumpen and apathetic. A smell of manure.

People were outside cleaning up after the storm. There was a fire burning in every yard and people hauling broken branches to feed to the fires. They paused and stopped pushing their wheelbarrows as Janatuinen drove past, staring expressionlessly, as if they sensed through the steel frame of the car that she was an outsider. Some lifted a hand in greeting, but Janatuinen didn't return it. She didn't know these people. She was sure that every one of them had a criminal record. Then the people and houses ended and forest rose up on both sides of the road. It continued for several kilometers. Just as Janatuinen was wondering whether she had missed Ylijaako's house, she came around a corner and had to stop, because there was an ancient tractor in the middle of the road.

It sat there and didn't budge, as if it had been put there by the local authorities as a roadblock. Great meadows stretched out on either side. There was a road across the meadow on the left that led to a now-familiar configuration of buildings—a veteran's tract house in need of paint, a barn, and a shed. Janatuinen had stopped ten meters from the tractor. Its windows were covered in a lumpy coat of dried gray mud. Janatuinen could just make out a figure in the cab. She got out of her car and walked toward the tractor. Yes, there was someone in it.

Janatuinen knocked on the door.

"Hello? Is everything all right?"

The figure in the cab gave a start. The tractor's engine started up with a puff of gray smoke from its smokestack, and the machine lurched forward. Janatuinen leaped into the ditch. The driver turned away from her and hit the gas. The antique contraption let out a comical whinny as it went into high gear. Janatuinen watched it go. When it reached the crossroads it slowed suddenly. It turned onto the meadow road and rattled toward the farmhouse.

Janatuinen drove after it. Throughout this whole episode the raskel sat demurely in his place and gave no reaction even when the car stopped and sped up again.

The tractor stopped in the farmyard next to the shed. Janatuinen parked beside it. An old guy in a gray fleece and billed hat climbed out of the tractor. He looked at Janatuinen with undisguised hostility and walked toward the house.

Janatuinen got out of her car.

"Hey," she said.

The old-timer turned around.

"What?"

"Is this the Ylijaako place?"

He spit on the ground.

"No."

"Could you tell me where the Ylijaako place is?"

The old-timer gave Janatuinen a weary look.

"I'm a police officer," Janatuinen said.

"Is this some kind of prank?"

"I'm Detective Janatuinen. I've come about a homicide."

"I see!" the old man said, with evident delight.

"Do you know what I'm talking about?"

He nodded, smiling as if the day had taken a new and brighter turn.

"The whole village knows."

"I'm looking for someone named Elina Ylijaako."

"Who?"

Janatuinen was about to repeat the name when the old man interrupted her and yelled, "Young Lady Ylijaako?"

"Yes."

"Well, listen. I'll tell you. Come on in."

The old-timer walked toward the house and turned to glance back at her.

"Did you know you got a raskel in your back seat?"

"I know."

"Let's go then."

He walked to the front door and Janatuinen followed. When she reached the steps, she turned and went back to her car, opened the door to the back seat, and said to the raskel, "Don't poo in the car."

The raskel's smile widened.

Janatuinen left the car door open and jogged back to the man. They took off their shoes in the spacious front hall and went into a large living area. There was a long table, a baking oven, a wood-burning stove, and a plank floor covered in long, colorful rag rugs. In the corner was a rocking chair and a grandfather clock.

There was another old fellow at the stove, stirring a pot of food. "Are you hungry yet?" he yelled, without looking up.

"We have company."

The man at the stove turned.

"Huh?"

The first fellow pointed at Janatuinen, who waved and said her name was Janatuinen.

"She's a cop," the old-timer said.

"Asko," the man at the stove said. "What'd you do?"

"I didn't do anything. She's come to talk about that witch Ylijaako."

The man at the stove wiped his hand on his jeans and put out his hand. "Efraim."

Janatuinen shook his hand.

"She's got a raskel in her car," Asko said.

Efraim stared at Janatuinen, then at Asko, and then at Janatuinen again. "I guess you know what happened to Elviira?"

"No."

"You'll find out soon enough," Asko said. "Have a seat at the table."

The grandfather clock had a long copper pendulum. The sides of the clock were decorated with carvings of enormous mosquitoes carrying off cows, horses, and people in their thin claws.

"Company first," Efraim said, setting a chipped bowl full of meat stew in front of Janatuinen. Bones and marrow, tendons and membranes. A few chunks of carrot and potato. Janatuinen dipped the tip of her spoon into the broth, raised it to her mouth, and tasted. Fatty. Meaty. She lowered her spoon and asked what the two men knew about Ylijaako.

"Just that it's high time the police took an interest," Asko said. He dug marrow out of the center of a bone with his knife and licked it off.

"Why is that?"

Asko put down his knife.

"She killed my brother."

Janatuinen took a notebook and pen out of her pocket and gave the pen a click.

"Your brother's name?"

"Auvo Unto Olavi Pasma."

"It's not for sure," Efraim said.

Asko nodded toward Janatuinen.

"She'll investigate," he said.

"The truth…" Efraim said, picking up his spoon and brandishing it in front of his guest like a piece of evidence, "can go through fire without burning away. Wouldn't you say, Officer?"

"Is it all right if I ask some questions?"

"No need. I'll tell you."

"I'd like to proceed systematically."

"It's all up here," Asko said, tapping a finger against his temple. "Systematical."

"Ha," Efraim said.

Asko turned to him.

"What?"

"I said, 'Ha.'"

"Could you please let me speak to our guest in peace?"

Efraim snorted.

"Thank you. My brother was the local police chief. A damn good, handy fellow. His widow Heta still runs the co-op here in the village. They got two boys. They're already out in the world now. Write down that Auvo was always ready to pitch in. He'd help with whatever he was asked to. And he worked hard for his family. Unlike Young Lady Ylijaako, who didn't do an honest day's work that anybody saw. A no-account child of a no-account family. But she happened to be born in stormy weather, at that planetary point when the spirit throng went thundering across the worlds till sparks were flying, and the land hunched its back like the billows of the sea, and the throng didn't spare a human child, just went right through her, like a flash fire. And they scorched and burned up all the innocence that's the blessing of birth for the rest of us and they soaked her through with magic powers and supernatural capabilities, and that's why she was an evil witch from the day she let out her first cry."

Efraim came to the table with a bowl of soup for himself.

"She was a con artist, just like you," he said.

"What?"

"I said she was a con artist, just like you are."

"A downright criminal is what she was. 'Member that time in the summer when she came walking past our place, looking in our yard? Giving the evil eye to Vekku? And then Vekku died."

"He died a year later."

"It wasn't a year. Six months, maybe seven. However long it was, Vekku wouldn't eat a bite or set foot out of the house, not even just to go for a run or do some rabbit hunting. And he was the best rabbit dog in the village."

"He was an awfully good dog," Efraim conceded.

"I tried to resurrect him," Asko said. "A dead spirit can be resurrected if you know the right tricks. I hollered Vekku's name in a dream. But he didn't answer. Didn't answer, no matter how I called and whistled. Then I knew that Ylijaako had tossed his soul into the belly of a pike, and even the Devil can't come up from out of that—or maybe only the Devil can."

"Around here," Efraim explained, "people believe that a pike can travel between this world and the other side."

Turning to Asko, he said, "I think he just died of old age."

"Into a pike's belly is where he went, damn it."

"Our Asko here is getting a little *köpö*," Efraim said to no one in particular. To his soup.

"How 'bout we start at the beginning," Asko said. "So our guest can get to the meat of the matter. From the time she was in diapers, Young Lady Ylijaako always had her nose in a book. That oughta've been a red flag that the Filthy One had been having his way with her soul. No normal person reads that much. And she didn't talk about what she was reading, either. It was like a storage chest where she was piling more stuff all the time, but when you opened the lid, there was nothing there. The chest was empty. Where'd all that knowledge go? To hell! See, she couldn't talk about any of what she was reading, because that knowledge in her head was ripening into a tool of darkness. One time, the other kids at recess were playing 'caught in the corner' while this one was sitting on the swings, reading some tome, and Arijoutsi, the caretaker, comes over and asks, 'Whatcha readin'?' and she stared that caretaker down so bad he nearly peed his pants. That's another one that comes to mind. It just so happens she gave him the evil eye, too, and it wasn't five years later he was dead and buried."

Asko stopped and looked at Efraim.

"Did ya hear that?"

Efraim ate his soup in silence.

"Arijoutsi tied a copper wire around his waist and tied the other end to a rock and threw the rock over the electrical wire. Zapped him right where he stood. Who would get it in his head to do something like that?"

"He had an alcohol problem," Efraim said.

"Nobody would, unless something possessed him. And anyway, everybody thought that girl's not so smart, she's a right dimwit, so how could she even fathom what it was she was reading? She never said anything in class, either, never raised her hand. So it was a real surprise to everybody when she finished school and waved goodbye and caught the train to apply to the university, and she got in. With the highest scores. That made some jaws drop around here. Super intelligent all of a sudden! But of course she did good on the test, since she had Old Nick looking over her shoulder and pointing out the right answers with his crooked finger. And her parents just shook their heads that their rag of a girl would throw her life away sitting on a school bench. Well, the girl liked to study, but she sure didn't like the city, 'cause it was swarming with people, like bugs they were, and when it comes to that, I agree with her. You can't even turn around in the city without knocking into somebody. So she walked up to the dean's office and told him she was chucking it in. The dean gave her the same look we used to give her when we were kids and he said, after all, the fun was just getting started. And she told him her mind was made up and she came back here that same evening. Her parents were awfully pleased. And they were about beside themselves with happiness when she took a look at one of the boys hanging around and drinking on the corner by the co-op, and it happened to be

Kauko Ylijaako. They got married and the first thing Young Lady Ylijaako got to work on was drilling a hole to hell there in the swamp and that's when things got rolling."

"Pike Pond has always been there, you know," Efraim said.

"Yeah, but she made it into her witch's cauldron."

"Hogwash."

"That was how she got a direct line to Satan. All of a sudden the Ylijaakos were succeeding in everything they set out to do. Kauko started up the sawmill and made a hell of a lot of money."

"It did go bankrupt."

"But it made a profit at first."

"They ran it for a year. Probably didn't even break even."

"Well, do you remember their fields?"

"What about 'em?"

"Never seen such top growth on spuds—in June!"

"They were perfectly normal."

"You could see those spuds growing right before your eyes. And such airs she gave herself, such airs. Waltzing around the village with her nose in the air, and if somebody spoke to her, she wouldn't say a word back to 'em. You could see from a mile away that she thought she was better than everybody else."

"She was just quiet."

"Proud as could be was what that bride of Satan was."

"And she did study agricultural science, after all. Don't you think it's normal that a woman who studied farming at the university would be good at farming?"

"Not with soil like they had. And now we come to this," Asko said, waving a finger. "Young Lady Ylijaako did not like it that there was another person in the village who was a big shot when it came to farming. And that was my brother Auvo. You see, Auvo wasn't just the local police chief. He was also the chairman of the village farm association. And out of the kindness of his heart he let this new potato princess into the association's government. And that sure didn't work out. In the very first meeting, this girl starts right in, advising them about how to sow their fields. Grown men! And of course they didn't listen to her. They just laughed in her face. And she got her nose bent out of shape. She even insisted that Auvo talk to them about how they ought to do things her way, but Auvo of course couldn't take her side like that."

"But it was pretty good advice, wasn't it?" Efraim said.

"Good advice?"

"Didn't she suggest they use less fertilizer? And pesticides?"

"Sure, she could grow her own spuds without chemicals— she had her devil buddy helping her out. Old Lucifer would scamper over those fields with his goat's hooves at night and stroke those potato tops and whisper to the spuds under the ground. So, naturally, they grew fat and sweet. I remember I once ate an Ylijaako spud and I thought to myself, if sin has a taste, this is it. It was such a good spud. But it was not Christian food. So anyway, Young Lady Ylijaako decided that she needed to clear Auvo out of the way."

"Can I ask you something?" Janatuinen said.

"That university dean traveled all the way here to try to talk her into coming back to the university. Can you believe it. That's how wily the Devil is. The dean came to the village with his fancy hat in his hand and tramped up those porch

steps built with spud money and rang the doorbell. They had
a doorbell, for heaven's sake. And that dean sat at the kitchen
table with his suit jacket and his combed hair, saying please
and thank you and pardon me and other nonsense. From what
I heard, he sat there a quarter of an hour, sipping coffee and
telling them how fine the house was decorated, and then he
got to the point and said that she ought to come back to the
university. Apparently he said that she was the most talented
student he'd ever seen and she had a fine future as a doctor and
a professor and who knows what sort of bigwig at the pinnacle
of science and that she had potential and she shouldn't throw
it away, not just for her own sake but for the world of science.
Young Lady Ylijaako absolutely refused. You shoulda seen
the look on the dean's face. First he paints a picture of all this
loveliness for her, and she just says it doesn't suit her. But what
does a human position mean when you've been promised the
highest seat in Lucifer's palace and a minister's post in hell?"

"How did she kill your brother?" Janatuinen asked.

"She threw his soul into a pike's belly."

"Ah. Like your dog."

"Vekku was just for practice. And, by the way, that's the kind
of magic you need a specialty level consultation for."

"I see. With Satan?"

Asko didn't answer right away. He pointed at Janatuinen's
notebook.

"You haven't been writing for a long time. Haven't written
anything I've said."

"I have a good memory."

"Or maybe you don't believe what I'm saying."

"To be honest, quite a lot of it sounds like complete rubbish."

Asko folded his hands on the table.

"How it sounds is not the point," he said. "And she didn't get her help from Satan. Satan has a wide range of work he does in this world. Loads of it. He's so busy keeping wars and torture and trouble going that he can't look after one witch woman all the time. Young Lady Ylijaako asked a friend for help."

"What friend?"

"Slabber Olli."

"Here we go," Efraim said.

"Who's Slabber Olli?"

Asko laughed.

"It's not a who: it's a what."

Elina walked down the farm road. She passed the place where she had turned into the swamp earlier. Light and warmth descended on her like a thick, radiant blanket. The little stones of the road crunched under her feet. Clouds of mosquitoes, like a disturbance in her field of vision. When she reached Big Inlet, she turned left into the birches and aspens. A path dotted with hare droppings wound through the trees. She came to the riverbank. There, among the water lilies, half drawn onto the sand, was Hoot's boat. It was actually Elina's boat. She bought it with reforestation money when she was fifteen and rowed it all the way home from the village.

If there was one thing she had done in her life, it was rowing. She had rowed that river downstream and up. She'd taken leisurely floats down the rapids, cast her fly, guided her lure through the counter currents, and pulled out bucketloads of brown trout and rainbows and graylings. Bushels of them.

Elina put the box of pie down on the boat's middle thwart and started to row. There was a spider under the left-hand oarlock, frozen in a star position, like a scar. It lived in the boat and had no say in deciding which destinations it traveled to. This arrangement suited the spider fine, because the boat was its home, not the worlds it traveled to.

The boat glided over the water lilies. When it reached deeper waters, the lilies ended, and that was where the waves began. They pummeled the side of the boat like little fists, becoming slightly larger fists the farther she went. Only the most eager mosquitoes were still along for the trip. Soon even those were blown away. Elina rowed toward Dead Man's Island. A puff of cold wind blew off of it. When she was halfway there, the wind started to blow in earnest and slowed the boat almost to a standstill. Elina hauled on the oars. She felt weak, and the harder she pulled, the harder the wind blew, which was not a coincidence. But it didn't even occur to her to turn back. The pie and meatballs shifted in her stomach, trying to find some space.

She dipped the oars into the waves and pulled, just about ready to vomit into her own lap. Suddenly the boat shot forward, as if she had broken through a wall. She lifted the oars and held them up as she slipped toward the shore, the flats of the oars' tips dripping with water like the bills of wading birds. Elina sat bent over, panting. She turned to look at the island. It loomed over her, black, another new test—how many were there going to be? The boat slid onto the sand and stopped.

.   .   .

Efraim cleared the table and Asko moved to the rocking chair. He pushed off with a foot and got rocking as he spoke.

"Slabber Olli was the hired hand at the Ylijaako place back in the 1880s. He got his name from when he worked as a roofer as a young man, putting shingles on barn roofs. Always had a handful of nails in his mouth. There were minerals in the nails that ate his teeth away, and after that he had a sloppy way of talking. Slabber Olli was a hardworking man. The tricks he came up with to get around problems seemed impossible until you saw them work. He was an awfully clever hand with the knacky. People say the two of them were seen playing cards on the riverbank many times. The knacky would just laugh sweetly even when it lost, and grab up whitefish for Olli by the fistful. Old Ylijaako profited by that, too. He would come back from fishing, grinning from ear to ear, his nets full of great big perch. Then, one time, Ylijaako found Slabber Olli leaning against a fence like a pitchfork. So he got mad and yelled at Olli, who wasn't usually lazy, always busy at something. But Olli still didn't move, so Ylijaako went over to him and saw that his face was all white. The old farmhand had died. Ylijaako took his hat off then and thanked Slabber Olli for his years of good service. Then he started to ponder what to do with the body. He didn't feel like taking it to the churchyard. And anyway, if he did bring it over there, the burial would cost a lot. So Ylijaako had him buried on Dead Man's Island. There were other dead buried there, too. But unlike the others on the island, Slabber Olli wasn't at peace there for some reason."

. . .

Elina pulled the boat ashore, tied it to a birch, and went inland. The slopes of Dead Man's Island were steep. She immediately had to start climbing, almost on all fours. She held onto the box of pie with one hand and with the other she grabbed birch and spruce branches and pulled herself up. She had to dig her feet well into the ground with every step and clamber up like a bear in a dense stand of spruce. Soon the ground leveled out enough that she could stand up. The spruce trees stood thick, dark green. They stood close together, tall ones and short ones, forming a tight knit that she made her way through. Under the trees it was shady and damp. Thick, lush mats of green moss grew on the ground, and wandering through it were springtails, potworms, and all sorts of earthworms and other creatures of decomposition that had been born and raised on the island. The island was the whole world to them, the water around it immeasurable, the land beyond nothing but a dream. Spiders had built webs between the spruce trees. Elina kept walking into them, brushing them off her face. After she passed, the spiders started spinning new ones.

She made her way toward the center of the island, where she seemed to recall there was a small clearing— and indeed there was. There was nothing in the clearing but grass and ferns, and light falling down from a space between the trees like in a shrine. Elina stood in the middle of the clearing and looked straight up. There was so much light that she had to close her eyes. She rested for a little while in that pose, and the mosquitoes settled around her face like a veil.

She headed northeast and studied the terrain, looking for old grave mounds. She found one, pressed her ear against it, and listened. Got up and kept going.

She came to a little moss-covered mound with blueberries and lingonberries growing on it. The plant life was so dense and lush in some places that she couldn't make out the graves. She knelt down and pressed her ear to the most promising spots, as if Mother Earth herself were pregnant and she would be able to make out the heartbeats of the new life developing under the dirt. She checked five mounds, all of them silent. Then she found one that was collapsed in the middle, as if something had been dug up there, or something had risen from it. She stopped, bent over the twig-strewn hollow, and listened for sounds of snoring. Nothing. She knew this was the right spot.

Elina sat down next to the grave and said, "Get up, Slabber Olli. It's a beautiful day." Then she set to waiting. She didn't feel like sitting, so she lay down on her back and closed her eyes.

"But the dead aren't like the living," Asko said. "They have their own kingdoms and hierarchies and councils. They grow and shrink and take on new forms. New jobs. Death itself doesn't necessarily mean anything. In death, you and I move into a different society, with different laws, and according to those laws the soul itself is a currency in a barter economy. Souls on the other side are like plastic that the Devil recycles. When somebody on this side shouts to the other side, there's no telling who will answer. The one they're calling for might be gone. They might be part of something else."

.   .   .

145

Elina may have fallen asleep. She sat up and brushed the leaves and needles and sprigs off her back. The light was different. Grayer.

She heard a rustle behind her.

She turned. The spruce trees were moving. No. Someone behind them was moving. Some thing. Steps, stealthy. Elina held her breath. She slowly got up and stood with her upper body twisted toward the sound. She didn't move her feet because she didn't want to reveal her location. She slowly inhaled. Two treetops trembled. Slowly exhaled. Spruce branches rocked. The trees parted.

She could see it now.

It was big, more than two meters tall. It was hard to say what it looked like because it felt like it had everything on the island in it. As if the core of the thing was a spirit so naked that it had gathered what it needed to function in this world from things it found around it. It looked like a root system, or a walking spruce tree. But you could clearly make out two arms and two legs made of some slender tree, maybe a rowan, and its footsteps were delicate and soundless, like those of an elk. Its head was a stump shoved down between its shoulders, shapeless, still forming.

It was just ten meters away. It reached out a hand, wrapped its fingers around a wrist-thick birch trunk, and snapped it in two like a matchstick. A dry, hollow, cracking sound. Woodchips and dust. It held the birch in front of it like a sword, or a cane for the blind, and waved it left, then right. The creature was feeling the trees and the ground in front of it, making a space for itself.

The head was nearly finished now. It looked like a human skull, but it had no eyes.

The creature spoke.

"Jestem leszy. Jestem las. Gdzie jesteś?"

The voice was deep and calm. Elina didn't recognize the language. The jaw of the skull didn't move, and the voice seemed to come from just behind it. As if the creature were a stage prop, and its real identity were hidden somewhere in the wings.

"Słyszę cię. Gdzie jesteś?"

Seven meters. Elina looked behind her, chose a spot, and took a step. The creature stopped. It tilted its dried snag of a head.

Elina still didn't breathe. The creature stretched the birch tree out toward her, turned in her direction, and stepped closer, over a fallen trunk. Elina backed up a step. The creature looked weightless. As if it were controlled from above, like a marionette, its feet just touching the ground as part of the trick.

"Gdzie jesteś?"

It couldn't be Slabber Olli. It was something else. Elina didn't know where it had come from or what it was capable of or how fast it could be. All she knew for certain was that the darkness that had made a nest inside her was denser and more horrible than the dry-stick god before her.

Elina said, "Who are you?"

The creature stopped and tilted its head again.

"What?"

It understood her. Elina concentrated on keeping her voice level and said:

"I'm looking for Slabber Olli."

"I've been called by that name."

The creature approached her, guided by her voice. It waved the birch tree as if blessing the ground in front of it. Elina backed up, keeping the distance between them.

"I'm Elina Ylijaako," Elina said. Then she thought for a moment and said, "You were a farmhand for my granddad's granddad."

"I once knew an Ylijaako."

"You are Slabber Olli."

The creature stopped for a heartbeat and Elina knew she was right.

"I need your help."

There was a sound like pieces of birchwood scraping together. Elina realized that the creature was laughing.

"I can see the mark that's on you. No one can help you."

"You can."

The creature didn't answer.

"I want you to drive the knacky away from Pike Pond."

"The knacky?" Slabber Olli laughed again, but now it was the way you laugh at an old memory.

"Will you help me?"

"I shouldn't."

"Name your price."

"Let me eat you."

Elina closed her eyes and shook her head.

"Name your price."

"You have nothing for me. Let me eat you."

They walked through the trees—Elina in front, Slabber Olli following.

Late-evening light filtered through the branches.

"Let me eat you."

The creature's mouth was filled with teeth hewn from chunks of granite, which it opened and shut with a loud clack. The sound of it boomed in Elina's body and sent ripples of terror through her that she could not allow to grow for even a second, not one instant.

So she lifted her head and looked right at Slabber Olli, right into his greedy mouth, and said in a loud voice, "I have something. Something I can give you. I brought rhubarb pie. You can have it. But I won't give you my life."

Slabber Olli stopped. Closed his mouth. Sat down on the ground, as if he were tired.

He sat with his knees bent, poking up in front of him, and suddenly he just looked pitiful and miserable, like a poor forest beggar attempting to disguise himself as a tree man.

He said, "You must really like to suffer."

"Yeah. Yeah, I do."

"Dziwna dziewczyna."

Elina waited.

"That curse of yours will make an end of you in a hurry. But in principle you do still have a little time left."

Elina waited for him to continue, but he said nothing more. He was perfectly still.

A great tit was flying above Slabber Olli's head. Elina could have sworn that he didn't move, not the slightest bit, but there was a sound like a whip's lash, a flash of green darted out of the skull like lightning, and the bird was in Slabber Olli's mouth.

Feathers floated around his head.

Slabber Olli worked his mouth, swallowed. Then he straightened up and spoke. He said that right after he died he wandered around Dead Man's Island, missing being with people. Every now and then someone would come to the island, but they couldn't see him, even when he spoke to them, shouted at them, tried to touch them. Then a serious little child had come to the island and looked straight at him and asked his name. Elina knew that Slabber Olli was talking about her mother. The child had asked questions that a child shouldn't ask, and Slabber Olli answered every question.

The child came to the island many times. They would sit together on the shore. Then she stopped coming. Slabber Olli had waited for her. He had started sleeping. He had slept and lain inside the earth and learned to think the earth's thoughts. He had calmed himself, preparing to dissolve into his original elements, but instead he had percolated down into chambers where demands were made. He had started to forget his own outlines, and it came as a surprise to him that there could be someone who still thought of him as a person, as someone who still had work to do. He didn't have much left to barter with.

Slabber Olli looked very small and fragile now. He looked like he'd had a terrible shock. As if a creature such as he was could be shocked by something.

He told Elina he had been sent to study worlds, those past and those to come, and the travel wasn't free—everything was for sale. He had already given up his eyes and even part of his soul, of which he had little left, and he needed more capital. He said there are still those great big mosquitoes in this world, and parts of them could be worth something in the places where he traveled.

"Stripefoots," Elina said.

"If you bring me the snout of a stripefoot, then I can arrange to have the water critter that you call the knacky stop bothering you. But it has to be a fresh snout. And if you don't bring it by tomorrow, then I get to eat you."

This was the second time in one day that Elina's very life was at stake, and she wasn't sure how long her luck would hold out. On the other hand, this wasn't a matter of a lucky hand of cards or a coin toss; it was about whether she was ready to do the work. Elina was good at work.

"Agreed."

Slabber Olli raised his head and opened his mouth. A thick green tongue slithered out to taste the air, as if it were checking the temperature.

"We have a deal," Slabber Olli said. "I'm afraid you won't be able to get what I'm asking for."

Elina looked at Slabber Olli. She wondered what he knew about other worlds, and this one. What kinds of wisdom he'd gathered on his travels. Then she probed her own will, which she and she alone controlled, and she told Slabber Olli she would prove him wrong.

He made no response to this claim.

"You said you had a present for me," he said.

"Yeah."

Elina went to where he was sitting, sat down beside him, and opened the box. Slabber Olli watched what she was doing closely, like an old man sympathetically watching a child at play.

"Cozy," he said.

Elina took out the plate of pie and handed it to the monster. With fingers that were branches, he picked up a piece, slowly and deliberately, as if he remembered the fragile, crumbly nature of pie. He set the piece of pie on the ground beside him. A swarm of ants seethed out of the ground and set upon the pie and ate it, crawling all over it.

Slabber Olli told her about the places he had been. He had been to the bottom of the sea and wandered endless gardens of stars in outer space. He said that human time as we know it was over. That the waters would rise and then fall, and then fiery waters would come. The earth would be reshaped into something new. Mud would flow. Boiling canyons would open up.

"The mountains are already starting to move," Slabber Olli said.

He told her about creatures that used to live in the sea, like reptiles with two mouths, a horizontal one and a vertical one. He told her about creatures at the bottom of the sea shaped like elm leaves, with five eyes and long, bendy elephant trunks and scissors on their heads. About sharks with anvils growing on their backs. Flightless birds three meters tall that ran after deer on graceful, muscular legs that bent and stretched, bent and stretched, their beaks opened wide. He told her about the rockets people would build to shoot themselves off to other planets, and how badly it would turn out. Humans would continue their journey. They would find doors to knock on and portals that wouldn't open when they knocked, and the humans would break them down, and the ones they couldn't break they would build keys for. And all the while, humans would be changing. Humans would be changed not just by time but by humans themselves, and before long you'd have to call them human derivatives, and then something else entirely. In the end, it was just matter rearranging itself over and over. What was the earth? Nothing more than an entrance hall where humanity had once briefly waited.

Slabber Olli talked about a lot of other things, too, and Elina listened and understood that the part of Slabber Olli that was still human wanted to wander and search for knowledge, just like anyone else. The evening advanced, the light softened. At some point, Slabber Olli disappeared. Elina went back to the boat.

11

"That doesn't sound like Christian talk," Efraim said.

"I put things together based on my own experience," Asko
said. Efraim looked at him like a man who had been listening
to another person's blather so long that he was out of reactions.
There was no light in the room. They sat in the dimness, the
dust rising and falling, and Janatuinen felt as if she'd gotten
lost on a film set where the funding had suddenly dried up
and everyone had left, except for two actors still waiting for a
signal from the director.

"How do you know all this?" she asked.

"About Slabber Olli?" Asko said.

"No, about Ylijaako."

"We went to school together."

"How is that possible?"

Asko glanced at Efraim, as if he didn't understand the
question.

"We just did."

"Are you telling me that you're the same age as Elina
Ylijaako?"

"No, I'm the same age as Markareetta Ylijaako."

"Who?"

"Markareetta. Marke. Maiden name Ala-Tokoi."

"It's spelled Mar-*ga*-re-ta," Efraim said.

"The person I'm looking for is named Elina Ylijaako," Janatuinen said.

"Right," Efraim said. "That's Marke's daughter."

Janatuinen dropped her pen on the table and looked at them. Looked at Efraim.

"We've been talking about the wrong person this whole time."

Asko and Efraim had nothing to say to this.

"But you said *Young Lady* Ylijaako."

"Well, that's true for him, because he doesn't remember that Elina exists," Efraim said. "Has Elina done anything wrong?"

"Where is this Margareta Ylijaako?"

"Marke Ylijaako has been dead and laid in her grave for nine years."

Janatuinen rubbed her face with her hands.

"It just keeps getting better."

Asko looked taken aback.

"Is Marke dead?"

Efraim tilted his head toward Asko and said,

"Didn't I tell you he was a bit of a *köpö*?"

Janatuinen sighed.

"What does *köpö* mean?"

"Like him. Slow on the uptake."

Asko stared at the table.

"Marke, dead."

"I should go," Janatuinen said. She scooted her chair back and stood up. "Thanks for the food."

"Why're you looking for Elina?" Efraim asked.

"She's suspected of a serious crime. Is that house just down the way the Ylijaako place?"

"Lord in heaven."

"Is it or isn't it?"

"It is. But you shouldn't head over there right now."

Janatuinen stood beside her chair.

"Why is that?"

"Tonight's a throng night."

"A what?"

"The night after a great storm. When the spirits walk abroad."

Janatuinen stared at him.

Efraim nodded toward the window.

"Look outside."

Janatuinen looked out at the dark farmyard. The river.

"I don't see anything unusual."

Asko roused from his daze and said, "Kusti, God rest his soul, went to use the outhouse on a throng night, and he never came back. Nothing left of him but his shoes and pants, left there in front of the privy hole when his soul was hauled off to the land of the dead."

"You're not serious."

"You can spend the night here," Efraim said. "But I can tell you that whatever it is Elina's accused of, there's gotta be some kind of mistake."

"Well, we're investigating it," Janatuinen said.

She knew she wouldn't sleep a wink if she stayed in this house. She went to the window and looked out over the field to the edge of the woods. There was a small cabin and shed there.

"Who lives there?"

"Hoot," Efraim said.

"A pleasant fellow," Asko said. "Even if he is always going in and out at the Ylijaakos'."

"Is there a hotel in the village?"

"Not in this village," Efraim said. "But there's an inn over in town."

"Well, I guess I'll spend the night there."

"Course, I don't know when the last time was that anybody stayed there."

"Thank you. I'm sure it's fine."

"Well, I don't really know."

"I'll be going now."

"Well, do it quick then. Hop in the car and get going. And don't stop anyplace, no matter what, just keep going till you get there. Although I do believe your car is a goner if you left that raskel in it."

Janatuinen put on her shoes and ran out the door.

Elina rowed away from the island. When she came ashore, a denser and hungrier cloud of mosquitoes joined her. She walked slowly down the farm road back to the house. The light was still strong, gold and gray. She had been in the south so long that she'd started to understand travelers who went to Lapland in the summer and ended up wandering around outside in the middle of a white night, addled from lack of sleep.

She wondered what kind of deal she'd just made. Hope flowed through her.

Everything was in motion again. Everything except the hours, repeating, always the same, hot and filled with mosquitoes, and she could feel time, and her surroundings, burrowing into her will, softening it, but the will was still there, and she used it to stagger through the bugs and the light.

There was a goldeneye feather lying in the middle of the road. In a state partly sunk in memory and partly in pain, only faintly conscious of this world, Elina bent down and picked it up…

HOW ELINA GATHERED A BACKPACK FULL OF BIRD FEATHERS AND JOUSIA PLUCKED A STONE FROM THE RIVER

They needed a game. They didn't know it themselves, but their bodies knew, so Jousia said that they should put on a play with toys. Elina thought it was a good idea. They gathered their dolls and teddy bears and barricaded themselves upstairs at Jousia's house and started acting out scenes from classic movies. Then they found that they weren't able to express the emotions deeply enough with the toys, so they started doing the acting themselves. And it wasn't very long before they were playing the parts of Scarlett O'Hara and Rhett Butler. With Elina as Rhett and Jousia as Scarlett, because it was funny, and Elina lifted Jousia's chin with her thumb and told him, "You should be kissed, and often, and by someone who knows how…" When Jousia said, "I suppose you think you're the proper person?", Elina kissed him.

"Oho," Jousia said.

They stared at each other.

"That's not how the scene goes," Jousia said.

"Isn't it?"

"No."

Suddenly the acting didn't seem so important anymore.

After that, they did everything together. Even household chores that had seemed deathly dull before, like raking, folding laundry, or tidying the woodshed, were filled with meaning if they did them together, just the two of them. Their parents took merciless advantage of this.

Elina and Jousia saw each other almost every day that summer, and the days when they were apart were the unbearable exceptions.

At the end of the summer, when the birch leaves were already yellow and there was a cold edge in the wind, Elina took Jousia to visit her neighbors, Asko and Efraim.

"It's about time," Efraim shouted from the porch when he saw them coming, and went in to make some pancakes. Asko shook Elina's hand in a formal manner, as if he had never met her. When she introduced herself, he flinched, turned his back on her, and went in to whisper something to Efraim, who parried him impatiently. Asko went to sit in the corner rocking chair. He rocked and glared at Elina and Jousia as they settled in at the table. Efraim asked Jousia how things were at Loon Spit. Suddenly, in a stony voice, Asko asked what sort of magic Elina's mother had been up to lately. When Elina didn't know how to answer, Asko started telling stories.

He told them about fetchers, helpful creatures, like familiars, that villagers would make in the old days. A fetcher could be made out of practically anything, even a skein of yarn. The fetcher's job was to steal butter, milk, and grain from the neighbors. If you caught a fetcher and broke it, the person who made it would be broken in the same way.

"Like this one," Efraim said, tapping his finger against his temple and nodding toward Asko as he brought the pancakes to the table. "Come and get it."

"Do people still make fetchers?" Jousia asked with his mouth full of pancakes.

"No," Asko said. "They made a pact about it between the villages. The things just bring trouble to everybody."

As they were leaving, Efraim nudged Elina on the shoulder. "Found yourself an awful good boyfriend there."

Elina and Jousia walked to her house. Elina said that Asko himself used to make fetchers in his day. It made the villagers angry, so they broke the fetchers, and Asko's memory with them. That was why Elina had to introduce herself to Asko every time she came over, but it didn't bother her, because Asko talked about the old days. Her mother never did.

"What about your father?"

"He says he doesn't remember anything because before he met Mom all he did was drink."

At a bend in the road they came to a little cabin on the riverbank. A man was sitting on the steps, sharpening a scythe.

"Who's that?" Jousia asked.

"Hoot."

"Weird name."

"I don't know him very well."

Elina and Jousia started high school as a couple. They walked hand in hand to the same schoolyard where they'd lived through the worst three years of their lives, because the high school was right next door to the middle school. They had prepared themselves for catcalls, mud-slinging, and gossip, but everything had changed because their tormentors had all gone to the vocational school.

They were together all throughout high school. Elina was amazed how a life that had been so lonely, dejected, and dreary was suddenly filled with love and light. Jousia's fiery speeches. Nights when it felt like the other person's embrace could go right through your skin.

Jousia listened to her and valued her opinions. Waited while she carefully dressed her ideas in words. Jousia was as preachy as he'd ever been. If he was caught making an error, he was dumbstruck, mortified. In practical matters he was a complete nitwit. Elina had to help him with the simplest everyday things, like cutting the grass or repairing the steps. Jousia's parents were used to his clumsiness and never gave him any chores where he might hurt himself.

But Jousia loved cooking. He baked ovenloads of rolls, sweet buns, and pies that they devoured late into the night.

After three years, Elina thought she knew Jousia inside and out. She knew beforehand how he would react to a surprise setback like a flat bicycle tire or a poor test score. Righteous indignation was Jousia's answer, every single time. Of course, they also clashed once in a while, because they were both stubborn, but all their disagreements ended the same way. They would lie down on the bed and stroke each other's eyebrows and whisper apologies. After every argument, their bond became stronger than before. So what Jousia had to say one day in the spring of their final year of school, on the first really warm day, when they were sitting in the yard at his house, playing a game of chess on an overturned potato box, came as a great shock to Elina.

Jousia said that they should see other people.

At first Elina thought: That must be why he's playing so badly. He had lost his queen on only the seventh move, which was very unusual. But this thought was followed by a choked feeling of horror as she absorbed the meaning of the words. What he was actually saying.

"You want to break up?"

Jousia tugged his hat bill lower on his head.

"Not really. Or... I mean... Yeah. But just for a little while."

Elina put her hands on her cheeks. Her face felt cold.

"Why?"

"Don't you think it's weird that we're planning to be together for the rest of our lives but we've never been with anybody else?"

"I think it's weird that you think it's weird."

"I wanna live."

"We're right here, living, all the time."

They had planned a future together. Jousia would go to art school and Elina to the school of forestry. They would graduate and move back here, build a house near the river, where there was a gentle wind. Jousia would use his art to change the attitudes of the locals and the attitudes of the whole society and become famous. Elina would do entirely new kinds of biological research on the local fish and wildlife.

But apparently the plans had changed. They talked about Jousia's suggestion all that day and the next, but Elina couldn't break through his resolve. She grew tired. She said, "Fine, then. That's what we'll do." She had thought her heart would break and the rest of her would crumble down on top of it, like a building with flimsy support beams. But that wasn't what happened. She didn't feel anything.

They hadn't done anything together for a week, which was the longest they had been apart since the first time she came to his house. Elina concentrated on studying for her entrance exam. She was applying to the school of forestry and was sure she wouldn't get in. The books didn't interest her one bit, but when Jousia called and asked if she could come over, she would have rather learned the name of every species of crane fly by heart, and she had to gather all her strength of will to say, "Yeah."

They had to talk.

Jousia was sitting on the steps, exhausted. He looked like the gerbil Elina had when she was little. The gerbil once managed to get out of its cage and went bouncing around the house until her father caught it with a fishing net. Once they got it back into its cage, the gerbil refused to eat or drink. It just lay in its sawdust nest, apathetic, and her mother said in a strangely flat voice that it had gotten a whiff of freedom and now it wasn't able to think about anything else, and no gifts or treats were going to change its mind. The gerbil died a week later.

Elina and Jousia walked to the shore in silence. Elina realized that she had to be the first to open her mouth.

It annoyed her.

"Let's just break up," she said. "If that's what you want."

Jousia nodded and took her hand.

"I'm afraid," Elina said.

"Remember what you said to me that first time?"

"No."

"You said that the world can't win."

"So?"

"So don't let it win."

Jousia said they could find a rock by the river and transfer their love into the rock, like it was in storage. Elina thought that was a childish idea. Jousia said that there was power in rituals, if you decide that there is.

Elina dug the toe of her shoe into the dirt.

"Whatever you say."

They searched the ground listlessly, unsure whether there was any sense in the idea, but as they searched they gradually became more enthusiastic. They picked up stones at the edge of the water one by one, rejecting each other's choices because they were too wrinkled or cracked or just seemed wrong for some reason. They tried to find heart-shaped stones. Finally, Jousia picked up a small, dark chunk of stone just beneath the surface of the water and let out a yell—"Here!"—and held it out it to her, and she turned it over in her hand and said that from a certain angle it didn't look anything like a heart.

"But that's a good thing. It means that our love has many faces."

"You're not actually serious."

"Are we doing this or not?"

Elina appraised the rock. It was very smooth and very blue.

"OK," she said.

They made up a simple poem that was like a spell. Jousia held the rock in his palm. Elina laid her hand on top of it. They murmured the words in unison. Then Jousia put the rock in his pocket and they talked about entrance exams.

"I'm in a bind," Jousia said.

.   .   .

The art school that Jousia was trying to get into demanded a sample of his work. He had made a variety of contraptions, but they all seemed stupid. He had to provide the sample within the next three weeks, and this morning he had rejected his last promising idea.

Now he had nothing.

Except for one idea.

"What?" Elina asked.

Jousia hemmed and hawed.

"Fine," Elina said, and Jousia told her he wanted to create a new species of bird that would symbolize the biodiversity of Lapland. He had gotten several meters of old chicken wire from his father to make the framework, but he also needed feathers to glue to it.

"What kind of feathers should they be?"

Jousia spread his arms.

"Long ones and short ones. Different colors. But I don't have time to collect them. I don't know where to get them. I'm gonna need a whole lot of them. Maybe I'll think of something else."

"No," Elina said. "It's a good idea. I'll get the feathers."

"Yeah? From where?"

"The woods."

"It's an awfully big task."

"You get the framework ready."

When Elina got home, she let her parents know they wouldn't be seeing her that weekend. She packed her frame pack with food and went out into the woods. She waded through the marsh, looking for water-birds' nests. She climbed up to bird boxes, collected mallard, teal, and goldeneye feathers and feather down. She wandered into a bog and found waders' nests, rambled the swamps and found a crane's carcass with lots of good feathers on it. She found feathers of meadow birds—black grouse, capercaillie, hazel hens. She packed them all in plastic bags, and when a bag was full she tied it shut, put it in her pack, and took another bag out of her pocket. One packful was four plastic bags stuffed full.

On her third feather-collecting trip, on the Sunday morning, she met Hoot, who was out inspecting the berry blossoms. Hoot came to visit the Ylijaakos now and then, to chat with her mother and father or to borrow tools. Once he had come for a cup of coffee and asked her father about birds. Her father told him his daughter knew more about birds than he did these days, and hollered for Elina to come into the kitchen. Elina came, bashful and mistrustful. Hoot had smiled in a kindly way and asked her if she had ever seen a horned lark. Elina wracked her memory. She mentally went through her Reader's Digest bird book, which she knew from cover to cover. Horned lark. It had a vivid pattern on its head. Elina said she hadn't, but she had seen a snow bunting and a redpoll.

When Hoot left, her father looked out the window and watched him get on his bike and pedal away and said that the world must be full of all sorts of crazy people counting birds when they ought to be worrying about putting bread on the table.

Now they were meeting in the woods, Elina and Hoot, and when the old man heard what she was doing he gave her a stern look and asked her how she was collecting them. Elina explained that she wasn't hurting any birds, or even disturbing them. She left the nests alone if she could see that they were still in use. Hoot approved her methods. He said that he was going to tell her something, and that it was secret knowledge that she could not reveal to her father.

"Of course not," Elina said.

Hoot looked around, although they were alone in the woods. There was a lone crow in the sky above the lake at Jurmusjärvi.

Hoot gave Elina a tip about the location of a goshawk's nest. He also gave her directions to the stand of spruce where the hawk hunted. Elina understood his caution. The people in the village hated the goshawk. They said it killed all the grouse and hares. They destroyed any nests they heard about. Elina thanked him and went on her way. She found the stand of trees and she had good luck, because she found the remains of a black grouse, a magpie, and a jay that the hawk had killed. She plucked them all bare.

On Sunday evening, Elina drove to Jousia's house in her parents' station wagon. She opened the tailgate and set the bags of feathers on the ground.

"What's that?" Jousia asked.

Elina opened one of the bags. Jousia was speechless.

"This oughta be enough," Elina said.

"This is fucking fantastic."

Jousia had constructed the form of a long-necked bird in chicken wire. It had an enormous head, like a pterodactyl. Jousia sorted the feathers by color and size and started gluing them on. Elina helped. They worked all night. Elina explained how to arrange them so that the bird's coat would look real. Sometimes they looked at models in the bird book, and sometimes they argued because Jousia didn't think that art needed to follow the laws of this world.

The project took a long time because every now and then he would think of an entirely new way to arrange the feathers.

We're not going to have it ready on time, Elina thought.

They slept for a couple of hours in the morning, and continued.

The bird turned out to be as big as a horse, colorful, and quite anatomically credible. It looked like a barn swallow crossed with a swan. The instructions from the school said that if the sample piece was large then it wasn't necessary to send it in—printed photographs would suffice. The photos just had to be very comprehensive and show the overall structure of the work, as well as all its details. Jousia and Elina photographed the bird from every angle, developed the photos in the high-school darkroom, and sent them in an envelope to the art school. According to the instructions, a postmark on the day of the deadline was acceptable.

Two weeks later, Jousia got a letter inviting him in for an interview. He traveled to the city and talked with the interviewer the way he would talk to anybody. Another letter came. He had been accepted.

Elina went for her entrance exams, too. The school of forestry was in a different city, not as far south and somewhat remote, where there wasn't a single building more than six stories tall. Elina thought she might actually like it there. She got on the second wait-list. A week before school was to begin, she got notice that there was a place for her.

They had a farewell picnic in Jousia's reading spot on the porch of the half-built cabin, and they had nothing to say to each other. They finished the picnic by declaring that they would get back together once they'd finished school and had a few adventures. Jousia painted a word picture of a wonderful future for them, and Elina watched his face, the face she loved, and wanted to believe him, but she couldn't.

12

The back door of the Toyota was still open. Three children were standing next to the car, staring into the back seat, where the raskel lay curled up, fast asleep. Janatuinen shooed the children away with her hand. They backed up, but stood watching as Janatuinen got in the driver's seat and started the car. She revved the engine and glanced at the raskel. He didn't stir.

The door of the house opened and Efraim appeared on the steps.

"Don't leave that animal in our yard," he yelled.

Janatuinen waved a hand to signal she understood. She got out of the car and closed the back door.

"Hey, lady," the biggest child said.

Janatuinen turned around.

"I mean, excuse me," the child said.

The crowd of tykes stood in front of her, solemn and in order of height, as if their parents had taught them to arrange themselves that way when talking to strangers.

"If you leave it someplace, just give it something that's yours, 'cause then it won't follow you," the child said.

"I see."

Janatuinen took a cigarette out of her pocket. The children looked at her disapprovingly. She put the cigarette away.

"What should I give it?"

"I gave it a Lego," the middle child said.

"Thanks for the advice," Janatuinen said.

The largest nodded.

"No problem."

It was only then that Janatuinen noticed that each child was holding the bottom rod from a plastic clothes hanger in one hand. Janatuinen nodded at them.

"What are those for?"

"Sheepooters," the smallest child squeaked, thrusting the plastic rod out in front of her, like a soldier at drills.

"I'll show you," the middle one said.

"No, I'll show her," the biggest said. The child pointed to the barn chimney. "See that chimney?"

"Yes."

The big kid reached into a pocket, took something out, and put it in her mouth. Then lifted the pipe to her lips, and blew. The shot clicked against the red brickwork of the chimney, clattered down the sheet-metal roof, and dropped to the ground.

"Like that," the child said. The middle and smallest child looked at the sharpshooter with admiration.

"Pretty good," Janatuinen said.

The child examined her pipe.

"You gotta use a hanger this early in the summer 'cause the cow parsley's not grown yet. Cow parsley's the best. They're long, and they're thin on one end. Daddy said it's like a shotgun. In the fall there's rowan berries. You can have a war. But now you gotta use little rocks and Daddy said we can't shoot each other with those."

"That's a good rule," Janatuinen said. She looked at the children. "You didn't shoot the raskel, did you?"

"We're not stupid," the big one said. The little one shook her head violently.

"Shootin' raskels isn't allowed," she said.

Janatuinen nodded.

"Thanks again. Goodbye."

"Bye-bye," the little one said.

Janatuinen got in her car and pulled out of the yard. She could see the children staring after her in the rearview mirror. Efraim appeared at the door again and shouted something and the children shot off at a run and disappeared behind the barn.

The car was filled with mosquitoes. Janatuinen rolled down the window and stepped on the gas. The mosquitoes were sucked outside.

The raskel in the back seat sat up. Janatuinen nearly drove into the ditch when his furry face filled her rearview.

"Good morning," Janatuinen said.

She examined the creature in the mirror. He looked fresh and rested. He yawned and she looked at his teeth. Little white knives.

Janatuinen turned onto the highway that led to town. Nothing but forest around her. After a few kilometers, she flashed her right-turn signal and pulled in at a bus stop.

Janatuinen got out of the car and opened the back door. "You should go now," she said. The raskel emitted an interrogative snarl.

"I can't take you to the inn."

The raskel didn't move.

"Shoo. Get out of there. Go back to the woods."

The raskel started trying to put on the seat belt. He tugged at the strap and growled peevishly when it wouldn't move.

Janatuinen shook her head.

"You can't stay there."

The raskel slowly clambered out. He stood next to the car and stared sadly at his feet. He swung his long arms, his knuckles trailing on the ground. Janatuinen made a broad gesture toward the woods and said he could go wherever he wanted to.

The raskel looked in the direction indicated without any enthusiasm.

"Wait a minute."

Janatuinen got the ice-scraper from the front-seat pocket and gave it to the raskel.

"Here."

The raskel took it, turning it over in his hands with wary interest. Janatuinen patted him on the shoulder.

"So," she said. "Bye-bye, then."

The raskel stared at the scraper apathetically. Janatuinen got back in the car, started it, pulled onto the road, and drove away.

She could see the raskel in the rearview standing at the bus stop. Just before the next curve she looked again. The bus stop was empty.

The evening darkened. Twice she saw a large shape cross the road far ahead, something that didn't look like a reindeer or an elk.

The inn was a wooden two-story house next to a few shops. Janatuinen pulled up in front of the building.

She leaned against the car and smoked a cigarette. It was cold, noticeably colder than when she left, and it felt good. An inviting light shone from the inn's windows. Janatuinen looked at the sign above the door. The letters were sawed from plywood and each one had a hole drilled in it and was hung from the porch roof by a thin chain.

Janatuinen dropped her cigarette butt in the ditch, got her pack from the front seat, and went inside. She expected to see a small lobby and a reception desk, but she walked straight into the bar. The place was empty, except for two men standing side by side at the other end of the room, playing fruit slots and coin pachinko, completely absorbed in what they were doing. The one playing pachinko was Simo the Shit.

Janatuinen looked for a bell to ring on the counter, but there wasn't one.

"Hello!" she shouted. The man at the fruit slots kicked the machine. Then he shuffled behind the counter and said, "You don't look familiar."

"I'm sure I don't, because I'm not from here."

"You don't say," the man said, sounding dubious.

"Do you have a vacant room?"

The man stared at her with his mouth open. Janatuinen repeated the question.

"A vacant room, you say?"

"Yes."

"They're all vacant."

"Great. I'd like a room for one, for one night, please."

"I see…"

"Yes?"

175

"It's just… There's a sort of a problem."

"What problem?"

"The rooms aren't ready."

Janatuinen looked at her watch.

"When can the room be ready?"

"Once I've cleaned it."

"How long will that take?"

The man screwed up his mouth. Looked around.

"First I have to find the broom. And the vacuum."

Janatuinen didn't know what to say to this. The man looked like he was expecting an answer of some kind.

"I see," she said.

"I'll no doubt have to look for them."

"Uh-huh."

"Listen," the man said, carefully weighing a suggestion. "Would you have a beer on the house while I look for the broom and vacuum and clean up your room?"

"That would be fine. Have you got nonalcoholic?"

"Have I got what?"

"Nonalcoholic beer."

"Nope."

"I'll take a lager, then, please."

"So, a regular beer."

"A regular beer."

The man took an enormous beer glass from the shelf behind him, filled it with beer, and set it on the counter.

"I don't know where that vacuum is," he said, and left the room.

Janatuinen was alone. She tipped the bowl of nuts sitting on the counter a bit and estimated the age of the nuts. She reached for the local paper behind the counter. It was a week old. The paper said that someone had dug up a body in the Vuopio cemetery and scattered the body parts around.

Below that was an item that said a sculpture by a local bird artist had disappeared from the same cemetery. It had an interview with "Old Lady Riipi," who was leading the investigation. She said the questioning of the trees was still ongoing.

Janatuinen tossed the paper on the bar, picked up her beer, and went to find herself a seat. The bar smelled like dust and salt pickles. The floor was covered with red wall-to-wall carpet. There were little mats on the tables with black burn holes in them. On the walls were black-and-white photos of groups of people logging or playing sports. Simo the Shit was sitting on a bench next to the coin pachinko machine, as if he and it were friends. He seemed to be sleeping. Janatuinen walked to the strip of room behind the counter and sat down in the corner with her back to the wall.

She had been waiting a quarter of an hour when the front door opened. She couldn't see the door from her seat behind the bar, but she listened. She heard two men talking quietly. A soft squelch as the refrigerator case next to the bar was opened, the faint clink of bottles, then the case closing and the men going to a table. Chairs moving. A cough. Two beer tops hissed. Sighs, puffs. Sleeves rustling against the table.

"Did you hear we've got a cop in town?"

"Can't say as I did."

"Yep. Looking into a murder, I hear."

"Oh yeah?"

"Goin' around Vuopio."

"Figures."

"Got quite a fright from a raskel, I heard."

"Course he did."

"It's a girl."

"What's a girl?"

"The cop."

"A girl policeman?"

"True story."

"The hell it is."

"Yep."

Silence. The men drank their beer.

"Did ya hear that a wraith got into the mayor?"

"Yeah."

"Now he just wants to eat all the time."

"That's how it goes with wraiths."

"You said it. I was there."

"You weren't."

"I was. I was on my way to see my mom at the old folk's home and I heard an awful racket in the yard at the town hall. So I went in. A bunch of people. Pertti was there, too. I asked him what was going on. He says there's a wraith in the rowan tree. I say, 'You're not serious.' Pertti says he is serious. I say, 'Are you drunk?' He says he is drunk, and there's a wraith in the rowan tree."

"Uh-huh."

"I shove my way to look. Old Lady Riipi and the mayor are up front by the tree. The one beside the town hall. You know it?"

"Sure."

"Well, there was some sort of little thing going back and forth up there. A little brownish bird. The mayor said he was on his way to work when he saw the bird in the tree. He wondered at it since it was a Siberian chiffchaff and you don't usually see those around here."

"How'd he know it was Siberian?"

"He's a mayor. They prob'bly know. But that's nothing. The bird was sitting there with its feathers all puffed up like it just woke up, or just got sucked through a jet engine. Saying as how it was awfully hungry. Like, 'I'm so hungry I could eat a whole hog.'"

"The bird said that?"

"Yep. The mayor was startled, naturally. Asked in a loud voice who was pulling a prank. And the bird said, 'There's a nice big hog. I could eat that.' And the mayor realized it was that little birdie talking. So he told it he would bring it a hog. The bird was glad to hear that. Said, 'Hurry up then, hurry up.'"

"Uh-huh."

"The mayor took off and went to get Old Lady Riipi. All she had to do was take one look at the bird. A tundra wraith. Then she walks around the yard three times backward and tells the mayor to pick her up and turn her upside down. So he goes to get the janitor and they pick Old Lady Riipi up off her feet and turn her on her head like a market pig. And she spits into the tree and says something that the mayor and the janitor couldn't make out. Then they turn her right side up. And the wraith was trapped."

"Old Lady Riipi knows her magic."

"Yes, she does. The wraith realized too late. She had made a jail for it. I showed up just when it started trying to get out. But it couldn't get out of that tree, no matter what it did. The outside limbs were like bendy prison bars and they set themselves in front of the wraith whichever way it tried to get through. And Dud was making a racket the whole time. Do you know Dud?"

"Who's Dud?"

"The mayor's spitz."

"Uh-huh."

"The dog's eyes darting every which way."

"Uh-huh."

"And we're in the crowd, yelling, 'Tell us if it can go into a person!' Old Lady Riipi says it can in principle, but it's extremely rare."

"Well, they are demons, wraiths are."

"Old Lady Riipi said they're the ghosts of thousand-year-old Yupiks. Powerful old witches, whose spirits have partly remained on earth. And the remnants of their spirits need hosts. They usually go into animals. Foxes and grouse. 'Cause their spirit life is less trouble than a human's. They don't fight back as much. Old Lady Riipi says wraiths are usually only seen in Siberia."

"She really gave a lecture on the subject."

"Well, anyway, the mayor's boy shoved his way to the front and threatened to get his rifle and shoot the thing. We laughed. You can't really shoot a wraith. I mean, you could, but it wouldn't do anything. After all, if a wraith wants something to get around in, it can just hop into somebody else. Like a person. Better to have a wraith in a bird than in yourself."

"That boy's a real numbskull."

"Sure is a big talker, anyway."

"So how did it get into the mayor? The wraith."

"Not there yet. Old Lady Riipi said she didn't know how to kill a wraith. For that you'd need a witch who understands all about Russian creatures. There was one in Savukoski apparently, and somebody'd already been sent to fetch him. So we just had to wait. But then the bird started flapping around even meaner than before. Moving awfully fast, too. And the rowan branches couldn't keep up. It looked like it was going to get through this one gap. Old Lady Riipi saw that and she yelled and said the wraith was gonna bust up her spell and she told them to turn her upside down again. But before the folks around her had time to pick her up, the bird exploded."

"What?"

"Yep. Feathers swirling around. It exploded when the wraith left it. And it got through Old Lady Riipi's jail."

"So where did it go then? Into the mayor?"

"No, into Dud."

"The mayor's dog."

"Yep. Dog fell to the ground like it'd been shot. Then it jumped up again. Started spinning like a top."

"Phew."

"Then it exploded, too."

"Uh-huh."

"Guts and everything flew all over us."

"Ugh! God…"

"The mayor's boy howls and leaps over to the wet spot where the dog used to be, but the mayor pushes him aside, saying, 'Don't. Don't.'"

"And then the wraith went into him."

"Yep."

"How?"

"He just sort of shook. Didn't fall down or anything."

"What did he look like?"

"Nothing much. He just got sort of an odd look to him."

"How so?"

"Well, I don't know. Stood where he was, rolling his eyes and twisting his face around. Then he said, 'Where's that hog you promised?' And we backed off quick, so the wraith wouldn't get the idea of jumping into us, and Old Lady Riipi started circling him, trying to put the wraith back in the cage. But it was on the loose now and it got its legs under it."

"Made a run for it?"

"Yeah. We saw it go. Never seen anything move that fast. And the mayor's got a belly on him."

"Yeah."

"Not exactly puny."

"Nope."

"But I'll tell you, he leaped over the ditch just like that. Like an elk. Old Lady Riipi yelled, 'Get him!' And we took off after him. The mayor dashed off like a bunny, getting farther ahead of us all the time. Then he was on the road. And a freight truck happened to come along. He ran right at it."

"No."

"Just like a shot."

"He didn't die, did he?"

"Nope. He came at it from the side. Either didn't see it or thought he could go through it. The driver saw the old guy in the road and braked as fast as he could. But you can't stop a rig that big in a second. Mayor smashed right into it, flew up, and fell on his back."

"Uh-huh."

"He was about to get right up again, didn't seem to be that bad off, just a little bloody nose. We jumped on him, men and women and all, in one mob. You never saw anything like it."

"Uh-huh."

"The wraith was dreadful powerful. Grabbed me by the neck hairs and tossed me in the ditch like a dried-up stick. Other people too. But there were a lot of us and after a while he settled down. The truck driver came over. He said an accident victim should never be treated that way, jumping him like that. We yelled that it was a wraith. He didn't get it. But when he saw people flying all over kingdom come, he threw himself into the mix. There were seven of us holding the mayor down."

"Then what happened?"

"We dragged him to the bank. Put him in the vault."

"In the bank vault."

"Yep."

"Who thought of that?"

"The bank manager. He was lying on the mayor's legs with two other people and he yelled, 'Let's put him in the vault!'"

"Too bad the cop wasn't there."

"Why?"

"The wraith could've gone into her."

"Well, there's that."

"We don't need any police around here."

"The truck driver brought a rope from the truck. We wrapped it around the mayor several times till he couldn't even move his little finger. Then we hoisted him up and carried him there like a Christmas tree."

"Or a coffin."

"What have you. We took him across the road to the bank and put him in the vault and screwed it shut. It has a thick door, by the way."

"Vaults usually do. Can't even get through it with dynamite."

"Have you tried?"

"Wish I had."

"Uh-huh."

"I'd quite like to see that cop."

"Would you?"

"Make it clear to her that she's not needed around here. We can keep the crooks and the wraiths in line all by ourselves."

Janatuinen finished her beer. She set her empty glass down and got up. She walked around to the other side of the bar and saw the two talkers at a window table, then went over to them and put her hand in her pocket. The men looked up.

Janatuinen dropped her identification on the table.

Chairs clattered as the men stood up. They weren't much taller than Janatuinen, but they had broad shoulders and the strength that comes from outdoor work. Janatuinen found herself standing between them. She'd realized the moment she stood up that she was drunk, but it never occurred to her to retreat.

One of the men looked her right in the eye and said, "I apologize."

"I'm terribly sorry," said the other.

Janatuinen crossed her arms.

"We had no idea there was anybody here but us and Simo the Shit."

"We were just saying whatever came into our heads. Just talk is all."

Janatuinen looked from one man to the other.

"Not very nice talk."

"No, it wasn't."

"Definitely not."

"I've had a long day," Janatuinen said.

The men nodded as if they were aware of that.

"I actually have a few questions. Would that be all right?"

"Absolutely."

"Of course."

The men sat down on one side of the table, Janatuinen on the other.

They insisted on ordering her a beer. Janatuinen declined. They insisted on ordering her a sparkling water on ice with a twist of lemon, and Janatuinen accepted. One of the men got up and went behind the bar to get a glass and spray it full of soda. He opened the freezer, chipped away some ice with a spoon, and dropped three pieces into the glass. He got a lemon out of a box, picked up a knife, and cut a pretty slice to put on top. He brought the drink to Janatuinen, who thanked him. Then he went back to the refrigerator and got two beers.

"Do you know Asko Pasma?" Janatuinen asked.

"Of course we know Asko."

"A reindeer man, like us. Auvo Pasma's older brother."

"A well-respected man, Auvo was, right to the end."

"Yes, he was."

"Would you describe Asko as trustworthy?"

"Well, he's a witch."

"What do you mean?"

"Well, you can trust him about as much as you can trust a witch. Which is not at all."

"He's become a bit of a *köpö*."

"And do you know the Ylijaakos?"

"Kauko, you mean?"

"Anyone in the family."

"We know everybody in Vuopio."

"Well, tell me something about Kauko."

"He did a little bit of everything. A bit fond of the drink. He died, what, seven years ago maybe. Not long after his wife did. Marke."

"What do you know about her?"

"She was a witch, too."

"A bit on the gloomy side."

"What do you know about their daughter?"

"I know she comes here every summer. I've seen her a few times. Looks like her mother. Lives down south. In some kind of environmental job, must be."

"What kind of person is she, in your opinion?"

"I don't know her that well."

"Me either."

"Whole other generation."

"I'd say she's on the gloomy side."

Janatuinen nodded. She sipped her drink.

"You spoke about witches. Do you believe in that?"

"In what?"

"Witchcraft."

The two men looked at each other.

"Yeah?"

"And wraiths?"

One man scratched at his beer label with a fingernail.

"I hope you don't take this wrong, but you ask some pretty weird questions."

"So, you do believe in it?"

The men stared at her.

"What do raskels eat?"

"You are an odd duck."

"It's important," Janatuinen said.

"Well. Berries. Mushrooms."

"But they have such enormous teeth."

"Well, they do eat meat sometimes, too."

"What kind of meat?"

"They might take a reindeer calf now and again."

"Taken 'em from me before."

"Me, too. And they could take down an elk."

"They could indeed. And they do. And they steal from birds' nests and scavenge carcasses, things like that."

"Do they eat people?"

"Not anymore, I don't think."

The innkeeper appeared. Red and sweaty, his hair standing on end. Out of breath. He looked happy.

The innkeeper greeted the men, who raised their bottles to him. He turned to Janatuinen and said, "Your room's ready, ma'am."

"Have a good evening," Janatuinen said, getting up from the table.

She fetched her suitcase from the car. The innkeeper was waiting for her at the counter.

"Let's just take down your information," he said. He opened a lower cabinet.

Then another. He crouched down and rummaged through the cabinet with both hands, cursing. Finally, he set a large ledger with battered corners and an old-fashioned, marbled cover on the counter. He opened the book at the ribbon marker. Then he lifted the book, examined the page, and nodded thoughtfully, as if its contents were news to him. He took a pen from a holder and asked Janatuinen for her name and home district and wrote it down in its own row in ornate cursive. Janatuinen saw the previous guest's signature and date. It was seventeen years ago.

The innkeeper led her to a stairway behind the bar and up to the second floor. They came to a hallway with doors on both sides. The innkeeper opened one of them and gestured for her to go in. The room had a single bed, a night table, and a desk with a chair and lidded wastebasket. A window that looked out over the back yard. The bed linens smelled slightly of mold. Janatuinen decided to sleep on top of them.

There was a broom and dustpan beside the bed.

"Let me just take these away," the innkeeper said, moving them into the hallway. On the wall opposite the bed was a small mirror, and hanging from a nail next to it was a yellow plastic device that looked like a rug-beater.

"What's this?" Janatuinen asked, taking it down from the wall.

"An electric paddle, for the bugs. It has a button on the back. Don't know if it's got batteries."

There was a fly in the window, buzzing feebly against the glass. Janatuinen gave the green, sun-bleached curtains a shake. The fly flew into the air. Janatuinen waved the paddle at it and pressed the button. The fly stopped as if it had hit a wall, snapped, and was roasted alive.

"Handy," Janatuinen said.

"Not too much," the innkeeper warned her.

The fly burst into flames.

"See what I mean," the innkeeper said, and Janatuinen let go of the button. She blew out the fly. A tiny, smoking wreck. Janatuinen stepped on the wastebasket lever and shook the carcass into the trash.

She took out a cigarette.

"There's no smoking here," the innkeeper said.

"I was going to go outside."

"No smoking out there either."

"Pardon?"

"Tonight's a throng night. Don't go outside. The toilet's down the hall. And the shower. There are earplugs in the drawer of the night table. On the house. Good night."

"What do I need earplugs for?" Janatuinen asked, but he was already gone.

Janatuinen opened the window and smoked, leaning on the sill and blowing the smoke outside. She decided to take a shower. She searched the room for a clean towel, but there wasn't one. She laid her suitcase on the bed, opened it, and took out a small towel and a travel-size bottle of soap, and went to the bathroom. It had a toilet and a fixed shower head attached near the ceiling. A gray, dirty shower curtain. Janatuinen checked to see if the door locked. It didn't. She got undressed, folding her clothes and laying them on the toilet lid, and got into the shower. She was careful not to touch the shower curtain. She turned the knob on the wall. The water that came out of the shower head was brown at first, then red, and finally more or less the normal color.

After her shower she went back to her room. She took out a folder, laid it on the desk, and read through the case information again.

Eero Wik, sixty-four years old, heard the sounds of a struggle in the attached house next door. Clattering furniture and breaking glass. Wik also heard groans and muffled shouts. Then it was quiet for about five minutes. Wik went into the living room.

He saw through the window that his neighbor's back door was open. Elina Ylijaako came out, dragging something behind her. Their yards are separated by a low picket fence. Through it, Wik could tell that the thing she was dragging was a body. He saw the arms dragging behind it. Ylijaako dragged the body to the back corner of the yard, at the edge of the woods. According to Wik, Ylijaako had a habit of burning her garbage there. Ylijaako went inside and came out again with a bottle of lighter fluid in her hand. She poured lighter fluid on the body and lit it on fire.

Wik was asked why he hadn't called the police. He said that he was paralyzed with fear.

According to Wik, Ylijaako had kept the fire burning for a long time, at least an hour, and kept adding firewood to it. Wik had watched her the whole time. When the fire was out, Ylijaako shoveled the remains of the body into a black trash bag and carried it away, presumably to her car. Wik heard the trunk of the car open and close. After that, Ylijaako came back into her house. About twenty minutes later, Ylijaako got into her car and drove away. The time at that point was six a.m. Wik was in shock. He called his sister. His sister advised him to call the police, but he was afraid it would get him into difficulties. According to Wik's statement, he had remained in his home, fearing that Ylijaako would come back and wondering what to do, until he finally called the police that afternoon.

A police unit arrived a half-hour after he made the call. The unit rang Ylijaako's doorbell, but when no one answered, they broke down the door. The unit stated that the home had been left in a hurry. There were signs of a struggle in the living room. Something had been burnt in the back yard, and the after-product had been shoveled away, just as Wik had described. Investigators at the crime scene collected evidence from the apartment, the back yard, and the place where the fire had been. Human fingernails were found among the ashes. The identity of the victim was unknown.

Eero Wik had lived next door to Elina Ylijaako for four years. According to Wik, Ylijaako was a quiet, almost reclusive person.

If he said hello, her reply was short, curt, almost hostile. According to Wik, Ylijaako seemed like a hard person.

Photos of the home and the remains of the fire.

Other information. Elina Ylijaako worked at the Environmental Center as a sampler. No living relatives. No criminal record. No significant financial assets. No record of identifying marks. She was ordinary, for a person originally from Lapland. Her colleagues at the Environmental Center didn't know anything about her personal life. No hobbies. No social network. All Elina Ylijaako's manager could tell them was that she took a vacation at the same time every year, in June, and spent a week in her hometown in Lapland.

Janatuinen closed the folder. She sat down at the desk and looked out the window at the sky. Gray clouds hung in a low, even layer, impenetrable, as if someone had laid a sheet of heavy steel over the world. As if someone wanted to seal it shut.

13

Hoot listened to Elina's plan with a fork in one hand and a knife in the other.

He had smoked them some perch. The fish lay fat and brown on a piece of waxed paper on the lid of the freezer. Hoot had already eaten one perch and was starting another. He shoved his fork into the slashed belly, pressed the tines against the fish's spine, and pried its ribs open with his knife. Steam rose from its insides. Hoot wedged the blade of his knife under the spine and lifted it, grabbing a rib with his fingertips and peeling the spine away. He raked the meat from the bones with his fork and popped the pieces into his mouth.

They were sitting at the table just as they had been the evening before. There was a perch in front of Elina, too, but it was untouched.

Elina said that, according to her mother's diary, stripefoots overwinter in hillside hollows in the woods, just like bears. They stumble out a little before midsummer and go on the hunt. In the old days, the stripefoots in Vuopio used to overwinter on the sandy ridges near Vaittaus. She and Hoot should go together to comb over the hillsides. With any luck they would find one, and if not they could try somewhere farther off. Of course, they would need something for bait. They could steal a reindeer from Asko. He kept a herd in a pen behind his house. If they went to ask with hat in hand at this hour, Asko would just ask questions. Better to just take a reindeer and pay him later. Elina had money. They could lead the reindeer into the woods and when they found a stripefoot's nest they could tie the reindeer up nearby and prepare an ambush. Before long, a stripefoot would come after it. They stick to their territory, like goshawks do, that's what her mother's diary said. The stripefoot would try to pick the reindeer up and fly away with it to some safer spot. But it would fail, because they would have the reindeer securely tied up. They would wait for the monster mosquito to give up and sting the reindeer, and start to suck it dry. Then they could walk right up to it and shoot it in the head with the shotgun. Best not to trust it to a rifle. The bullet would just go right through it and make the mosquito angry. They had to shoot its head completely to pieces. Or they could chop it off with an ax. After that they could remove the stripefoot's snout and bring it to the guy who had promised to help her with the knacky.

Hoot had one side of his perch filleted. He turned his plate a hundred and eighty degrees and started on the other side.

"What are you on?" he asked.

"What do you mean, what am I on?"

"What drug?"

"Nothing."

Hoot lifted a forkful of fish, plucked a bone from the meat with his fingers, wiped it on the edge of his plate, and put the fork in his mouth.

"Where to begin…"

"I could go by myself."

"First off, it's a throng night."

"That is a big minus, of course."

"Second, there aren't any stripefoots anymore."

"There might still be some."

"And then there's the card game with the knacky. For God's sake. That was such an incredibly stupid thing to do."

"I know."

"If I had known."

"The idea just came into my head."

"You were damn lucky. Real beginner's luck."

"I know. But now we have to find a stripefoot."

"Third, Asko and Efraim don't keep reindeer anymore."

"Oh, they don't?"

"They got rid of their reindeer last fall."

"I see."

"Fourth, I heard that some police officer has been in the village, asking questions about you."

Elina rubbed her eyes. Now this.

"A police officer, you say?"

"Yeah. So what did you do?"

Elina looked out the window. It was darker out than usual. Mosquitoes banged against the windowpane as if they were begging to be given asylum.

"Nothing."

Hoot sighed.

"I mean, I was in a fight."

"What fight?"

"Just a fight."

"Is that why you're limping?"

"Yeah."

"How bad is it?"

"It's a little thing. When did the cop get here?"

"I don't know. I heard she had some difficulties. If you were just fighting or something, then it's no big problem for the police to ask about you, I suppose. Right?"

"Yeah."

"You don't sound very thrilled about it, though."

"It's fine."

"Listen. Who did you make this deal with about the stripefoot?"

"Just this person."

"Uh-huh."

Hoot's meal was finished. He pushed the skin and bones into a neat pile at the edge of his plate and shifted the plate a little farther away. Elina looked at her perch, its eyes roasted to brown buttons. She had an odd feeling in her stomach.

Hoot nodded at her fish.

"Want me to filet it for you?"

"No need."

She picked up her knife and fork. When she had stared at the perch for a full minute, Hoot grabbed her plate, slid it to his side of the table, and started to filet it.

He worked on the fish, deep in its guts, and asked, "Was it Slabber Olli?"

Elina was silent.

Hoot put down his cutlery.

"Holy hell."

"I had no other choice."

"No other choice."

Hoot raised his eyes toward the ceiling, looking for answers, but there weren't any. He let his gaze fall on Elina again. Breathed. Started to speak.

"You run around here, making insane deals with ghosts that nobody really knows anything about."

"My mother left good instructions in her diary."

"That's old information. All for one pike. OK, I know it's not just ordinary fishing. That you have some important reason. But could it possibly be that important? You're going to get yourself killed. Do you hear me?"

Elina looked down at the oilcloth stapled to the table. It had cuts through it in places where she had learned to slice bread as a child.

"But if we can find a stripefoot…"

"There aren't any!"

Elina looked up at Hoot, startled. He seemed worked up.

"There aren't any. Do you think I haven't been all over Vaittaus this spring? From here to Jurmusjärvi? All through those woods? I have. When I say there aren't any, there aren't any."

"Uh-huh."

"You should tell me what this is about."

"I don't have to tell you anything."

"I'm worried about you."

"I'm sure everything will be fine."

"It won't be fine."

Hoot sliced at the perch so irritably that he tore the skin. He looked sadly at the tattered fish.

"Whatever devil's got you riled up is going to be the end of you. Are you listening? Even if you could manage to find a stripefoot, which I seriously doubt, it'll still be the end of you, one way or another. And I can't support that. Do you understand?"

Hoot looked up from his plate.

"I couldn't live with myself if that happened. So, I'm asking you: tell me."

Elina held her head in her hands. Her whole body felt prickly. "Can we just let it go for now?"

"No. You're going to tell me."

Elina picked a pen up from the table and hurled it down the hallway. Hoot was startled. She quickly jumped up, fetched the pen, and shook it in front of Hoot.

"Stop making demands of me!"

She dropped the pen on the table and put her hands over her face.

"I'm sorry."

"Are you in such terrible trouble?"

"Yes… No… I'm sorry. I'm sorry, I'm sorry, I'm sorry."

"Calm down. It's all right."

Elina peeped from between her fingers. Hoot was working on the fish again. After a moment he shoved Elina's plate toward her.

"Oh, well. Eat your fish."

Elina ate. She waited for Hoot to say something, but he just watched her.

"It involves another person," Elina said.

Hoot nodded.

"Do you mean that if you tell me about this problem of yours you'll be revealing someone else's information?"

"Yeah."

"But does this problem put your mental and physical health in danger?"

"Yeah."

"Then you can tell me."

"I don't want to cause trouble for anybody," Elina mumbled. Hoot waved a hand dismissively.

"I haven't told anyone about it," Elina said.

"Listen. Tonight there's every kind of horror you can imagine out and about. And some you can't imagine. I think your story will be a very appropriate addition to the lineup."

Elina finished her perch.

"Thanks for the dinner," she said.

"No problem."

The trees, bushes, and buildings standing in the dusk of the yard had lost their shapes. The ceiling light was still on in the kitchen. Suddenly they realized how visible they were to anyone watching from outside. Hoot got up and turned out the light. He fetched some matches, struck one, and lit the candle. Elina went to turn out the light in the back entryway. Hoot said that the light was still on in the mud room. Elina went to turn that one off, too. Finally the whole house was dark, except for the candle on the kitchen table. Soon it seemed too bright, and Hoot moved it to the counter.

They could start to make out the details in the yard now. The mosquitoes had disappeared. There was no wind.

"How about if I make some tea?" Hoot said.

"Some tea?"

"Yeah. And then you tell me. All about it."

Elina whispered something.

"What?"

"All righty."

Hoot got up and put some water on to boil.

Elina remembered what Slabber Olli had said. She said it out loud.

"No one can help me."

"Hogwash. That's not true. There's always something to be done. Are you terminally ill? Is that it? Do you have untreatable cancer?"

"Worse."

"What could be worse than that?"

"Well, it's a really long story."

"There's plenty of tea. And we have wine, too."

Elina sat with her eyes closed. The water in the pot started to boil. Hoot got some mugs from the cupboard and put teabags in them. Picked up the pot, poured the water.

Elina started to talk.

WHAT JOUSIA DID TO THE ROCK, OR HOW ELINA'S LIFE WAS RUINED

They would graduate after five years. That was their plan.

During their first year, Elina and Jousia had little to do with each other. That was Jousia's idea. He thought they should concentrate on making new friends.

Elina was able to rent a cheap furnished studio apartment in a building at the edge of town. On her first night in her new apartment, she sat in the armchair with her arms around her knees. She felt like she was living in a dresser drawer that might be pulled open at any moment.

Elina decided to participate in everything. She went to pre-parties, after-parties, nightclubs, and pub quizzes. All of her classmates were interested in her because it was rare to meet an actual Laplander in the south. People gushed to her about the beauty of the north and clicked their tongues at its dangers. When Elina didn't have anything to say to these comments, she was asked to recite all the words she knew for snow.

"Well, there's slush and powder, and crust. Not that many," she told one classmate.

"I thought there were like a hundred."

Elina asked her where she got that idea, but the classmate had already turned to a friend and explained that, according to her uncle, you can't even close your eyes in Lapland, because the locals will steal the clothes off your back.

Elina even got onto the governing board of the student association, although she had always avoided any sort of collaborative undertaking. She kept up this social activity for two months. Then, at the beginning of November, hunched in the back booth of a bar and well into the second hour of discussing what theme they should have for the annual Christmas party, she declared that she couldn't do it.

The other students went silent. The entertainment director, an aspiring alcoholic, poked his head out from the center of the group and asked her if she was talking about the Christmas party. Elina said that she was talking about the student association.

"I'm very ill," she said, and stood up. She was sitting at the back of the booth, and the other students hurriedly made way. She pushed her way out almost violently, because she suddenly couldn't bear these people a second longer.

No one yelled after her as she marched out of the bar.

The city was black, wet, and snowless. Lighted advertising signs shone red and green. Elina walked past the signs and wished she was in Vuopio, where there weren't even any streetlights. Where the land was white.

The next morning at nine, Elina's doorbell rang. She opened the door a crack and saw a thin strip of the student association entertainment director standing in the stairwell.

"I brought ginger snaps."

Elina asked the entertainment director where he had gotten her address. The boy's name was Jari or Lari—she could never remember which. Jari or Lari said that everyone in the association had given out their addresses. Didn't she remember?

Elina told him her illness was contagious, so she couldn't be with anyone right now.

Jari or Lari sniffed and nodded.

"OK."

"OK," Elina said. "See you later."

"See you later," Jari or Lari said.

He didn't move from where he stood. Elina sighed and opened the door, and Jari or Lari came inside.

They ate the ginger snaps in the kitchen. The entertainment director's name turned out to be Jari. There was nothing for them to talk about.

Jari said he was hungover. He still had his coat on.

After three ginger snaps, Jari pulled a half-empty bottle of cut brandy out of his pocket, expertly twisted the cork off with the same hand he held it with, and took a drink. He was about to put the bottle away when he remembered his manners and offered it to Elina.

"No, thank you."

Jari put the bottle back in his pocket.

Elina wondered whether these were the sorts of adventures Jousia was talking about.

Jari asked if they could watch television. Elina said that she didn't have a television.

Jari nodded.

"An excellent principle," he said.

After a while, Jari asked if he could sleep a little. Before Elina could answer he had already stood up, walked to the couch, and lay down, still wearing his coat. In three seconds, he was asleep.

Jari woke up an hour later and reached for the bottle. Elina said that she actually had work to do. Jari nodded understandingly. He wandered to the door and said he'd see her at school on Monday.

"Goodbye," Elina said, closing the door and watching out the window to be sure that the entertainment director found his way out. She felt like calling Jousia, but she suppressed the urge, as she did every day, and instead went to lie down on her bed and wait for another horrible twenty-four hours to be over.

Elina went home for Christmas. She arranged to meet Jousia on Boxing Day.

Before they were to meet, Elina was nervous. She thought that she had failed at keeping their agreement from the very outset. She didn't know how to enjoy life. She feared that Jousia, on the other hand, had succeeded too well and would flaunt all of his conquests. And all Elina had to show was the bizarre and unpleasant breakfast with Jari.

Elina drove to Loon Spit and she and Jousia went for a walk. To her relief, he talked mostly about art school. About what a wonderful place it was. He talked about a guy who painted nothing but straight lines, had dedicated his life to them. He talked about a conceptual artist who spent evenings dressing up as a snow leopard and going around town trying to spread awareness about the endangered animals. Jousia said that all the students were courageous and represented every possible art style. They wanted to change the world and they disdained anything old and everyone who preceded them, like their teachers.

Jousia's energy and conviction felt homey to Elina. I'll ask about our agreement, soon, she thought.

"How have things been going for you?" Jousia asked.

Elina flinched.

"Fantastic."

She told him she was on the board of the student association. She went to parties and hung out with Jari.

Elina hoped this information would make an impression on Jousia, but he just said, "Good."

She couldn't bring herself to ask about the agreement.

During the spring term they talked twice on the phone and both times Jousia sounded hurried. Elina was hurt that it didn't seem to be at all difficult for him to say, "Have a good day," and hang up.

Elina could have listened to his voice for hours.

"Tell me more about the leopard guy," she asked him, but he said he had to go because there was an exhibition opening that evening.

Elina sank into gloom and focused on her studies. Her favorite teacher was a bald, severe-looking lecturer, who began the course on evolution by saying that the study of biology has two phases.

"Phase one: falling in love. You learn to understand what beautiful animals wolverines are, and woodpeckers, and butterflies. And silverfish. Listen to me—you will fall in love with silverfish. I guarantee it. You may hate silverfish now, but three years from now you will practically be praying to see them zipping around your bathroom. Just so you can stare at them. They belong to the bristletails, an order of insects that has been on this planet for more than three hundred million years. Think about the fine-tuning, the pinnacle of functionality. If you're not in love with silverfish within three years, you're in the wrong field.

"Phylum, class, order, family," the teacher recited. "Genus. Species. The stunning complexity of carbon-based life will open up to you, one taxonomic level at a time. Suddenly you'll see unbelievable ingenuity all around you. Plant life that crushes stone. Birds. All you need to do is look at birds! Birds alone have adaptations that exceed our powers of comprehension.

"Phase two: This knowledge, this third eye punched into the middle of your forehead, will become a source of chronic pain. That's what happens when you comprehend that people, fellow members of your own species, are working tirelessly every day to destroy the biosphere. Humans kill animals to extinction as easily as going to the store. That is the truth. Do you know what extinction means?"

He wadded his notes into a little ball and threw it in the wastebasket.

"It means that a species has irrevocably disappeared from the world. But in such a way that it leaves a reminder. A painful wound. You know what I mean. Skeletons. Pictures.

"In the second phase, you can't go to natural history museums anymore. The museums that were exciting places for you as a child become mausoleums, right before your eyes. The exhibits change, but the theme is always the same. Loss. Grief. Destruction. How painful it is to look at the skeleton of a Steller's sea cow. How painful to look at photographs of a Tasmanian tiger.

"You will learn to love something beautiful," he said. "And then it will be immediately snatched away from you. That is the truth."

In November, Jari announced that he had dried out and he asked Elina to the movies. She didn't have the strength to say no. They sat quietly side by side through two hours of crashing action.

To her surprise, it was rather pleasant.

After the movie they went for a walk. Jari talked about his father, who had left him and his mother years ago. Elina was only half listening. She was focused on Jari's attractive qualities: the calm rhythm of his speech and his leisurely way of walking. She invited him to her place. They made some food together and then they went to bed.

The relationship lasted three weeks. The reason for Jari's teetotaling turned out to be an ulcer, and his doctor had forbidden him to drink alcohol. When the ulcer improved, Jari celebrated the end of his dry stint by renting a cabin for the weekend with some friends. The cabin burned down. Jari returned from the trip plastered, his clothes reeking of smoke. Elina wouldn't let him into her apartment. Jari refused to leave her doorstep, yelling through the mail slot that he needed to borrow some money. Elina asked him to go away. Jari said he needed the money for the damages. Elina took all the bills from her wallet and dropped them through the mail slot. Jari immediately left. The following evening, he came back and pounded on the door, raving about his feelings of love and asking for more money. Elina said she was calling the police. Jari left.

Visiting home in the fall of her second year, Elina saw Jousia by accident in front of the service station in town. She told him that she'd had a brief relationship with a classmate. Jousia nodded and lit a cigarette. The cigarette smoking was new. Jousia said that he'd had several relationships. They hadn't meant anything, of course; it was just for fun, and inspiration. Elina felt unendurably miserable and jealous and wondered at the source of this welling-up of feelings, what reserves they were coming from.

In the spring, Elina tried again to take an interest in people. First she tried to take an interest in men, then in women. But though she did make a few friends, she didn't feel attracted to anyone. She felt herself sliding into the same muteness she'd had in middle school. And she wondered where she came by her melancholy, her cheerlessness, her desire for solitude. The answer was obvious—she got it from her mother. She only liked people when she was with Jousia, and she cried, because Jousia was slipping ever further away.

She started to take long walks in the woods surrounding the town. The forest there was different from Lapland. The trees were tall, the rivers small, and there were plant and bird species all around her that she had never seen before. Handsome old beech trees, bright yellow orioles.

Elina had read about blackbirds and their song in bird books. She had expected to see them in the south, but she hadn't found a single one. She asked the bald lecturer about it, and he said that there used to be blackbirds just ten years ago.

"Now they've disappeared from southern Finland entirely. Why? No one knows. Researchers aren't getting funded anymore."

He said that the living world was flashing broken traffic signals now, with colors that changed at random, and no one knew what to do about it. Everyone was just praying that the damn thing wouldn't burn out for good.

Elina brought a fishing rod from home, got a permit, and went fishing in some nearby rapids. The more anxious she felt, the more often she walked to the shore with the rod in her hand. She caught brown trout and rainbows, and buckets of graylings. She delivered them to grateful, surprised classmates, and when they said they already had enough, she brought them to her teachers. The teachers accepted the fish, making it clear that this would by no means alter her grades.

Gradually, Elina's misery faded to an ache, and continued melancholy. And melancholy was familiar to Elina, so before long she had made a quite satisfactory recovery.

In her third year of studies, Elina didn't see Jousia even once, but she heard from a mutual acquaintance in Vuopio that he had started partying furiously and may have been using drugs. Elina was surprised at how little this information moved her.

She got a temporary gig as a sample taker for the Environmental Center. It was pleasant work. She rambled through the woods collecting bottles of water from ponds and rivers to be tested in the lab for their levels of iron and nitrogen and their bacterial content. One day followed another more or less bearably until the end of October. Then she got a message from her father that her mother wasn't well. She called Jousia in a panic. The phone rang for a long time before Jousia's roommate answered. The roommate said that Jousia had gone to a party a couple of days before and he hadn't seen him since.

Elina got time off from work and traveled home, where her father told her that her mother had lung cancer.

And that wasn't all. According to the doctors, there were signs in her system that she'd had cancer before. In her liver, large intestine, even her pancreas. Aggressive tumors that were fatal nine times out of ten. She had recovered from all of them, until this last one, which was finally breaking down her body's defenses.

Elina and her father sat in the living room, silent. Her father ran his trembling hands through his hair.

Elina knew that they were both thinking the same thing. They had always thought that he would die first. Her carefree, accident-prone father, who drove too fast, went net fishing drunk, and didn't eat enough vegetables.

What they didn't know was what her mother was thinking. This was a painful fact. They hadn't got around to getting to know her.

Her father had never understood her mother. Elina had heard him say this, many times.

"I don't understand you, not one bit," he would say.

Still, he and her mother had always been inseparable. Her mother was like a post driven into the ground and her father was like an eager dog tied to that post, dashing around in a circle as far as the rope allowed, reacting to every stimulus, but sleeping at the foot of the post every night, content in the safety and stability that it offered.

When Elina first told her parents she'd been accepted to the school of forestry, it was her father who got tears in his eyes. Her mother's expression had been impossible to decipher. She had helped Elina find an apartment and wished her a good trip, but also said that Elina didn't have to visit home if she didn't feel like it.

"Of course I'll visit," Elina had told her.

"You can come if you have time. It's up to you."

Bursts of emotion were alien to her mother. Social activities were repugnant to her. Her only friend was Heta at the co-op. Her mother couldn't stand people's idle chatter, but she would listen to Heta's babbling with rapt attention, a cigarette between her fingers.

Elina had warned her mother about smoking many times, and so had her father, but her mother would just smile, lift the cigarette to her lips, and breathe in the smoke.

Elina went to see her in the hospital and told her she would survive this.

"Show your father how to use the dishwasher," her mother answered.

The cancer treatments started immediately. Elina went back to the south, but she couldn't concentrate on her studies. After a month, her father called her again.

"What now?" Elina demanded when her father couldn't get the words out, and he said that her mother had only weeks left. Or maybe days.

Elina left immediately. The next three weeks were spent in the hospital, where her mother lay yellow and shrunken, almost a ghost, struggling for breath. They only conversed a little. Most of the time her mother slept. When she wasn't sleeping, she stared at the ceiling, her eyes hard and bright. Elina kept watch at her mother's bed, just as silently. Her father came to visit every day, but only briefly. He talked the whole time, whether her mother was sleeping or not, grew frustrated at her silence, and left, muttering to himself. Sometimes he only came as far as the door. It often happened that Elina would look up from the textbook she was reading and see her father in the doorway, staring at her dying mother. Staring, and then leaving.

One morning at the hospital Elina read in the newspaper that Jousia had won first prize in the national young artists' biennial. She stared at her lap, lost in a large, scattered cloud of thought. She roused herself and glanced at her mother, whose eyes were open. Her mouth was open. Elina called to her, but she didn't answer—she was dead.

"Wait a sec," Hoot said.

"What?"

"Look."

They were sitting in the dark kitchen. The candle had gone out ages ago. Hoot was staring out the window. His eyes wide. Holding his breath. Elina followed his gaze. Near the swamp side of the barn stood a dark figure whose head was about as high as the peak of the sauna roof. It was a frakus. Watching the yard, the house. Resting one hand on the porch beam of the old sauna, like a landowner inspecting his holdings. The frakus had slaughtered an elk, skinned it, and wrapped the bloody hide around himself. The dead elk's hooves dangled from his shoulders. No one knew how the frakuses lost their culture. They had at one time been herders and planted forests and harvested them, shaping the world to their desires. But something had gone wrong.

The frakus let out a long, mournful sigh. He looked behind him, as if someone had called to him. He turned and walked down along the hillside. Hoot and Elina got up and tiptoed to the living-room window that looked out over the swamp. They watched the frakus plod through the bog, stride over the ditch, and plunge into a willow thicket that reached up to his armpits. He meandered through the brush, holding his arms up on either side.

After the willow thicket there was a thick stand of spruce. The frakus pushed the trees aside to make a channel for himself and stepped through. The only sign of his passage was the waving of the treetops as he passed. Then the trees stopped moving, and the brute was gone.

Hoot and Elina sat down on the sofa.

"That was something," Hoot said. He looked at Elina. "Go on."

Elina hadn't expected Jousia to come to the funeral. She was surprised when she saw him come in and take a place at the back of the chapel, looking haggard. He'd lost weight. His eyes were sleepy and turbid. At the memorial at the house, Jousia didn't sit still for a moment. He kept going in and out to smoke, bumped into guests, dropped part of his sandwich torte on the floor, stepped on it, picked up his foot, and burst into strange, mirthless laughter.

The other funeral guests avoided him. There were a lot of people because her mother was a figure who provoked a lot of questions and fear, and her departure was of interest all the way to town. Efraim was there, too. Efraim tried to say hello to Jousia, but he walked right past without speaking. Eventually Elina pulled Jousia into her old room and told him he should shape up or leave. Jousia said he wasn't bothering anyone.

"Yes, you are. People are keeping their distance from you because they're scared you're going to push them over."

Jousia mumbled something Elina couldn't catch.

"You've got your collar turned up, too."

Elina stepped closer and straightened his coat collar.

"You've always looked after me," Jousia stammered.

"Don't be silly."

"And you collected the feathers."

Elina looked him in the eye and asked, "Is our agreement still on?"

Jousia looked baffled. As if he didn't understand the question.

"Of course, definitely."

He opened his arms and clumsily tried to hug her. His insincerity disgusted her. His untidiness. His smell. She thought of Jari's bouncy, free-floating childishness, his avoidance of responsibility. She pushed Jousia away.

"It's all right," Jousia said. "No problem with that."

"Do you even know what I'm talking about?"

Jousia stared at the walls.

"Stay here for a while," Elina said. "And if you're not up to being with other people, then leave."

Elina walked into the living room. She sat down next to her father. He had been hunched in a corner of the sofa throughout the whole gathering, staring at the cracks between the floorboards.

Her father, who had always believed things would get better. When her mother died, the optimistic parts of him blackened and curled up, like the leaves of a frostbitten dahlia. He dedicated himself to drinking and never left the house anymore.

Two years later, he had a stroke and died. It didn't come as much of a shock to Elina. In a way, she had lost both parents at once.

Elina made a deal with Hoot that he would take care of the home place while she finished her last year of school. Or until she thought of what to do with her life.

In the fall of her fifth and final year of study, a month after her father's funeral, Elina had just left a mind-numbing forest-utilization planning lecture when she was stopped by a boy in a gray hoodie in the foyer. He introduced himself as Tuomas and said he was a new student. Tuomas's tutor had promised to show him around, but he'd been waiting for half an hour. He told her his tutor's name. Did she know him? Elina said that unfortunately she didn't know anyone except the students in her own year.

Tuomas smiled and thanked her. Something about his way of saying that simple thing—"All right, thanks for your help"—made her hesitate. She thought about how she was once again alone, going home, where there was nothing for her to do.

She said that she could show him around the department. If he liked.

"I'd say so," Tuomas said.

Elina laughed.

"That's what we say at home. In Lapland."

"OK. I'm from the west coast, though."

They took a thorough tour and then went for coffee.

In Lapland, Elina was used to people looking at your feet or past you when having a conversation. At the wall, the sky, the yard. But talking with Tuomas, she examined his face the whole time. It was like a clean, bright window. Elina felt like she could see right through it into him, into his core, and at the same time see a reflection of herself. And what she saw wasn't entirely unpleasant.

She told Tuomas about the death of her parents and about Jousia and the stupid agreement they'd made. Tuomas didn't judge her; he just said it sounded awful.

"Yeah," Elina said. "It's really awful."

She tapped her empty coffee cup with her fingernail.

"Y-y-yep."

She started to laugh.

"What?" Tuomas asked.

Elina couldn't stop laughing. Tuomas held out his napkin. Elina wiped her eyes with it. She said that she'd had a terrible, lonely time—that was why she was laughing. Said that she didn't really like to do anything but read her course materials and walk and go fishing.

"I guess I'm kind of boring," she said.

"I like fishing," Tuomas said.

They marveled at this lucky coincidence and decided to go to the river the next day.

They didn't get a single bite, but when she got home, Elina realized that she was in a good mood for the first time in a long time. They started to meet several times a week. Elina thought that maybe even she could have something nice, for a little while. Maybe there was a little bit of happiness reserved for her.

She saw Jousia at the New Year, and told him about Tuomas. She didn't expect any reaction from him, but he seemed pleased. He said it was about time Elina started going wild. That word he used—wild—confused her, because she didn't know how to connect it with Tuomas.

Jousia looked better than he had in a long time. He told her he'd quit drinking and drugs and affairs and started making art again.

"I just needed to experience things," he said. "I needed to experience it all, down to the bottom. Now I don't need to go back to it anymore."

They were sitting at the service-station café in town. Pertti was dozing at the table behind them with an empty pint glass in front of him. He had the same knit hat and quilted coat that he'd been wearing winter and summer for as long as Elina could remember.

"So this is what it feels like," Jousia said.

"What?"

"To know that you have someone. It feels terrible."

"Yeah. That's what if feels like."

When Elina went back south, Tuomas was waiting for her at the train station, and he asked if she wanted to move in together. Elina couldn't think of any reason not to.

Three months later, before their schooling ended, Jousia

called Elina and said that he had wonderful news. "About what?" Elina asked, glancing into the kitchen where Tuomas was making a salad. Jousia said he had come to the decision that the entrance project he had made with Elina was the best thing he'd ever done. All he had done in art school was regress.

"What about your pieces for the biennial?" Elina asked. "You won. What were they again? Little models of living rooms made of sand?"

"Studios. Models of artists' studios. It was a calculated entry. The sort of thing the panel likes."

Jousia felt that art school itself had set him back.

"Being a real artist is just unlearning."

He said he thought the city environment wasn't good for him. Too many temptations. So he had decided to take up where he had left off before he got into school.

"You understand what I'm saying?" he asked.

"Well, tell me."

Jousia said that he was planning to make an entire series of imaginary birds. He had already made some sketches.

"And now comes the best part."

He said that he'd got in touch with the district council, and they said they would fund the project. So he was going to be a hometown boy, with pay and everything. The council was going to place the sculptures in prominent locations.

"They probably want to show off to people from Savukoski," he chuckled.

Although he pretended otherwise, Elina could tell that the hometown recognition tickled him.

"Congratulations," she said.

"I'm moving back this summer. You should, too. You can finish your final project. Or something. I know you've moved in with Tuomas, but you can leave him."

"I can what?"

"I said, you can leave him now."

Elina stammered. She said she was doing her final project on the ecosystems of streams. The streams she was researching were here, not in Lapland.

"Oh. Well, how long will it take?"

"I don't know. Three months or so, for sure."

"Then come after that. I've gotta go there right away, because of the grant."

"OK."

"I love you."

"What?"

"I love you. Do we have a bad phone connection?"

"OK," Elina said. "Bye-bye."

"Who was calling?" Tuomas shouted.

"Hoot."

Jousia got a two-year grant from the district council. He moved to an empty farm on Loon Spit, a kilometer from his childhood home, where his parents were still living. He called Elina every couple of weeks and asked how her project was going. Elina was evasive. Jousia reminded her that she should leave Tuomas as soon as she graduated. Prolonging it would only make it worse. He knew this from personal experience, both as the leaver and the leavee.

"Say your piece and leave, and don't answer his calls or letters or anything," he advised.

"Right, right."

When fall came, Elina ran out of excuses. She had dragged her feet on the written part of the project as long as she could, but when the Environmental Center, which had funded the project, started pestering her, she had to send them her work.

Seven months after Jousia moved home, Elina went to visit him at his new place.

He'd had the old barn converted into a studio. Jousia showed her the first three pieces in his animal series. A swan-eagle, a woodpecker-crane, and a winged tortoise. They were impressive, she had to admit. People in the village hauled over more feathers than he could use. The old feed room was stuffed with them.

"Who'd've thought?" he said. "In an art-hating place like this…"

Jousia was his old sharp, quick self. Filled with passion and certainty that the world would settle into the shape he wanted.

It felt so familiar that Elina's body was tingling.

"Well," Jousia said as they sat down for coffee in the house. "How'd it go with you and Tuomas?"

Elina had been waiting for this. She looked at the table. It was almost the same as the table she'd stared at in Jousia's parents' house years ago. She felt just as shy and miserable and unsure what to say.

Jousia repeated his question.

Elina said, "I haven't told him."

Jousia bounced back up from the table in one sudden motion. He walked once around the room and sat down again.

Glanced at Elina, grunted, got up again, and made another round of the room. This time he puffed and muttered to himself. He sat down again, sought her eyes with his, as if he were hunting down a fish in the water, and asked her if she thought he was going to wait forever.

"You don't have to wait for me."

"But I want to."

"You don't have to."

"Is it that you don't love me anymore?"

Elina stared at him.

"Is it?" Jousia asked.

"No."

"Then what?"

Elina didn't know. He had too many questions.

"Can you say something, please?" Jousia said.

"Let me think a little."

"Think and think."

Jousia got up again. Paced back and forth.

Elina looked at his stance. Angry, so familiar. Of course I love you, she thought.

"I guess there is something."

"What?"

"Some kind of responsibility."

"Oh, it's about responsibility?"

"Yeah."

"Toward who?"

"Well... Tuomas."

"Oh, for God's sake."

"I'm sure it'll all settle down."

"Oh, God damn it."

"I just need some time." Elina nodded. She got some certainty in her voice. "I just have to arrange things a little."

Jousia stood with his hands on his hips, staring at the window in front of him. "It doesn't sound good."

"I'll take care of it."

"Doesn't sound good at all."

"Yeah. This whole thing just came right at me. Sort of sudden."

Jousia laughed darkly.

Elina got up from the table.

"Give me time. I'll figure it out. I should go now."

Jousia didn't look at her.

"Two months, maybe," she said.

Two years passed. Elina graduated and got a permanent job as a sampler at the Environmental Center. Tuomas started his master's program. Jousia's grant ended, but he got another one, for three years, from the state. The district installed a series of seven birds next to the center of the village, but moved them six months later when two of them fell over and someone tried to burn down another. The birds were put along the forest nature trail.

Jousia and Elina chatted now and then on the phone. Elina had feared he would continue to pressure her, but to her surprise he never referred to the break-up idea again.

Elina knew that she had to make the decision. Sometimes, in a burst of energy, she would place Tuomas and Jousia on the scales in her mind, go on a long walk, and come back as uncertain as she'd been when she'd left.

Elina was vexed, from morning to night. She started going fishing alone again, explaining to Tuomas that she needed her own space.

Jousia called and told her he'd started spending time with Janna Keippana.

"The Janna who threw my hat in the tree," Elina clarified.

"The very same."

"All right."

"Whaddaya mean all right?"

"Just that."

"You're not serious."

"Really, it's nothing."

"Nothing. Clearly."

Elina ended the call in a grumpy mood. Was this something new, a warped way of pressuring her?

That evening she had a furious fight with Tuomas. Things had already been bad between them for a while. They wrangled over tiny things. The right way to load the dishwasher, to fold the clothes.

The transparency that had delighted her in Tuomas had become a burden. Tuomas couldn't bear any anxiety, not Elina's or his own, for more than a minute, and always tried to solve any differences as soon as they arose. He got angry when it didn't work.

Elina felt like she was living in a house with windows she could never pull the drapes over.

She had also realized that she simply didn't like living with another person. She didn't feel like being attentive, discussing things, adjusting.

The kindling for the fight was something that Tuomas had said. He had said he wanted to get married and have children.

"Shut up," Elina said.

They were eating dinner. Tuomas looked at her over the macaroni casserole, shocked.

"What did you say?"

Elina got up from the table and went into the mud room and started putting on her sneakers. Tuomas followed her.

"Where are you going?"

"Don't ask me questions," Elina said.

"Well, I am asking."

Elina got one shoe tied.

"So you're just going to leave again," Tuomas said. "That tells me you don't wanna be with me. Do you want to break up?"

Elina laughed. Marry, break up. Like pulling the petals off a daisy.

"What are you laughing at?"

Elina couldn't answer. She held her stomach and laughed, with one shoe on.

They didn't break up that evening. They did it a week later. Tuomas offered to leave her the apartment, but she insisted he keep it. She would take some time off from work and go to Lapland, get her own place. It was all her fault, after all.

Tuomas didn't argue with her.

On the train, she wallowed in self-pity and noted that she had broken up with the only person she might ever be able to have a more or less bearable life with.

In the morning, as she waited at the train station for the bus to Vuopio, she felt relief.

She didn't have to make a choice anymore.

When she reached her parents' place, she called Jousia and asked if they could see each other. Jousia said he didn't have time. Maybe later.

Elina looked out the window. Partly cloudy morning. She ate and went out into the yard. Grabbed the fishing rod and thought it had been a long time since she checked to see if the pike was in the pond.

She was already heading behind the barn, toward the farm road, when she heard the sound of a car. She walked back around the barn into the yard. Jousia got out of the car.

"Hi," he said.

"Hi."

"I came after all."

"So I see."

"What're you doing?"

"What does it look like."

"On your way to the pond?"

"Yeah."

"Oh."

Jousia looked around the yard. Then at Elina again. "Can I come?"

"Of course."

They got him Hoot's rubber boots from the mud room and set out. They talked about the weather. About what the weather was like in the south, about what it was like in the north. Elina remembered Jousia once saying that the world was killing itself talking about the weather, but he nevertheless remembered that as late as a couple of weeks ago the nights were still frosty. And when Elina told him that the trees in the south were already in full leaf, he nodded solemnly, as if she'd revealed a painful, deeply personal secret.

They walked side by side through the bog, single file through the willow thicket. It felt good to her to hear another voice nearby, a traveling companion. They came to the pond. It looked like a neglected wishing well. White clouds bobbed in place above it, like ships at anchor, ready to embark. They approved of Elina's plans.

Elina said that she had good news. Jousia gave her a questioning glance.

"I left Tuomas."

"Uh-huh."

Elina felt this answer lacked enthusiasm. She dangled the fishing rod in her hand. Waiting for more.

When nothing more came, she snapped, "Don't you have anything else to say?"

"No."

"I see."

"I mean, yeah, I do."

"Well, what?"

"Janna is pregnant."

"Whose is it?"

"Mine, silly."

The fishing rod suddenly felt heavy. It was hard to breathe. Elina dug the toe of her boot into the muck. A bog bogey tried to get hold of her boot. She jerked her boot away and stamped her foot. She wasn't a corpse yet.

The bog squelched. This was no doubt a good time to say something.

"Well, congratulations."

"Thanks."

They stood side by side. Jousia looked tense.

"How far along is she?" Elina asked.

"Three months."

"Well then. All I can do is wish you the best."

"Thanks."

"That's great."

More silence.

Jousia pointed at the pond.

"You haven't checked. To see if the pike's here."

Elina made a mumbling noise. Jousia coughed and said, "This is so fucked up."

"What is?"

"Don't you think the whole thing's terrible?"

"Yeah."

"Then why are you saying, 'That's great'?"

"I don't know what else to say."

"What do you really want?"

"What does it matter now?"

"D'you think I wanted things to happen this way?"

"You think I did?"

"Sorry, what?"

"Nothing."

"You're the one who ruined everything."

"Me?"

"Yeah, you. Why didn't you keep our agreement?"

He'd said it now. Elina didn't answer.

"Why couldn't you just immediately leave that shithead?" Jousia asked.

"Tuomas isn't a shithead. And what about you? Why couldn't you leave your hometown bride before you knocked her up?"

Jousia looked at her with a crooked smile.

"Whew. You've learned to talk shit."

"Fuck off."

"You fuck off. It's because of you that everything's fucked."

Elina stared at the pond. The clouds lifted their anchors and hurried away.

"Help," Jousia said. "I can't breathe."

He was doubled over. Elina dropped her rod. She put one hand on Jousia's back, the other on his chest, and slowly straightened him up. She held him between her arms as if his upper body was about to collapse in a heap.

Jousia breathed. In. Out. He calmed down.

"Does Janna know how to do this?" Elina asked.

"Of course."

Elina lowered her arms. They stood silently, at a loss again.

"How did things happen this way?" Jousia said.

"I don't know."

"I should've gotten away from here."

"You did."

"But then I came back. What kind of crazy person does that? Goes back into the trap he just got out of? And now there's the kid."

Jousia kicked the bog with his boot.

"I would have liked to be here with you."

Elina didn't answer.

"Everything's different now. Now I'm stuck here. With Janna Keippana and her kid and some shit art."

He looked like he might burst into tears. Elina had never seen him this despondent.

"Hey. It'll be OK," she said. "It's all right. I'll come and see you."

Jousia shook his head.

"Don't come."

"Of course I'll come. This is just the way things worked out."

Jousia raised his head and looked at her.

"I mean it. Don't come."

"Don't even say that."

"This isn't 'just the way things worked out.' The way things work out is up to us. Why didn't you tell me the agreement didn't mean anything to you?"

Elina squeezed her eyes shut.

"I thought you didn't care about it."

"When did I ever say anything like that? It was always clear to me what the point of the thing was. The whole time. I was as consistent as I could possibly be. Why didn't you believe me? Is that how little you trust me? The point was to get a look at the world. I was looking. The point was to gather experiences. I was gathering them. I was done with it two years ago. And what did you do?"

"What did I do?"

"You waited and waited. And then, when we could've finally been together, you decided to start playing house."

"You led me to believe that we didn't have an agreement anymore."

"Led you to believe, how?"

"At the funeral."

"What about the funeral?"

Elina spread her hands.

"Well. You were really messed up."

"Don't start. I was having horrible withdrawals right then. Pardon me if I was in a bit of a bad mood."

"I asked you if our agreement was still in effect and you didn't even know what I was talking about."

"As I remember it, I said that it was in effect."

"Uh-huh."

"If I'd wanted to break the agreement I would've told you. Told you well in advance. Before one of us had time to ruin the other one's life."

"I didn't want to ruin anyone's life."

"But you have ruined mine. What do you say to that?"

Elina didn't say anything.

"You. Have. Ruined. My. Life. Period. I could've gone any-where. You know what? Let me tell you a story. I was offered a year's stipend in New York after the biennial. A fucking year. I said no. Didn't even think about it. I had it clear in my head what we were gonna do. Move here…" Jousia turned his back on her and said in a choked voice, "and start a family."

"I didn't know."

"Why couldn't you just say you weren't interested? I would have left right then. Now I'm stuck here in a goddamn *swamp*!"

He shouted that last word. He look around, spooked. Looked for something to throw. He didn't see anything. He snatched up some moss and flung it around.

"Fuck!"

Then he sank to his knees and cried.

"I didn't know," Elina said again.

A sinking certainty came over her. She had betrayed Jousia. Elina took off her cap and ran her hand through her hair.

"It can't be," Jousia muttered. "It can't be. All those years."

"People change," Elina said. "You can't expect me to wait for you till the end of time."

Jousia wiped his eyes.

"But that was the agreement."

"No, no, no," Elina said, twisting her cap back down on her head.

There had to be a way out of this.

"And anyway, you can't just think that you could've been in New York," she said. "Or had a career."

"Why not?"

"You can't do it," Elina said. "I'm the one who gathered the feathers for you. Without me, you wouldn't have gotten into that school. Listen to me—without me you wouldn't even be an artist."

Jousia's face froze.

"OK, I'm sorry," Elina said.

Jousia didn't answer. He was pale, staring at Elina with black eyes drained of all feeling.

Elina put her hands to her cheeks. She rubbed the delicate bones under her skin.

Why did everything always go wrong?

"I said I'm sorry. You're scaring me."

Jousia put his hand in his pocket and took something out of it.

"'Member this?"

He was holding a rock in the palm of his hand. Elina recognized it immediately.

"Of course."

"You don't have to do anything for me anymore."

Jousia lifted the hand with the stone high into the air and said, "I curse this stone."

"What are you doing."

"I revoke our love."

"Don't."

"It never existed."

"You don't know what you're doing."

Jousia recited:

> *"Into this pike's twisting entrails*
> *Deep within the fish's belly*
> *I now cast this cursed stone."*

Jousia threw.

The stone flew, and fell. The pike leaped out of the pond. It rose completely above the water, gulped down the stone, paused midair at the apex of its leap, and dropped back into the water head first, splashing as it plunged under the surface and startling the water skippers patrolling the horsetails near the shore. They moved as a swarm a meter away, buzzed around for a moment, then reconstituted their ranks and returned.

A wave moved across the muddy surface. Then the pond was still again.

14

When Elina finished, it was nearly midnight.

"Right," Hoot said.

He got up from the sofa and closed the blinds. He pulled the curtains closed, too, and the house was almost pitch dark. Hoot was only faintly visible, a dark silhouette making his way from one window to another. He said he was going to go lock the doors as well.

Elina took the quilt from the sofa and wrapped it around herself. She listened to Hoot moving through the house. Heard the scratch of a match in the kitchen. A feeble ray of light appeared in the hallway. The glimmer grew stronger and Hoot came into view, returning to the living room with a candle on a small saucer. He put the candle down on the coffee table carefully, as if it were part of a ritual, and asked, "What happened then?"

"Everything all right with the house?" Elina asked.

Hoot sat down.

"Yeah. What happened then?"

"I told him that he didn't understand what he had just done. That he had just condemned us both."

"In other words," Hoot said, "Jousia cursed you."

"Yeah."

"And himself? You were both in the stone."

"Yeah."

"How'd he know the right words to use?"

"He saw them in my mother's diary. I showed it to him once, and he remembered the words somehow."

Hoot sat and thought. Let out a long sigh. Elina could tell what he was thinking. Don't panic.

"Does that mean he's in just as bad shape as you?" Hoot asked.

Elina fiddled with the corner of the quilt.

"I guess."

Hoot ran his hand through his hair.

"OK then."

He asked what Pike Pond had to do with it. Elina said that it had happened there before. "In what way?" Hoot asked, and Elina told him that there was an entry in her mother's diaries that said she had performed the same curse at the pond years ago. The pike wasn't in that pond every spring by accident. It was there because of magic. Who or what had caused it, even her mother didn't know, but she'd said that the pond was an old altar to witches, maybe even frakus witches, for centuries. The pond was bottomless. It just looked shallow. Her mother tested the depth with a pole, shoved the stick through the layer of silt, and saw that pole kept going down as long as it could reach. She had guessed that there was a hole at the bottom leading to the depths of the planet, and in the depths there was some kind of opening into another reality. And the pike was a messenger, moving between these two worlds.

"And the other world is no doubt a place of the dead," Hoot said.

"Well, among other things. According to my mother, the magic could only be done in the spring, once the floods had brought the pike to the pond. The curse itself had two parts. The first spring you had to feed the pike some personal item. Hair, fingernails, or in this case a stone with magic in it. That marked the target of the curse. You didn't catch the pike; you let it go and it took the cursed personal item with it. There was no harm to the one cursed, for the time being.

"The next spring, there was a black pike in the pond. This pike held the soul of the one who was cursed, and if the pike wasn't taken out of the pond within a year after the spell was recited, the pike would take the soul to the land of the dead.

"If the pike was caught and killed, the imprisoned soul was set free for another year. The next spring was the same thing all over again. And the next."

"What does that mean?" Hoot asked in a hoarse voice. "For the soul to be taken to the land of the dead."

"You die."

"You and Jousia."

"Yeah."

"When is your time up? It must be pretty soon."

"Tomorrow at nine p.m."

"Damn."

"Yeah."

"Have you asked for help from anybody?"

"Well…"

"You don't have to mention Slabber Olli. Listen. Are you really sure the curse is still in effect?"

"Yes," Elina said, and threw up on the living-room floor.

Hoot leaped to his feet. Elina threw up again. Hoot went to get a rag and a bucket. He handed the bucket to Elina and asked if she was all right. Elina nodded, holding the bucket.

"I'm sorry."

"Don't be silly."

Hoot led Elina to bed. He went to clean up the vomit, then came back.

"I'm cold," Elina said. Hoot helped her under the covers. She was shaking. He fetched the quilt from the living room, came back, and sat down at the foot of the bed.

"Rub my feet," Elina said.

"What?"

"Rub my feet."

Hoot gave her feet a rub.

"Better?" he asked.

"No."

They sat in silence.

"We should go looking for that stripefoot," Elina said. "But I'll just rest for a minute."

"We're not going anywhere tonight. How'd you think of Slabber Olli?"

"My mom's diary."

Hoot rubbed his eyes.

"If I'd known what she wrote in those diaries, I don't know if I'd ever have given them to you."

"Yes, you would."

"Yeah, I would. I promised your mother."

"Have you got any ideas?"

"What if I talked to him?"

237

"To Slabber Olli, you mean?"

"Yeah."

"That's about as dumb an idea as the one I had."

"He might understand."

"He'd more likely rip your head off."

"Maybe."

They thought for a moment.

"Wait a second," Hoot said. "I know where you can get a stripefoot's snout."

"Where?"

"Old Man Ala-Kaltio has one on his sideboard."

"That thing's at least a hundred years old."

"It'd be about fifty."

"It's supposed to be fresh. From this year."

"Would a raskel do, d'you think?"

"Too ordinary."

Hoot scratched the back of his neck.

"I know why he asked for a stripefoot. They're not supposed to exist anymore. And they don't. Hell, hell, hell! That's some agreement you made."

"I can't get out of it now."

"Maybe Asko would know. What we should do."

Elina didn't answer.

"Did you hear me?"

"I doubt he would help me."

"Course he would, if it's a real emergency."

"I don't feel well."

"I believe it. Which foot's your good one?"

"This one."

Hoot wrapped his hand around Elina's toes and squeezed.

"Aah."

"Does that hurt?"

"No."

"My dad used to do this when I was little."

"Do it again."

Hoot obeyed. Then he said, "Go to sleep now. We'll see what we can do in the morning."

Hoot listened to Elina breathing. The room was dark. From the yard came a peculiar sound, unlike anything Hoot had ever heard before. He felt frightened and cold. He waited until Elina was breathing deeply and evenly, then counted to sixty, for good measure. Then he stood up, went out of the room, and tiptoed through the house to his own bed.

The raskel reached the inn a little before midnight. He was still carrying the ice-scraper. He tried the front door, but it wouldn't open. Then he climbed the drainpipe to the roof of the inn and sniffed around, looked into the chimney. He stood on the peak of the roof and looked down at the blanket of fog that lay over the river like mold. The raskel climbed down the drainpipe and went into the back yard. He lifted the lid of the trash can, climbed in, and pulled the lid back on. By midnight, all the windows and doors in town were locked, the blinds drawn, the lights turned out. Dogs that would normally be asleep in their kennels had been brought indoors. They whimpered and crawled under beds and behind sofas. That was a sign to their owners that it was time to hurry to bed and

239

pull the blankets up to their ears. The weather had been stiflingly hot for the last few nights, but tonight it was cold. Only
one person was outside—Simo the Shit, lying in the ditch in
front of the drugstore, snoring, with a piece of cardboard for
padding and Father Shit clutched to his breast. A lone hare
came out of the woods and raced through the village for dear
life. What was it running from?

Out of the trees came sneaky sprites, blue mist maids, and
kuippanos, the green kings of the forest. Out of the trees came
pixies and frost fairies and the demons known as hittolaiset.
Out came creatures without any names, without any shapes.
One by one they wafted into view and one by one they wafted
out again, melding into the night. They climbed onto the roof
of the inn and sat atop it in a row, like crows. Soon they were
on the roofs of all the buildings, keeping watch over the night.
There was a straight row of domovois on the roof of the town
hall, so many that when one of them climbed up to join them,
another one fell off at the other end. They sat motionless,
as grotesque and patient as gargoyles, looking to the north.
Toward the road. Then came the diseases. They came one
by one and two by two with plague and measles at the front,
wrapped in ratty furs and filthy bandages. They scattered and
circled the houses, knocking on doors, calling out to people
in mellifluous voices. Simo the Shit awoke to their beckoning.
He knew immediately what was happening, and pulled off his
trousers to put them over his head. Tuberculosis bent low over
the ditch and examined the shape of Simo the Shit. It didn't
recognize the wino in disguise as a human and withdrew, con-
tinuing on its way. Simo the Shit peeped out through the fly of

his trousers, saw tuberculosis retreating, and thanked Father Shit three times. Tuberculosis had been trying to get him in its clutches for years. The next to come into view was leprosy, letting its terrifying face shine upon Simo. He closed his eyes and prayed. The occupying army of monstrosities on the roof-tops turned their eyes upward. Enormous creatures were taking shape against the sky—the giants known as daidarabotchi in Japan. And still stranger things, unclassifiable colossi, given license on this night to walk the land. They were like upended whales with feet, their heads jutting upward at the sky like the heads of clams—small and lumpen, with intelligent eyes on either side, like portholes into the hold of some sort of ship. The diseases moved on to the next village. Then the roads filled with human forms. They crowded the main roads of the village in one transparent mass. The monsters on the roof peaks watched as they passed, human ghosts looking for their old homes. And farther off, on the river, in the dense fog over the rapids, the knacky sat on a stone, playing the accordion and singing an old, old sad song. The water around the knacky was a river of bodies. There was no water now, only bodies moving upstream as if tugged by invisible strings, all of them blank-faced, dead. Only the most hard-blooded witch could bear to watch the carnival of throng night, but there were no hard-blooded witches in this village anymore. Even Old Lady Riipi knew her limitations and was lying in her bed in a house on the outskirts of the town, among a dense stand of spruce, with a black blindfold over her eyes, listening in fright as claws scratched at her tin roof and scaly, feathery, chitin-covered bodies rubbed up against the walls.

Elina was awake, too, in her own bed in Vuopio, with a vomit bucket on the floor beside her. She had opened the curtains. She saw the silver light of throng night falling on the walls and welcomed the terror that flowed into the room with it, because fear was a welcome change from sickness. Without going to the window, she knew that her parents were standing outside looking into their old home.

THE THIRD DAY

15

Janatuinen lay in bed and thought.

She was trying to decide whether what she had experienced the night before was something she should forget about—a drunken nightmare, a hallucination—or something that she should give some weight to.

She had awakened to the sound of trumpets. She had gone to the window and looked out at the back yard. A parade was going by. It was led by a bear who was carrying a naked, lion-headed woman on its back. The woman was holding a viper in one hand and reins in the other. Behind her came a thing that walked on stocky spider's legs and had three heads—the heads of a cat, a crowned man, and a frog—attached in a broccoli-like formation. Next was a Minerva owl on long heron's legs, and last of all a child-faced humanoid on a dromedary's back.

Janatuinen had stood at the window until the cat head turned toward her like the gun turret on a panzer. It looked at her and meowed. Janatuinen drew back from the window, took a sip of water from the glass on the bedside table, shoved the plugs in her ears, and went back to bed.

Now there was nothing in the back yard and no track or trace of the parade on the ground.

Janatuinen went downstairs. The innkeeper was behind the counter and called out, "Good morning!" He asked her if she'd like some coffee. The guest book was open on the front desk, as if he'd been reading it all morning. Janatuinen nodded. The innkeeper poured her some coffee and asked if she'd slept well, since throng night can be a little restless. Janatuinen said she'd woken up once. She opened her mouth to tell him more. Then closed it again.

Janatuinen asked whether the inn offered anything else for breakfast. The innkeeper looked startled, as if this were the first time he'd ever heard that such a thing was possible.

He said they didn't, apologizing with many and varied turns of phrase.

"That's all right," Janatuinen said. She paid for her night's stay and said goodbye.

"What's the reason for your trip, Miss?" the innkeeper asked.

"To arrest a crook."

Janatuinen could see from a long way off that there was a dent the size of a fist in her driver's-side door. The village appeared normal. Empty. She looked at the inn and wondered whether she should go ask the innkeeper about the dent. She opened the car door, got in, and pulled out of the yard. She stopped at the edge of the road and looked left, glanced in the rearview mirror, and gave a shout when she saw a hairy ogre running after the car, waving his hands over its head. It was the raskel. He came up to the car and started tugging on the back-door handle as if in fear for his life. Janatuinen reached back and unlocked the door before he could tear it off its hinges. The raskel wrenched the door open and clambered into the car. He smelled like mettwurst and gravy. He was still holding the ice-scraper in its hand.

The raskel stared out the window, as he had the day before, evidently trusting her judgment about where they should go.

"First we'll go to the grocery store," Janatuinen said.

The store was closed, though the hours posted on the door claimed otherwise. Janatuinen stood on the steps in front and wondered where else she could get some food. Across the street, at the service station, a woman was standing with her arms straight at her sides, as if drugged. Janatuinen wondered why you only saw a handful of people at any given time in Lapland. It was as if they took turns going outside.

Janatuinen went back to her car and took a chocolate bar out of the glove box. It was, like her, from the south, and, like her, it had been baked a little soft and lost its original consistency. She tore the wrapper open, wolfed down half of it, and tossed the rest to the back seat. The raskel snatched it out of the air.

Elina turned on her side. It didn't help. It hurt to breathe. Her head ached. Her toe ached. She sat up in bed and waited for the dizziness to pass. She looked at her toe. It was a black parasite attached to her foot, sucking the life out of her and repaying her with a throbbing pain as steady as a radio transmitter.

She set a goal of putting on her trousers and shirt. She succeeded.

"Now let's go into the kitchen," she commanded herself.

She felt like a miserable shipwreck that had been hoisted up from the bottom of the sea and ordered to set sail. Hoot was sitting in the kitchen, solemn, as she dragged herself to the table and braced her palms against it to lower herself carefully into a chair.

"Good morning," Hoot said.

"Good morning."

"How you doing?"

Elina described her condition.

"Want me to look at your toe?"

"No need."

Hoot nodded.

"I'll tape it up," Elina said.

The yard looked the same as before. Not at all like a place where creatures out of every possible and impossible nightmare had passed through. Hoot told her the car tires had been slashed during the night. That wasn't unusual on a throng night. He was going to replace them. She could have something to eat and drink in the meantime. Then they could go, if she felt up to it.

"Go where?"

"To Ala-Kaltio's, to ask him about his stripefoot snout."

"It won't work."

"We don't have any other options."

Elina didn't answer.

Hoot drummed the table with his fingers.

"I can go by myself."

"I'm coming with you."

"That's what I thought."

Hoot went out. Elina poured some coffee into a mug. Something caught her attention. Some sound. Birds? No. The refrigerator? Then she realized what it was. Someone was approaching in a car.

Judging by the sound, the car was coming onto the straight stretch that led to the house. It had just come around the bend and was picking up speed. Elina put her mug down on the counter and went into her room, where she could see the road from the window. An old red Toyota flashed past between the trees. A car she'd never seen before. Elina went back into the kitchen. She couldn't see the turn from there, but she could hear the car slowing down. The moment of silence as the driver shifted into second and made the turn. Sped up again. Three seconds, maybe four until it reached the house.

Elina waited.

The car pulled into the yard. Elina took hold of the window handle and opened it a crack. A car door opened outside. The driver had parked at the end of the barn, out of sight. It was by the old house, next to the road.

Elina moved away from the window. She watched the yard. A figure appeared between the old house and the barn, an ordinary-looking woman in blue jeans and a gray T-shirt, a small pack over one shoulder.

She must be the policewoman Hoot was talking about.

The woman looked around the yard. She seemed to make a note of Elina's car, parked in front of the barn, the new tires in a stack beside it.

Hoot was nowhere to be seen.

The policewoman looked at the house, the windows. Elina drew back into the dark hallway. The policewoman started walking toward the porch, to the front door that Hoot and Elina never used.

The porch was on the west side of the house. Elina went in the opposite direction, to the kitchen entrance.

She crouched down as she crossed the kitchen—there was a clear view from the porch into the window. She heard the thud of the woman's shoes as she walked over the porch flooring.

Elina reached the mud room. She put on her sneakers. She grabbed the frame backpack from the corner, the one that she packed the night she arrived, and put it over her shoulder. God, it was heavy. There were two doors to the outside at this end of the house. The mud-room door, and another one at the back of the mud room. The red metal door that opened on the mud room was to her right. She opened it.

She didn't go in. She remembered something she had forgotten.

Her mother's diaries.

They were on the night table in her room.

"Go. And don't look back," she said.

Elina put the pack down by the door again, slipped off her shoes, and went back the way she came.

She didn't know if the porch door was still locked. Hoot had locked it the night before, for throng night. But if the policewoman had come inside, she would have heard her. The door was heavy and noisy. When she got to the kitchen, she crouched down again.

Had the woman tried the door handle?

Elina's breathing was heavy, through her mouth. Walking in a crouch hurt her thighs. The porch was quiet. Maybe the woman was trying to look in through the windows.

A high, clear sound. *Prinnng. Pronnng.* She was ringing the doorbell.

Elina's room was directly across from the porch door. She crept into the room, grabbed the diaries, and turned around. As she went through the doorway, the pain bent her double. She went down on her knees, put the diaries on the floor in front of her, and tried to breathe deeply, in, out. She looked at the porch door. The handle was moving downward.

"Be locked," Elina begged.

There was a tug on the door. It didn't open. Elina stretched out her right leg and pushed herself up. There was a stabbing pain in her gut. She got upright.

When she reached the kitchen, she had to crawl. She clutched the diaries to her chest with one hand. There were two hollow thumps from the porch, the second fainter than the first. The soft rustle of shoes meeting grass. The policewoman had left the porch and was walking around the house, headed east. Toward the kitchen. She would see the kitchen entrance the moment she came around the corner. Elina crawled faster.

She was in a race with the woman walking beside the house.

Elina got there first. She reached the entryway and stood up, panting, tucked the diaries under her arm, and picked up the backpack. She heard the policewoman climbing the concrete steps to the kitchen door. It was a meter and a half in front of her, and almost certainly unlocked. Elina stepped toward the mud-room door and opened it. The door was perfectly silent because it didn't have a latch or a lock, just a fixed wooden knob. She stopped just inside the door and held it open a crack with her heel. She listened. The kitchen door handle jerked. It turned. A creak. The door started to open. Elina moved her foot and let the mud-room door close. She walked over to the boiler, turned left, and passed the firewood cart. When she reached the door to the outside, she stopped to listen, just in case, but there was no sound. She pressed the handle down and opened the door as silently as she could. She poked her head out into summer as hot as a greenhouse and craned to see the kitchen door. It was closed. The woman was inside the house. Elina opened the door all the way and stood at the top of the steps. She would first have to get to the barn and find Hoot. She turned to close the door and saw the policewoman standing behind the door next to the steps, less than two meters away, with a pistol pointed at her.

"Put the books down on the steps," the woman said.

She spoke slowly and calmly, as if she were lulling a baby to sleep. Elina squatted down and put the books on the steps.

"And the pack."

Elina slid the pack off her shoulders and put it down beside her.

"Put your hands up and come down the steps."

Elina took one step down. The woman took one step back. She was holding the gun in both hands.

Sweat dripped into Elina's eyes. She was afraid to make any sudden moves.

She's not going to shoot me, she thought. She's a police officer.

"Are you Elina Ylijaako?" the woman asked.

"Yes."

The barrel of the gun rose a little.

"Hey, listen," Elina said.

"I'm Detective Janatuinen. I'm arresting you on suspicion of murder."

"Wait a minute, now."

"What have you got in that pack?"

"Some clothes."

"What are those books?"

"Those are my mother's diaries."

"All right," the woman said. She took one hand off the gun and took a pair of handcuffs out of the back pocket of her jeans. "Turn around."

"I think I know what you're here for."

"I said turn around."

"Could you wait a second?"

Twenty meters behind the policewoman was the root cellar, a tall mound with raspberry bushes growing on top. Hoot appeared from behind it. Elina saw him stop and stare. He picked up the heavy wooden brace on the cellar door and began to creep toward Janatuinen, who still stood pointing her pistol.

Elina kept her eyes on Janatuinen. The detective furrowed her brow. She had noticed the change in Elina's expression.

"Is there anyone else in the house?" she asked.

"No. Can I sit down?"

Elina didn't wait for permission; she just sat down on the steps. She pressed her hands against the pale concrete. This was where she used to sit and listen to the springtime sounds, when the swallows had just arrived and the mosquitoes hadn't yet come.

She closed her eyes and put her head between her legs. She was dizzy. For the first time, Elina felt like she might give up.

"Are you all right?"

"No, I'm not."

The worst of the pain passed. Elina lifted her head. Hoot was ten meters away now, and getting closer.

Hoot looked ridiculous. The way he held his makeshift club, it wasn't clear whether he meant to threaten the woman or strike her with it. He seemed to be switching his intention with every step. Hoot looked at Elina like he was asking for advice, but there was nothing she could do.

"Are you injured?" the policewoman asked.

Elina's eyes kept wanting to look to the right. Hoot was four meters away now. Then another figure appeared behind the root cellar. A hairy black bullet, like an enormous dog or a bull, shot after Hoot.

"Look out," Elina shouted, leaping to her feet.

Janatuinen and Hoot turned at exactly the same moment, as if they were in a play. Hoot dropped the stick. Then the monster was upon him, lifting him into the air on straightened arms, like a weightlifter. It was Elina's fault, all of it, and with this thought her mind dropped, layer by layer, into that incomprehensible jumble waiting at the bottom.

16

The raskel held Hoot high in the air and spun around in a full circle, as if he wanted to show the whole world what he had caught.

Janatuinen pointed her pistol at the raskel and ordered him to put the man down. The man shouted. The raskel dropped him, first into his arms, gently, like a parent playing with his child, then carefully let him slide to the ground.

The man held his right hand to his chest. His thin white straggle of hair was standing straight up. The man put his left hand on the raskel's shoulder.

"You startled me," the man said.

The raskel smacked himself on the cheek and strutted around.

"What's going on here?" Janatuinen asked. She aimed at the man. "Who are you?"

"Hoot."

"Who?"

"Hoot."

"What's your real name?"

"Juhanijänis Hili Pili Ylikriipi."

"What?"

"Hoot's better, don't you think?"

"Do you know this raskel?"

"Yeah. His name's Musti."

The raskel jabbed a finger into Hoot's shoulder.

"Stop it," Hoot said.

Janatuinen didn't lower her weapon.

"What were you planning to do with that stick?"

Hoot glanced at the stick on the ground.

"Well, um… It gave me a scare when you pointed a gun at Elina."

Then Hoot saw Elina, who was lying on the ground on her side at the foot of the steps.

He ran to her and kneeled down next to her. Spoke to her. No response. He felt Elina's pulse and pressed his ear against her chest.

"She's in a bad way," he said.

Janatuinen put her gun in her waistband.

"Do you know what's wrong with her?"

"There's a curse on her, and it's killing her. Help me a little, will you? Let's carry her inside."

Janatuinen clicked her tongue.

"I should take her to the police station."

"Can't you see that she can't even stand? Help me out here."

Hoot pulled the door open and carried the backpack and diaries into the back entryway.

"Those books are evidence," Janatuinen said.

Hoot didn't answer. He went back to Elina, put his hands under her armpits and looked at Janatuinen.

"Come on."

The raskel stepped up to Elina and took hold of her ankles. He lifted her feet into the air as if he were trying to help her perform some sort of gymnastics maneuver.

"Knock it off," Hoot said.

Janatuinen tapped the raskel on the shoulder. The creature let go of Elina's legs and Janatuinen took hold of them. They lifted her and carried her into the house.

"Which way?" Janatuinen asked when they were inside the door. She was walking in backward.

"Forward," Hoot said.

They went into the kitchen.

"Forward," Hoot said.

They carried Elina into the living room and put her on the sofa, arranging her on her side. Hoot sat down next to her.

"You've got to go for help," he said to Janatuinen.

"A doctor?"

"Nothing like that. Asko. Our neighbor. I can give you directions."

"I know the place."

"She's not getting any better. Go right now."

Janatuinen seemed to be thinking about it.

Hoot sighed.

"If you think we're going to escape, just look at the state of her. I'm an old man. I can't carry her to the car. And besides, we only have one car, and it doesn't have any tires on it."

"All right," Janatuinen said, and turned to leave.

"And take him outside," Hoot said, pointing at the raskel, which was standing on the other side of the room. He was looking at the bookshelf, holding Elina's parents' wedding photo in his hand.

"Let's go," Janatuinen said to the raskel, who turned, still holding the photograph. Janatuinen told him he couldn't take it with him. The raskel put the picture down on the floor, like a toy that was too expensive.

He refused to wait in the yard, so she let him in the car. She looked at him in the rearview and said, "So, your name is Musti?"

The creature's tufted ears trembled.

They reached Asko and Efraim's house and she parked in the same spot next to the tractor. She turned to face the back seat and shook her finger at the raskel.

"Stay."

The raskel watched her gestures and facial expressions with rapt attention.

Janatuinen went up the steps of the house. There was a broom leaning against the front door. Janatuinen stood in front of the broom. She thought about Asko and wondered if he was a person who might set a booby trap.

She didn't touch the broom. She went back down the steps and peeped in through the windows. The house was empty and dark. She checked the other buildings—the sauna, barn, and woodshed. She peeked in the door of each, and listened. She glanced at her car. She could see the raskel in the back seat, an impenetrable black shape, sitting like a dark avenger, patiently waiting for his driver. Janatuinen went into the back yard. There was nothing there but the sloping riverbank and a boat at the shore. She looked at the river. She turned, and Asko was standing in front of her.

"Good Lord," Janatuinen said, putting her hands on her heart.

"Whatcha lookin' for, Officer?"

Janatuinen couldn't fathom where the old man had come from to appear behind her so quickly and quietly.

She took a breath and said:

"Elina Ylijaako is sick. The man—Hoot, I mean—said you would know how to help. Apparently it has to do with some kind of curse."

"Of course it's a curse," Asko said, and started walking toward the house.

"Hey," Janatuinen said, running after him. "Where are you going?"

Asko stopped and turned around. Janatuinen stopped, too.

"To get my things," he said.

"Oh. All right."

Asko kept walking. He went around to the front and up the steps, grabbed the broom, and leaned it against the porch rail. He told her it would only take a couple of minutes. He opened the door and went inside.

Janatuinen waited at the bottom of the steps, smoking. Seven minutes later, Asko came out. He was carrying a brown leather case. He stopped at the top of the steps and thought for a second, then put the case down and went back inside. Janatuinen lit another cigarette. Two minutes later, Asko came out, leaned the broom against the door, picked up the case, and walked to the car. Janatuinen stubbed her cigarette in a flower pot and ran after him.

"Needed to leave a note for Efraim," he said.

Janatuinen opened the passenger door for him, closed it, went to the driver's side, got in, and started the motor. They pulled out of the yard.

"You know you got a raskel in your back seat?"

"I know."

"All right, then."

Hoot stroked Elina's hair. She tossed and turned feverishly on the sofa. She begged forgiveness from her mother, her father, Hoot, and Jousia. In that order, over and over. At the end of each of these litanies, Hoot answered that she hadn't done anything wrong. And anyway there was no need to worry because help was on the way.

Hoot looked at the clock. Janatuinen had been gone for twenty minutes.

"Hurry up," Hoot said.

Elina mumbled something about Hoot, and a monster, and a warning. Then she asked for forgiveness.

"It was just a raskel," Hoot said. "Just old Musti. You remember Musti, don't you?"

Half an hour later, Janatuinen's car pulled into the yard. The front door opened. Hoot could hear Asko's slow footsteps and Asko's voice saying proudly that he'd never set foot in this house before. Janatuinen's sharp tone as she ordered the raskel to stay outside. Then Asko and Janatuinen came into the living room. Asko was clutching his case to his chest and staring around him at the walls, the ceiling, the hall mirror, as if he could see through them and understood the house's true and shocking character.

"She's still breathing," Hoot said.

Janatuinen nodded.

"The patient's on the sofa," she said.

"Hi, Hoot," Asko said. He looked at Elina. "Who's this?"

"Elina, lamebrain. Help her."

"Bring me a seat."

Hoot got a stool from the corner and set it next to the sofa. He stood by to watch. Asko sat down on the stool. He laid his fingertips on Elina's chest and held them there, feeling. He muttered and scowled as he took his hand away.

"Her heart won't last much longer."

"It's a curse," Hoot said. "Some pike-belly thing."

"Yeah. I can see that."

"Is there anything you can do?" Hoot asked. He had tears in his eyes. "Say there is."

Hoot and Asko had been neighbors for more than twenty years. They cast their nets in the river together every spring. Hoot had seen Asko put the limbs of a reindeer fawn hit by a car back in their places and a moment later had seen the fawn get up and run away. He had seen when Kauko Ylijaako staggered into Asko's yard white as a sheet after he cut off his thumb in the wood-splitter, holding the nearly severed thumb on tight in his good fist, and how Asko reattached the thumb with two words. Asko forgot who Hoot was about once a week, would stop sometimes in the middle of what he was doing, and just stare into space, perhaps to remind himself who he himself was, but Asko was the most powerful witch Hoot had ever met, if you didn't count Marke, and it was just a malicious trick of fate that the two of them had crossed their skis ever since they were kids.

Hoot searched Asko's eyes for hope. They were frighteningly empty.

"Now, listen carefully," Asko said.

Janatuinen and Hoot bent toward him.

"I need a glass of really cold water."

Hoot glanced at Janatuinen, who sighed, went into the kitchen, and came back with a glass of water. Asko took the glass, drank a swallow, and set the glass down next to the stool.

"And then," Asko said, looking at Hoot. "You got any whole milk?"

"There's some."

"What about whipping cream?"

"No."

"It doesn't matter. Have you got any cinnamon sticks, whole vanilla, nutmeg, and eggs?"

"Might have."

"No rum, I suppose?"

"We've got some."

"Good."

Asko snapped his case open. Rummaged inside it. He took out a small bottle with a screw-on cap. It was filled with red flakes.

"Hey, Officer."

"Yeah?"

"I need you to do one more thing for me."

"Say the word."

"Put three hundred milliliters of whole milk and one stick of cinnamon in a pot. Get a vanilla pod, split it down the middle, and scrape the seeds out with the tip of the knife. Toss out the pod and put the seeds into the milk. Sprinkle in half a teaspoon of nutmeg. Add one teaspoon from this bottle. Heat the milk until it's just about to boil. Stirring constantly, so it don't burn

SUMMER FISHING IN LAPLAND

on the bottom. When the milk's hot, take the pot off the burner. Put in a good splash of rum. Put in another splash. Take three eggs. Separate the yolks from the whites and put them into two different bowls. Stir two teaspoons of sugar into the yolks and whip them. Pour the whipped yolks into the hot milk. Stir constantly. Take out the cinnamon stick. Whip the egg whites and stir them in. Pour it into a mug and bring it in here."

"All right," Janatuinen said, and headed into the kitchen.

Hoot watched her go.

"You sent her to make you an egg toddy?"

"Yeah."

"What's in the bottle?"

"Dried raspberries. They give it a nice flavor. I like them."

Asko took another bottle out of his case. It was filled with a yellow-black liquid. He held the bottle out at arm's length, like a grenade, and pulled out the cork as warily as pulling the pin. A horrible, pungent smell spread through the room.

"Phew! What the hell is that?"

"Frakus pee. We've gotta make the girl drink it. She'll fight it. But if she doesn't drink this, she'll die."

"Got it."

Asko drank down the glass of water, poured two fingers of the pee into the glass, put the cork tightly back into the bottle, and stashed it in his case again. He looked at Hoot.

"Ready?"

"Yeah."

Hoot lifted Elina's upper body. Her eyelids fluttered. She called for her mother and father. For Jousia. Hoot lifted her head a bit more and Asko held the glass against her lips and tipped it. Elina twisted her head to one side. Asko pulled the glass away. He ordered Hoot to hold her head tighter. Hoot sat down on the sofa and put her head in his lap. He lifted her and wedged her head into the gap between his arm and his armpit. Asko brought the glass up again and ordered Elina to open her mouth. Elina tried to say something. Asko poured the drink in. When Elina got the liquid in her mouth she started to cough and spit the drink down the front of her shirt.

"Again," Asko said, and tipped the glass.

Elina spit. Hoot asked if they should mix it with water.

"No. Again."

Hoot spoke to Elina. He told her she was going to be all right, but she had to drink this. The caustic fumes from the liquid made both Asko's and Hoot's eyes water. Elina refused to drink it one more time, but then she swallowed it.

Hoot stroked her hair and praised her. Asko tipped the glass once more. Hoot told him not so fast, but Asko just said, "Hold her head." They did this four times. Then the glass was empty.

"That'll do it," Asko said. He set the empty glass on the floor. Elina's breathing leveled. Asko got up and opened the ventilation window.

"I'd say she's got ten more hours."

"How d'you know?"

"Auvo lasted ten hours."

Hoot stared at him.

Asko nodded.

"This is the same shit that killed my brother."

"Oh, hell. Hell, hell, hell."

"Yeah. But this house might give her more time."

"This house?"

"There's power in these walls," Asko said, resting his palm against the wall and smiling. "That mother of hers. Damn her."

Janatuinen came back into the living room holding a mug.

"All ready. What's that smell?"

"That's the smell of good luck," Asko said, taking the mug and tasting it. "Excellent. Come on, Hoot. Let's go in the kitchen and have a toddy."

Elina walked into the kitchen. Hoot, Asko, and Janatuinen were sitting at the table.

"My mouth tastes like shit," Elina said.

Hoot made room for her on the bench.

"Sit here."

He put a mug in front of her.

"Have some of this."

Asko and Janatuinen sat across from them. Everyone had a steaming mug in front of them.

Elina was terribly thirsty. She touched the mug with her fingers.

"Why is this hot?"

"Just get some in you."

Janatuinen took a swig of hers, staring at Elina without blinking.

"It's awful good," Asko said. "Give you some strength, now that the medicine's done its work."

Elina took a drink. Then another. She looked at her watch. It was a quarter to twelve.

"Nothing to worry about," Hoot said. "You were out of commission for maybe fifteen minutes."

"We've gotta go see Ala-Kaltio," Elina said.

Janatuinen cleared her throat. Hoot scratched the side of his nose.

"Yeah, we should," he said. "But we've got another problem. Listen. This police officer says she's here to arrest you. She thinks you killed somebody."

Silence. Elina sipped from her mug.

"Did you kill somebody?"

"No."

Hoot slapped the table.

"What did I tell you?"

"We have an eyewitness," Janatuinen said.

Elina took another drink of her toddy.

Janatuinen crossed her left leg over her right. Without looking at Elina, she said that, according to the witness, Elina killed someone and burned the body in back of her row house three months ago.

Hoot stared at Janatuinen.

"You've gotta be making this all up."

Then he looked at Elina.

"Tell her she's making it all up."

Silence.

"Well?"

"It was a fetcher," Elina said.

Janatuinen closed her eyes. In a very weary voice, she asked, "What's a fetcher?"

Hoot explained the operating principle of a fetcher. Then he asked with a groan who in their right mind would make a fetcher in this day and age.

He turned to Elina and asked what the fetcher looked like.

"A sort of a crane with arms."

She said the fetcher tried to steal her television. She had a fight with it and managed to pin it to the floor. Then she took out its heart, which was a piece of rye bread, and dragged it into the back yard and burned it, and that must be what the witness had been describing.

Janatuinen pursed her lips and nodded. As if she expected to hear something like this.

"They did find traces of a bird in the yard," she said. "But all the feathers were black. Cranes aren't black."

Elina mumbled something the others couldn't hear.

"Speak up," Hoot said.

"It was made with black woodpecker's feathers."

Hoot scowled.

"Hold on. That's Jousia's sculpture. The one that was stolen from the cemetery two weeks ago. Why didn't you say so? That means the fetcher was made here. Who around here still knows how to make a fetcher?"

He looked at Asko. Asko didn't say anything.

"Did you know whose it was?" Hoot asked Elina.

Elina didn't say anything. Hoot looked at each of them in turn:

"Somebody say something."

Then he understood, and fixed his eyes on the culprit.

"For God's sake, Asko."

Asko glared at them.

"It was supposed to steal something from Marke."

"Marke's dead, you dope."

"She owes me."

Hoot buried his face in his hands.

"You're not serious. You mean that dog?"

"He was a good dog."

"This again. Jesus."

"I wanted compensation. The fetchers were supposed to bring something for me."

"What do you mean 'fetchers'? Is there more than one?"

"Three," Elina said.

"And you didn't say anything about it."

Elina didn't answer.

Hoot waved his arms at Asko and Elina.

"This cop ought to arrest the both of you. You've both gone nuts."

Elina scratched at the breadbasket on the table with her fingernail.

"I didn't want to cause Asko any trouble."

"Cause *him* trouble?" Hoot said.

"The fetchers were harmless."

"They framed you for murder."

"I didn't think of that."

"Are you hearing this?" Hoot asked Asko. "This girl has sat at your table who knows how many times when she was a kid. She knows that you forget who she is the second she walks out the door. And that you hate her mother. And to top it off you send fetchers after her. And still she didn't say anything. She could've reported you to the village association. Lord knows what I would've done. You know how high the fines can be for making fetchers. What the hell is wrong with you, Asko? You and Efraim could lose the roof over your heads."

Asko reached for the candle in its saucer on the table. He turned it counterclockwise. As if he wanted to turn back time. He turned it clockwise. He let go of the candleholder, laid his palm on the table, and looked at the others as if he just now comprehended what he had done. Or remembered it.

"I didn't mean to…" he said.

"Shut up, Asko," Hoot said.

"I'm sorry."

"It's all right," Elina said. "Everybody, calm down. It's OK. I should have said something earlier. It's my fault."

"Could you please stop blaming yourself? And you," Hoot said, turning to Asko. "Maybe you really didn't realize that Elina is the last Ylijaako. There isn't anybody else. And you specifically told the fetcher to get something from Ylijaako. So it went after Elina."

"I'm sorry."

"And when a fetcher is taken apart, it breaks whoever made it, too. Did that fact occur to either one of you? Because it does occur to me that could be why Asko's head has rotted off that much more, since he built the fetchers and Elina has apparently destroyed them."

"I save their hearts," Elina said. "That way no harm comes to their creator."

Asko looked at Elina like a man with a life sentence who's just been pardoned.

"Or not as much harm, anyway."

Hoot glared at them.

"I see. Well, let's do a little dance, then, since everything's turned out so great."

Elina opened her mouth to say something, but then Janatuinen raised her hand. They suddenly realized whose approval all this depended on.

Janatuinen chose her words carefully.

"I read in the news that someone dug a body up from the cemetery." She turned to look at Asko. "Was it you?"

Asko sat silent with his hands on the table. He studied the backs of his hands with a sad, thoughtful look.

He said, "Yes."

"OK," Janatuinen said, and stood up. "I'm going to go have a smoke."

She went out. She appeared a moment later in the yard just outside the window and looked in, as if to make sure no one had escaped. She lit a cigarette. A lone horsefly teetered toward her from the lilac bush, as if out of a sense of duty, and started diving at her. Janatuinen swatted at it and missed, which worked like a magic trick because suddenly there were three more of them buzzing around her.

"So you dug up Kalevi Räsänen," Hoot said.

Asko fidgeted in his chair.

"You never cared for Kalevi, either, did you?" he said.

"Well, no. But I don't think that's a reason to go digging up somebody's grave."

"I just needed some arms for the fetcher."

"Of course you did."

The raskel tottered over to Janatuinen and stood next to her, as if awaiting orders. Janatuinen didn't look at him. She stared out at the swamp, smoking. The raskel turned and looked at the swamp, too.

Hoot said, "Listen. If you could just remember from here on out that Marke is dead…"

"Yeah, you said that."

Hoot started to hold up a finger, but Elina said that they really ought to get going to Ala-Kaltio's house. They didn't have much day left. Asko asked why in the world they wanted to go there. Elina told him about her deal with Slabber Olli. When she said Slabber Olli's name, Asko's eyes widened. He bent over and started chuckling.

"You made a deal with Slabber Olli?"

"Yeah."

"Have you met him?"

"Yeah."

Asko then began a long rambling story. He said that when Marke was in school she used to brag that she had a new friend who lived on Dead Man's Island. Hoot said he was sure Marke wouldn't brag. Asko admitted that he'd actually heard about it from Esko. "Whatever," Asko said with a wave of his hand. In any case, he had guessed immediately that her friend was a ghost, because who else would live on Dead Man's Island? And he'd rowed over to the island to look for the ghost, because he wanted to make friends with those in the land of the dead. Those on the other side could bend the laws of nature in a way that those among the living could only dream of. And Asko wanted to learn how. He examined all the graves there and recited all the magic words he knew, but he never got even a glimpse of such a creature. So he started rowing back home, disappointed. But when he was halfway across the water, he saw a tall figure walking on the shore of the island. He called to it and immediately turned his boat around, but by the time he came ashore the island was empty again. He started rowing home again, twice as depressed as he was before, and the figure appeared on the shore again. So he turned around one more time and searched the whole island, and found nothing. And he rowed away again, this time with his eyes closed, so he wouldn't end up being lured back again. He heard later that other people from the village had seen this figure. Old Lady Riipi knew that his name was Slabber Olli, and where he came from. And then Asko said that everybody knew that Marke got her knowledge from Slabber Olli, while he himself had acquired his power by listening to stooped old witches and through study, and Hoot interrupted and told him to get to the point, and Asko said that the stripefoot snout wouldn't work.

"Why won't it work?"

"It doesn't have any power left in it. You might as well foist an old stick on him."

"I told you!" Elina said.

"Would a wraith work?"

The voice came from outside. It was Janatuinen, out in the yard, talking through the ventilation window.

"A wraith," Asko said, tasting the word. "It very well could. It's a plenty supernatural critter."

"Good," Janatuinen said. She took one last drag of her smoke and held the butt up. "Where should I put this?"

A minute later she was sitting at the table, telling them what she'd heard from the men in the bar at the inn.

Hoot held onto his skull as if he had a headache.

"Do we even know how to catch one? They're pretty horrible creatures."

"Mom saw one in the woods once and she managed to scare it off," Elina said.

Asko waved a hand.

"A child could scare a wraith *away*. But don't you worry. We've got everything we need to *catch* one."

He paused a moment. The others waited.

"First off, we've got a bag of tricks," he said, holding up a thumb and jabbing it against his chest.

"Then we've got a tough guy," he said, nodding at Janatuinen.

"And we've got the bait."

It took Elina a second to realize why everyone was staring at her.

17

On the outskirts of Bologna, on the last day of March, 1561, Giacomo de' Medici, a pupil of Paracelsus and younger cousin of Cosimo the First, the Grand Duke of Florence, tried to turn mercury into gold in an alchemical operation and blew himself and his laboratory sky high. The first person to arrive in the aftermath was Sofia Alfano, de' Medici's resentful housekeeper, who made a careful examination of the remains of the lab and put away everything that looked valuable. She found an intact glass flask with a smoking tatter of de' Medici's soul curled up at the bottom. Alfano cursed the piece of soul three times and tossed the flask into a sack. She sold the sack's contents that same day to Alfons Lumicelli, a competitor of de' Medici's. Lumicelli was interested in de' Medici's research into perpetual-motion machines and thought he might be able to isolate the fragment of de' Medici's soul and distill the information from it. But when Lumicelli submerged the flask in boiling water, the piece of soul absorbed energy from the boiling water and changed into an evil spirit—a wraith, that is—and took possession of Lumicelli's body. Lumicelli hanged himself from a chandelier. The wraith escaped through a window and went rushing through the streets of Bologna, overturning pedestrians and fruit carts, shocked by its own existence, until a priest named Gaspare Bombieri was summoned and trapped the being in a spirit-proof ebony box. Bombieri dispatched the box to the Vatican, where it was shut up in a section of a vault reserved for dangerous creatures. The wraith spent a hundred years in the vault. Then Cardinal Daniello Coscia, who had gambling debts, sold the box to a Flemish merchant named Jan Hooft. Coscia didn't know what was in the box, but he told Hooft that it wouldn't be wise to open it. Hooft wrote in his inventory that the case contained a sensitive occult substance that could be injurious, and with this description sold the box to a British auction house that specialized in esoteric objects, and the auction house in turn sold it to a Russian mystic named Moshe Botvinnik. Botvinnik, a lifelong collector of supernatural paraphernalia, was able to interpret certain carvings made on the outside of the box and deduce what was inside. He opened the box at his home in Moscow. Using a rudimentary spirit-herding spell, he succeeded in directing the wraith into his pet rat and was so happy with his success that he clapped his hands together in delight. This unraveled the spell, and the wraith was blown out of the rat and into the mystic. Botvinnik hanged himself from his living-room rafter. The wraith then returned to the rat, escaped into the yard, let itself be caught by a passing cat, possessed the cat, and ran out of town. The wraith moved from there into a fox, and then a reindeer, a wild boar, a wolf, and a vole. It wandered in the wilderness. It started missing its original body—de' Medici's body—and also fretted over the fact that it wasn't even an entire soul, but more like a memory of one, and the only means it had to alleviate its distress was to eat. It gorged its animal bodies till they burst or ran them to death, and sometimes wandered

275

for weeks without a host, an icy phantom rushing across the land. It drifted ever farther north, drawn by the magnetic pole. It hung around with others of its kind on the frozen seas and pack ice for the next two hundred years.

"What about me?" Hoot asked.

"You're the extra pair of hands," Asko said. "Every operation needs those."

They stuffed themselves into Janatuinen's car. Janatuinen was driving, Asko sat in the passenger seat, and Hoot and Elina were in the back. The raskel stood in the yard and watched them drive away. He was holding a road map that Janatuinen had given him.

As they crossed the bridge and turned toward the town, Hoot cleared his throat, searching for words.

"So, hey, Officer… You're not really gonna arrest anybody, are you?"

Janatuinen turned onto the highway, accelerated, and shifted into fourth gear. She rested her elbow on the edge of the open driver's window and leaned her head on her fist.

"If I told you that last night I saw a naked man climb out of a garbage can, and he had the head of a unicorn and wings and he spread his wings and took off and flew away like a magpie, would you think I was completely crazy?"

A quiet fell over the car. Then Hoot said,

"Stranger things have happened."

"Right. That's what I figured. So, why not go and see this wraith of yours?"

. . .

One day, a storm blew over the Arctic and snatched the wraith up with it. In the midst of the winds, the wraith met a Siberian chiffchaff, took over its body, and went whirling over the border into Finland, where it got stuck in a tree next to a town hall in eastern Lapland. The wraith went into the mayor's dog and then into the mayor, whose constituents locked him in a bank vault. They put a notice on the door of the vault that read: "Do not open: wraith inside."

In the morning, the first person to arrive at the bank was a loan officer. It was her birthday. When she saw the note, she believed that it was a birthday prank, and she thought that there was some sort of surprise for her, perhaps a raise, in the vault. So the loan officer opened the vault, at which point the wraith shoved her aside and almost ran her over, because it was pretty tired of the trap it was in. It wanted something to eat. It ran out of the bank and saw a grocery store.

Timo Leppänen had opened the grocery a little late, because of the throng night. He had only been in the shop half an hour when the mayor walked in. Leppänen decided that the store had been open long enough and he hotfooted it out of there.

He ran across the road to the service station, shouting that the wraith was on the loose.

The wraith sprinted past the fruits and vegetables. It didn't so much as glance at them. It stopped in the meat section. There was meat in slices, rolls, and chunks. Why? the wraith wondered. It took a package of Russian mettwurst off a hook and asked for advice from the mayor's fingers. The fingers found the corner tab on the package. The wraith pulled the package open and a pungent odor came flooding out. The wraith used the fingers to grab the entire leaning tower of sticky, smashed-together slices of wurst and crammed one end in its mouth. It chewed. Spicy and tasty. The wraith ate some more and howled with happiness. It dropped the rest on the floor and grabbed a pack of boiled ham, then smoked ham. It kept going until it had eaten every kind of meat product, from honey-baked turkey to salt pork. With a stomach full of meat, the wraith walked to the dairy aisle. It opened the door to the refrigerator case. A cool wind blew out over its face and it remembered the lonely, endless years in Siberia. It shook its head and closed the door. It opened the door again. It took out a tub of margarine, dug out a handful, and crammed the fat in its mouth. It opened the case again and took out some cheese. Edam, Gouda, and a kilo of Oltermanni. It unwrapped some cream cheese from a gold-foil package, held the soft chunk in both hands, growled, and wept, it was so moved. On the tundra it had gnawed on frozen seeds. The wraith vomited on the floor, wiped its mouth on its sleeve, and continued. The mayor's stomach was so full now that it hurt to walk. The wraith came to the freezer cases, pulled aside the sliding door, and took out some ice cream. It probed an oval tub of mango ice cream, found the tab, and pulled. The lid popped off. The wraith tried to dig out some ice cream with its fingers, but it was too hard. It lifted the tub and licked the ice cream straight out of the package. It opened packages of berry, salted chocolate, cranberry fudge, Neapolitan, and licorice ice cream. It dropped them all on the floor and walked on. It found the potato chips and tore the bags open. They exploded like cluster bombs, scattering their contents on the floor. The wraith sat down among them and scooped them into its mouth. Rustic chips, ranch-flavored chips, and vinegar chips. It licked the salt and fat from its fingers, wiped them on its shirt and trousers, and lumbered to its feet. It tried the drinks. It opened soft drinks and mineral water—but it didn't drink the latter, only took a sniff. It opened a liter bottle of Coca-Cola and poured some into its mouth, then some more. It swung its head from side to side like a dog and laughed. The wraith swept its hair back with one hand—which must have been one of the mayor's habitual gestures—and went to the candy shelf. It ate some chocolate bars. It tore open a bag of fruit chews, shoved a hand in, grabbed a sticky gob of the candies, and crammed them into its mouth. The gob got stuck in its throat. The wraith coughed. It dropped to its knees and gacked. Its face started to turn red, then blue. It jumped up again. The thick veins on its neck and temples bulged. The wraith wheezed, on all fours on the floor, its mouth open as if it were in labor pains. The slimy glob slid out. The wraith spit mucus on the floor and moaned. It threw up. It wiped its mouth on the back of its hand, then threw up again. The wraith groped for the glob of sweet, found it, and put it back in its mouth. When it started to slide into its windpipe again, it dropped it out of its mouth and onto the floor. A long string of spit led from the wraith's mouth to the candy. The wraith blew a spit bubble. The bubble popped. It stood up and the spit string lengthened, broke, and fell like a thin ceremonial sash across the wraith's chest. Then it went to the fish counter, laid its hands against the plexiglass guard, and peered at the salmon and pike perch.

It was just picking up a blue-cheese salmon roll when it heard the door of the grocery store open. It dropped the fish on the floor and raised its head as if it were trying to smell the newcomer—or newcomers. There were several of them. The wraith listened. Two people had stopped just inside the door, and a third continued into the shop, toward the wraith. The wraith came out from behind the fish counter. It wanted to see the newcomer, to get a closer look. It started to run. It ran down the aisle and around the corner, and it saw the person. At that moment, the world swung ninety degrees. The grocery aisle was suddenly a vertical chasm with the person at the bottom, and the wraith began to fall uncontrollably, wrenching itself away from the mayor's nauseated body, heavy as a wet bathrobe, and shot like a rock toward the woman, who held her hands up in front of her.

Elina's head slammed against the shelf behind her and she slid on her back to the floor. Kilo bags of wheat and barley flour teetered for a moment on the shelf above like hesitant suicides, then fell on her one and two at a time. Elina raised an arm to protect her face. Thwump. Thwump. Puffs of flour drifted into the air.

Hoot and Asko, waiting at the counter, hurried to her.

"He came at you like a pig on a pumpernickel," Asko yelled.

Hoot helped Elina to her feet and dusted the flour off her.

"You all right?" he asked.

Elina nodded. She handed the box, carved from burled wood and as big as a large matchbox, to Asko.

"There you go."

Asko turned it around in his hands and chortled.

"He's not going anywhere. Did you hold onto it right?"

"Like this," Elina said, putting a fist in front of her chest. "Just like you said. As soon as I felt it go in the box, I slammed the lid shut."

"You did great."

Hoot looked warily at the box.

"Are you absolutely sure it can't get out?"

"My great-great-grandpa stayed in there for a hundred and fifty years," Asko said.

"What happened then?"

"Efraim opened it. We must've been cleaning for a week after that."

Hoot wanted to know why Asko was so sure the wraith would try to take over Elina. Asko said that active magic attracts spirits like moths to a flame. Elina's curse was still particularly strong. It radiated for a mile around.

"In the old days, witches would curse their youngest child specifically to lure wraiths and shadow spirits so they could catch them in a jar."

"What did they do with them?"

"Let them loose at the neighbor's house."

"What for?"

"To be a nuisance."

There was a moan from the aisles. The mayor was trying to stand up. They went over to him. Asko told him that he should get up and move if he felt at all able.

"Am I dead?" the mayor asked.

"No."

"I feel like I might be dead."

"You've gorged yourself till your stomach's nearly burst, that's your trouble."

They helped the mayor to his feet and led him outside. Janatuinen was standing on the steps in front of an enormous crowd, her arms spread like Christ on the cross.

When Asko, Hoot, and Elina had first gone inside, Janatuinen had sat down on the bottom step in front of the entrance. She smoked and watched people gawking from the service station across the road. More people gradually arrived. The first of them had already been there when Janatuinen parked the car in front of the bank. More had arrived while Hoot, Elina, and Asko were questioning the distressed loan officer, who pointed them in the direction of the grocery store. They drove to the store. While they were in transit, the audience doubled.

When Janatuinen finished her cigarette, the people started crossing the road. They came in their ugly trucker hats, their track jackets and track bottoms. Men, women, children, youths. There was even one elderly man being pushed in a wheelchair. The crowd was boisterous, emboldened by their numbers and the justness of their errand. That was nothing new for Janatuinen. She climbed to the top of the steps and waited. The people formed a semicircle around her. Those without hats shaded their eyes with their hands, and she looked at them, their sour expressions, and felt like a sheriff in an old Western, confronted by townspeople demanding that a prisoner be lynched. The crowd chattered and glared at Janatuinen, who didn't avoid eye contact with any of them. She waited for Simo the Shit to take a place in the back. Then she said that there was nothing to see here, or to try to see, and in particular nothing to gossip about, and everybody could go back to their homes.

Someone in the crowd replied that they didn't need the police ordering them around. Janatuinen said that she wasn't ordering anybody to do anything, just looking out for their safety. There was laughter. Someone said that this parish had taken care of its own safety for hundreds of years. Janatuinen said that was something that they might want to reconsider.

"Nobody here likes you," somebody shouted. "And I don't like you, either," Janatuinen said. "Where's your gun?" "In the car." "Are you a bit stupid?" "Probably about as stupid as you are."

"Boy, if we still had Auvo Pasma as police chief…" someone said.

There was a bustle among the crowd. People were making way for someone. Some two—a little old woman and an even littler, older man were pushing their way to the front. The woman was wearing a neon-green tracksuit and running shoes. The man was wearing a white shirt with a small plaid pattern, like an engineer, and trousers that were too large, held up by a black leather belt. He had an expression on his face like a person who has no idea where he has ended up.

The woman peered at Janatuinen and seemed to be waiting for her to speak first.

Janatuinen remained silent.

"Do you know who I am?" the woman asked.

"No."

"That's Old Lady Riipi," someone in the crowd yelled.

The woman glared in the direction of the yeller.

"I am Helmi Riipi, this village's certified witch."

"Congratulations."

Old Lady Riipi nodded toward the man next to her.

"This is Naru-Taavetti, my colleague from Savukoski. He is an incredibly renowned spirit-fighter."

The renowned spirit-fighter blinked fearfully, as if startled by this appraisal.

"We can take care of that wraith," Old Lady Riipi said.

"Thanks for the offer, but we already have an expert working on it."

"Asko, you mean? We saw him go in. I wouldn't trust it to him, if I were you. Him and that wraith are a bad combination. Real bad. And the wraith is inside our mayor. We're worried about his health."

The crowd murmured in agreement.

"So, if you would just let us in there."

"That won't be possible."

"Listen," Old Lady Riipi said. "If you don't let us in then Taavetti and I will have no choice but to turn you into a toad."

The crowd cheered.

Janatuinen put her hands on her hips.

"Go ahead."

There was a stir in the crowd. Everyone was looking at Old Lady Riipi.

"What?" the old woman said.

"Go ahead."

Old Lady Riipi glanced at her colleague from Savukoski. He had closed his eyes, as if it were a way to escape the bewildering situation he was in. Old Lady Riipi raised her hand. She fluttered her fingers at Janatuinen and mumbled. Janatuinen looked at her. Old Lady Riipi lowered her hand.

"Aren't you afraid at all?"

"I don't have time. I'm working."

There was an altercation at the edge of the crowd. The two men Janatuinen had talked with at the inn the previous evening were exchanging heated words with the people around them. The men said they knew Janatuinen and that the villagers should listen to her. The crowd was shocked. The shouting increased and Janatuinen raised her hands and told everyone to calm down.

The door of the grocery store opened and Asko walked out. Behind him were Hoot and Elina with the mayor between them, supporting him in his stumbling steps. The crowd leaped two meters backward. Asko said that the wraith had been driven out. The mayor smiled hesitantly and raised one hand. The crowd cheered. Janatuinen went down the steps with her arms wide and cleared a channel through the mob. Asko, Elina, Hoot, and the mayor followed in her wake.

Old Lady Riipi looked on in disbelief.

"Where's the wraith?"

"In a safe place," Asko said. "Look who's here! Hi, Taavetti. They giving you time off from the care home nowadays?"

The spirit-fighter from Savukoski looked at Asko with a furrowed brow.

"The wraith should be destroyed," Old Lady Riipi said.

"Everything in its time."

They gave the mayor over to his family's care and pulled Old Lady Riipi and Naru-Taavetti aside. Hoot gave them the general picture of the situation.

They asked a favor of the two witches.

Asko took a bottle out of his case and gave it to Old Lady Riipi. He told her that Jousia Mäkitalo was under a curse that required attention without delay. He needed to drink at least fifty milliliters of this liquid.

Old Lady Riipi held the bottle up in the sunlight to look at it.

"Is this what I think it is?"

"The very same."

Old Lady Riipi and Naru-Taavetti got a ride from the mailman. Elina, Hoot, Asko, and Janatuinen set out for the Ylijaako place. In the car on the way there, Elina started to feel worse. Janatuinen pulled over. The others sat in the car and waited while Elina crouched on the shoulder with her hands braced against her knees.

She kept her eyes closed and breathed deeply the rest of the way.

Asko said she would improve once she got back to the house. Not a lot, but a bit.

When they were a kilometer from Vuopio, Asko grunted and started tugging at his seat belt, demanding to be let out of the car. Hoot put a hand on his shoulder and told him calmly where they were, and why.

Asko nodded.

"Oh yeah," he said.

When they reached the house, there was a surprise for them in the yard—a white Ford Escort. Hoot recognized it as Keijo's car. As they parked next to it, Keijo and Heta, who had been on the porch keeping lookout, came down the steps to meet them.

The raskel came, too, from behind the sauna. He was clapping his hands together so hard that the noise echoed across the yard.

"Afternoon," Keijo said as Janatuinen, Asko, Elina, and Hoot got out of the car.

Hoot nodded.

"Hi."

"Sure are a lot of you here," Keijo said. He nodded at Janatuinen. "Miss Police Officer."

"Afternoon," Janatuinen said. She gave the raskel a scratch behind the ear, and he purred with happiness.

"You and that raskel have become quite the bosom buddies."

Janatuinen made no reply. For a moment, everyone just stood and sized one another up. Finally Heta spoke.

"What's going on here?"

"What do you mean?" Hoot asked.

"That one there," Heta said, pointing at Elina, "has been up to something at the pond. Even though she's got no business being there."

Elina opened her mouth, but Asko beat her to it.

"Her spirit's gone into a pike's belly."

Heta clapped a hand on her forehead.

"I knew it."

A vole ran out from under a lilac bush and dashed across

287

the yard, a dark stub of a thing as wide as your hand, headed toward the riverbank. The raskel took off after it.

"I don't have time for this," Elina said. "Slabber Olli's waiting."

"Slabber Olli," Heta gasped.

Keijo led the shocked woman over to the sauna steps to sit down.

Asko took the box out of his pocket.

"Do you mean to go alone?" he asked Elina.

"No, Hoot's coming too."

"I could go with you."

"It's a narrow boat. Shouldn't put three people in it."

Asko screwed up his mouth.

"It's just that it occurred to me that if you have a deal with Slabber Olli for a stripefoot's snout…"

"Yeah?"

"…and you bring him that wraith instead… It is a good payment, nothing wrong with it, but you can't just change a deal with a spirit. What if I were to come instead of Hoot? To negotiate."

Asko turned the box around in his hands nervously as he spoke.

"I wanna see him!" he cried.

Elina took the box.

"Don't worry. You'll see him all right."

Hoot rowed. Elina sat in the rear with her arms wrapped around her stomach. The box was on the bottom of the boat in front of her.

288

Asko had rubbed some salve on her toe to ease the pain, but when they left the house the ache in her stomach grew worse again.

"If you're feeling that bad, how are you going to get up the ridge on the island?" Hoot asked.

"I'll be fine."

"Maybe it'd be better if you stayed in the boat and I took the wraith ashore. What do you say?"

There were two mosquitoes on the back of Hoot's left hand. They were the fastest, strongest, and shrewdest of the thousand-head swarm that had followed them to the boat and now out onto the windy open water. Superior warriors readying to collect their spoils. They stung.

Hoot blew them away.

Elina didn't answer. Hoot rowed. They were halfway between the shore and the island.

"This is where we caught that big pike. Remember?" Hoot said. "Or almost caught it. Snagged it with your fluorine red Rapala."

"It was the orange Hi-Lo," Elina said.

"Was it?"

"Yeah. And you said you'd eat a hat full of shit if we caught anything with it."

"Did I?"

"Yeah."

"I see. Well, that pike must've been ten kilos."

"Might've been five. Then it broke the line."

"Or did the line come untied?"

"My knots don't come untied."

"Well, at least I didn't have to eat that hatful."

"I caught some pike with it later, too."

"Did you?"

"Yeah."

"I see. Listen…"

"What?"

"We're gonna catch this pike."

"You think so?"

"I don't think so—I promise. I'll dive in for it and get it for you myself if I have to."

"Hoot…"

"Don't believe me?"

"Hoot!"

"I can still do things."

"Look over there."

Elina pointed at the island. Hoot lifted the oars and turned his head.

On the shore of the island there was a big pile of brush, on two legs.

"Oho," Hoot said.

They pushed the boat ashore a short distance away from Slabber Olli. He was still motionless.

Elina gestured to Hoot to stay with the boat. She approached Slabber Olli with the wraith box held in front of her.

When she was two meters away, Slabber Olli turned his head. He lifted one foot, then the other, slowly, as if he'd been waiting for a long time and gotten stiff.

Slabber Olli rotated and faced Elina. Even bent over, he stood two and a half meters tall.

Elina could hear Hoot brace himself against the boat. An oar clattered.

Stay there, she thought.

"Elina Ylijaako," Slabber Olli said.

"You look better," Elina said. "Bigger."

"I've been eating squirrels," Slabber Olli said. He raised an arm. "I'm starting to grow leaves."

There was a faint trace of green buds on his gnarled forearm.

"That's great. Listen. I don't have a stripefoot snout for you."

Slabber Olli didn't say anything for a moment. Then he said, "Oy-oy-oy…"

"But I have a wraith."

Elina held out the box.

"A wraith," Slabber Olli said, turning the word over in his wooden mouth like a sour candy. "We agreed you'd bring a stripefoot's snout."

"This is better," Elina said. She heard Hoot's footsteps approaching behind her. Slabber Olli didn't take the box.

Hoot came up next to Elina and asked if there was any problem.

"The thing is," Slabber Olli said. "I already sold it to someone."

"Sold what?" Elina asked.

"The snout."

Elina and Hoot glanced at each other.

"Who'd you sell it to?"

"A certain party."

"Why?"

JUHANI KARILA

"It's a good thing you summoned me here," Slabber Olli said. "Very good. It gave me a chance to hide. Get stronger. But I still owe that snout. To a certain party."

Elina shook the box.

"Maybe this friend of yours would take this instead."

"It's not a friend of mine."

"The buyer, then."

"This is bad," Slabber Olli said, and sat down on the ground. "Real bad."

He opened his mouth, which was as big as a washtub. He closed it.

Then nothing happened.

"What's he doing?" Hoot whispered.

"Wondering whether he should eat us."

"I see."

Hoot glanced behind him, at the boat.

"Don't do anything," Elina said.

They waited. A beetle crawled up Slabber Olli's cheek, spread its wings, and flew away.

There was a crash. Slabber Olli had moved. Hoot grabbed Elina's arm.

Slabber Olli stood up.

"Yeah," he said. "I got time. I accept the new deal. I'll take the wraith, and chase off the knacky."

Hoot let out a long breath.

Slabber Olli put out his hand. Elina gave him the box.

"You should probably be…" Hoot began.

Slabber Olli opened the box.

"…a little more careful with that."

The wraith shot out of the box in a screeching electric arc. Elina and Hoot clapped their hands over their ears. Slabber Olli's hand shot straight out.

A cloud of sparks like a living flame wriggled in his fist.

Slabber Olli lifted his fist to his mouth.

His head caught fire.

The flash was so bright that Elina and Hoot instinctively put their hands over their eyes. Slabber Olli's head was blinding flames, a bright, white torch. The empty eye sockets and mouth rippled and warped in the bonfire. In a few seconds the flames subsided and condensed into a small, glowing halo around his head. Slabber Olli swallowed. The ball of fire slid into his depths, then went out.

"It's good," he said.

The flexible wooden branches that his limbs were made from began to move like snakes. They bumped together and moved over and under one another, becoming stronger, wrapping into tight braids and growing longer. Rowan leaves burst from the buds on his arms and legs. His head, a charred black stub of log, changed color: first the orange of fresh wood, then the green of the inner bark and cambium. On top of this sturdy structure, a thick, reddish-gray layer of pine bark formed, with mouth- and eyeholes like the nest holes of little birds. White clover, daisies, and catbells in full bloom burst from the top of his head and a spruce seedling covered in bright green needles grew in the middle, like a crown.

Slabber Olli stood three and a half meters tall now. He looked at his hands, large as road signs, and squeezed them into fists.

"I feel strong," he said. "See you at the pond."

He stepped into the water, waded a few meters, sank sound-lessly into the depths, and disappeared.

Hoot scratched his head.

"Heck of a thing."

"Let's go," Elina said.

As they rowed back, they looked at the water around them, but they didn't see any sign of Slabber Olli.

When they came ashore, Elina looked at her watch. It was seven p.m. She had two hours left.

18

Elina was first to step off the farm road into the swamp. Behind her were Hoot, Asko, Janatuinen, and, lastly, the raskel. There was no bribe that could get him to wait in the yard. He walked along intently, as if he understood that this trip could solve everything.

A cuckoo called from a wooded fen island like the first bird of the morning. The tussocks trembled under their feet, apt to give way at any time.

The horizon was bright and clear. The swamp was brown and wet and scruffy.

There was an appalling quantity of mosquitoes all around them.

Before they'd left, Elina had said that this was probably a suicide mission. Nobody was obliged to go with her.

"Yeah, yeah," Hoot had said, coming out of the mud room in rubber boots. He handed another pair of boots to Janatuinen. Asko rubbed bug repellent on his neck. Heta and Keijo wanted to go, too, but Elina talked them into staying behind, in case there was a call from Jousia's house.

Elina was carrying her spinning rod. Asko had his medicine case. Janatuinen had her pistol shoved in the back of her waistband, although Elina had told her that a pistol was no use against a knacky.

They finished the first leg of the trip and came to the Back Pond. Janatuinen, who had already fallen down four times, asked hopefully if this was the place. Elina said it wasn't. Janatuinen let out a string of curses. They trudged through the willows that surrounded the Back Pond. Some of the branches were dry and gray and exceedingly unyielding. They labored on under a blinding blue sky, like a march of the downtrodden, with no reprieve and no spark to set them aflame. When they had made it through the underbrush and stood at the edge of the bog, catching their breath, Janatuinen pointed to a stand of spruce about a hundred and fifty meters to their right. She asked why they hadn't gone through there. Elina explained that it was nothing but swamp, with a fen island about two hundred meters across, floating in the middle, and the rest was pools, fens, and open marsh for miles. They were on the most direct route, Elina assured her, and Janatuinen said that this was the most unbelievable dungheap of a place she had ever seen.

When they were getting ready to go, Janatuinen had turned down the offer of a cap and bug spray at first. When the others told her she wasn't going anywhere until she put them on, she slapped some of the repellent haphazardly on her cheeks and hands and let Hoot put a trucker hat on her head. But the skin on her temples, the edge of her hair, and behind her ears was unprotected, and the mosquitoes swarmed to those spots as though it were Crazy Days at the department store. Janatuinen let out little cries and scratched until Hoot grew tired of listening to her. He ordered her to close her eyes and hold her breath, took a spray bottle out of a cargo pocket, shook it, and sprayed a gray cloud of it in the air all around her.

"You can open your eyes," he said.

Janatuinen blinked amid the powerful stink. She stared past Hoot and asked, "What's that?" Everyone turned to look. About three hundred meters off to the left, they saw Slabber Olli. He was walking slowly through the swamp on his long legs, upright, bristling with sticks and twigs like a big fuzzy bird, a tufted swamp ruff grown to monstrous proportions. Fresh, bright rowan leaves rustled on his mighty shoulders.

When Elina explained what the apparition was, Janatuinen just nodded. Asko squinted eagerly in Slabber Olli's direction.

"Finally, finally," he murmured excitedly.

The raskel sullenly turned his back on the giant, as if he'd met a competitor.

They started moving again and kept their eyes on Slabber Olli, who was coming roughly in their direction and getting closer with every step. Just before they reached Pike Pond, their paths merged.

Elina's troops trudged in a line, like the last survivors on the planet. Alongside them, as if remote-controlled, walked their only weapon, a miraculous creature made from a brush pile of assorted trees, his striking power as yet unknown.

Pike Pond came into view. They could easily spot it because the knacky had built a tower on the opposite shore.

The fish-trap throne was gone. In its place was an old black rowboat and a four-meter aluminum Buster motorboat with a decorative blue fish-pattern, both standing on their ends and leaning against each other. The structure looked like a mid-summer bonfire. At the top of the tower, where the bows of the boats met, was a platform made from a weathered wooden loading pallet. On top of the pallet was the tattered driver's seat from the motorboat, where the knacky sat, watching them approach.

It was anybody's guess what tools or powers the knacky had used to get the boats so far into the swamp. There were no signs that they had been dragged to the spot, and no moving equipment. He was sitting on the boat seat with one hand thrown over the backrest, like a carefree captain. When they came closer, he stood up and put his hands on his hips, smiling broadly. His posture conveyed incontestably superior strength, and Elina realized that bringing the others here was a terrible mistake.

"Welcome to my kingdom, travelers," the knacky said, spreading his arms in a cordial greeting. He glistened silver in the sunlight, as if he'd coated himself in chrome paint from head to foot, like the leader of some wilderness cult. "Have a seat, everyone! Unfortunately, all the seats are damp."

"You all should leave," Elina said to Hoot. "Right now."

"Don't talk nonsense."

The knacky giggled and jumped up and down until the tower shook. "Wonderful!" he said. "Wonderful, wonderful, wonderful."

Elina was breathing hard. The walk to the pond had used up almost all her strength.

The knacky stepped to the edge of his stage. He stood on tiptoe and rocked forward and back, looking at each visitor in turn. He looked at Slabber Olli for a long time. Like an old acquaintance whose name he couldn't quite remember.

The knacky rocked back on his heels.

"Olli Yliniemi," he said. "I must say that time has not been kind to you, old friend."

Slabber Olli remained silent.

"What brings you here?" the knacky asked.

Silence.

The knacky smiled.

"I think I've hit a sore spot."

Hoot bent closer to Elina and nodded toward Slabber Olli.

"Why isn't he doing anything?"

"I don't know."

"D'you think you should say something?"

"To Slabber Olli, you mean?"

"No, to that one." Hoot nodded toward the knacky.

Elina glanced at the others. Asko was swaying in place, his eyes half closed. The raskel squatted nearby, with his arms spread and his fur standing on end. He looked like he was waiting for permission to run at the tower and knock it down, knacky and all. Next to the raskel was Janatuinen, wet and dirty. It was hard to tell as she stood staring at the knacky whether she was overcome with dazzled admiration or abject dread.

"Is everything all right?" Hoot asked.

"Doing great," she said.

"My guests are whispering among themselves," the knacky said. "It's very impolite."

Hoot nudged Elina. Elina cleared her throat.

"So, um…"

The knacky's sparkling blue gaze, under hooded shark-gray lids, met Elina's.

299

"Yes?"

Elina cleared her throat again. She tried to stand up tall.

"I came to get that pike."

The knacky smiled.

"I told you what would happen if you came back here. I was very, very sad after your last visit. When you tried to cheat me like that. I hoped that I wouldn't ever have to endure the sight of you again. But looking at this delegation…"—here the knacky made a sweeping gesture with one hand—"…I'm really not sorry at all. Not at all. It's nice to see that Asko Pasma has also worked up the courage to leave his yard after all these years. And after I tried so many times to lure him head first off the riverbank. Isn't that right, Pasma?"

Asko didn't reply.

"Though it's hardly likely he's even aware of where he's wandered to."

No one answered. The knacky nodded.

"I could just sit and chat with all of you for such a long time."

A crow alighted on a branch at the edge of the fen island and cawed.

"Say no more," the knacky said. He pressed his palms together. "Any last wishes?"

"Hand over the pike and no harm will come to you," Elina said.

"What a delightfully bold attitude! But I'm afraid there's nothing you can do to get out of this alive. Nor can any of you, for that matter."

"There's no need to bring the others into this."

"But of course there is. It would be such a shame for them to go to all the trouble to come here for no reason."

And, having said this, the knacky crouched, dropped down from the top of the tower as lightly as a bird, and started walking around the pond.

Elina ordered the others to move back.

"What's happening?" Janatuinen asked, and Elina told her that the knacky was coming to kill them.

"I'll shoot it," Janatuinen said, and reached for the gun in the back of her waistband.

"No. Whatever happens, don't shoot."

Slabber Olli still stood where he was.

"This would be a good time," Elina told him.

The knacky was nearly all the way around the pond when he suddenly stopped about fifteen meters from them, and seemed unable to go any farther.

"What's this?" the knacky said. His head swiveled.

Everyone had backed up except for Asko, who, like Slabber Olli, stood firm, as if frozen in place, his hands in fists at his sides.

The knacky walked back and forth behind an invisible barrier.

"Clever, Asko Pasma. Very clever. You must have started building this the moment you arrived. These abilities of yours are something I've wanted to talk to you about. If you had only accepted my invitation and dropped in at my villa at the bottom of the river…"

The knacky rubbed his chin.

"How to get through…" he said, placing a palm against the air, like a mime. He moved his hand. "How to get in…"

he said, stroking the obstacle in front of him. "Ah, here it is." He pressed his fingers against the air as if punching in a code and Asko gasped and fell to his knees.

"That was rather easy," the knacky said, and started walking again.

The raskel spread his arms and made a dash at the knacky. The knacky chuckled jovially and lifted his hand, as if in greeting. The raskel drew back his right fist and then threw it forward with a force that could have put a hole in a log-cabin wall. The knacky swung his head slightly to one side and the blow passed an inch from his temple. The raskel followed the blow forward and fell, and the knacky walked past him with an affectionate smile, as if he were passing a dear acquaintance on the street. His hand paused at the raskel's face, as if he were plucking a speck out of his eye. Then the encounter was over, and the raskel was standing behind the knacky. The raskel took a sudden breath and started to scream. The knacky didn't turn around. He walked toward the horrified group and raised a hand to show them the raskel's eye, like a medal. Then he put the eye in his mouth and ate it.

The raskel had one hand over his eye socket. With the other hand he scrabbled at the moss, yelping.

"Who wants to be next?" the knacky asked.

"Out of the way," Janatuinen said, and pulled out her gun.

"Don't," Elina shouted.

Janatuinen fired. She held the gun in both hands and shot in a quick, trained rhythm, as she'd done thousands of times in practice. The knacky just kept walking, bending his body as he went, as if he were doing stretches.

Janatuinen's gun clicked, empty. Not one bullet had hit its mark.

"Fantastic," the knacky said, and reached out a hand to grab Janatuinen.

Slabber Olli's tongue shot out five meters like a projectile, like sticky green lightning. The knacky bent forward. The tongue zinged past. The knacky was holding the tongue in both hands. The sequence of events was so fast that it seemed as if the knacky had wished for the green sausagey thing and his wish had been granted at a slightly awkward moment.

Janatuinen, Elina, and Hoot pulled Asko back. The knacky watched their efforts.

"Don't go away," he said. "I'll be right back."

Slabber Olli stood in the swamp, his tree-trunk legs spread wide. He jerked his head, his mouth wide open, trying to get his tongue back.

"This is mine now," the knacky said, and gave the tongue a yank with both hands. Slabber Olli slumped to his knees. The knacky wrapped the tongue around his wrist.

"You gave it to me," the knacky said, and yanked again. Slabber Olli fell on his face in the swamp. The knacky let go with one hand and sliced the tongue in two with a fingernail.

The end of Slabber Olli's tongue spun in the air as it snapped, like a live snake. The knacky dropped it into the swamp and walked toward Slabber Olli, who tried to stand up. Slabber Olli launched his right hand toward the knacky. The motion was almost as fast as his tongue, but the knacky just stepped aside, and the punch shot past it. The knacky took two brisk running steps and was behind Slabber Olli.

"How can he move so fast?" Hoot said.

Slabber Olli turned to face the knacky, but the knacky matched his movements and remained behind him, like a shadow, guffawing like a drunk. Then he grabbed a bit of stick on Slabber Olli's back and pulled him backward with one quick jerk. Slabber Olli tried to get up, but the knacky put a foot on him and held him down. He climbed up on Olli's chest and pinned his left arm in the swamp with his right foot, then took hold of Olli's right arm and started twisting it clockwise. The wood creaked and the fibers sputtered apart one by one. The knacky tore the limb off entirely and threw it over his shoulder like any old stick. He lifted his foot and Olli started flailing at his torturer with his free arm, but the knacky dodged his ludicrously flapping hand. Then he tired of this and grabbed Slabber Olli by the wrist. He twisted the other arm off, and tossed it aside. Slabber Olli lay still now, as if resigned to his fate, his legs lying straight. The knacky whistled a tune. He probed Slabber Olli's torso with his fingers, found a sturdy piece of juniper wood in the giant's leafy chest, took hold of it, and started to pull. The wood screeched and the thicket of branches that made up Slabber Olli's body started to stretch and break apart.

Then Slabber Olli's head vaulted forward, as if it were on a spring.

The knacky's grip came loose.

His head was in Slabber Olli's mouth. Slabber Olli crushed the skull in his jaws.

He stood up, using only his legs. The knacky hung limply from his mouth. Slabber Olli lifted his chin toward the sky and gobbled his prey down like a heron does a frog.

Janatuinen rushed over to the raskel. Hoot went over to Asko, who was already able to stand on his own.

Elina had only one thought in her head.

The pike.

19

Slabber Olli was leaning a bit backwards, as if he had fallen asleep upright. With no arms.

Janatuinen considered all the murderers she had met in her career. She realized she would need to create an entirely new category.

"It'll heal up," Asko said.

Janatuinen turned.

"What?"

"It's a clean hole," Asko said. He pointed to the raskel's empty eye socket. "I gave him a compound. To ease the pain."

The raskel looked relaxed. Janatuinen stroked his back.

Slabber Olli's serenity annoyed her.

"Hey," she shouted at him. "What was the problem? Why couldn't you just kill the knacky straightaway?"

A voice came from inside Slabber Olli, like a recording:

"I had to make the knacky believe he had the upper hand. That's when he would start to get careless."

"A lot of stuff happened while you waited."

The middle of Slabber Olli's body started to tremble.

"What's happening?" Janatuinen said.

"I'm sorry," Slabber Olli said.

.   .   .

Elina walked along the pond on legs that felt borrowed from someone else. The water was still and quiet. She had no idea if the pike was still in there.

She looked at her watch. Eight-thirty. She didn't know how strictly curses followed schedules.

The rod felt as heavy as an iron bar. Elina focused, and cast. She nearly flew into the pond after the lure.

"Take it easy," she told herself.

She reeled the line in, ready for a bite.

It never came.

She gathered her strength and cast again. The tip of the rod looked like two tips. It was hard to stay upright.

"Here, let me," said someone beside her.

Hoot was there, holding out his hand for her fishing rod.

"Don't," Elina said, snatching the rod farther away. It was only Hoot's hand on her shoulder that kept her from falling over.

"Would you let me be?" Elina said.

"You're about to tumble over."

Hoot didn't let go of her. Elina swayed. She felt like she had to sit down. Maybe that was a good idea. Maybe she could actually fish sitting down.

"Don't get mixed up in this," she said, and slumped to the ground.

"You can't even cast," Hoot said.

Janatuinen stood in front of them.

"What do you want?" Elina asked.

"Something's happening to Slabber Olli."

"This is not really a good time."

Janatuinen pointed.

"Too bad. Look for yourself."

Slabber Olli's thickety body was swelling and growing denser. New, green willow branches were pushing their way out of his torso and blossoming with pussy willows, then leaves. From the holes where his arms had been, spruces were emerging, intertwining, thickening, and lengthening until they were as sturdy as roof beams. They twisted together into mighty arms, mighty hands, fingers as stout as sticks of firewood. Slabber Olli's legs were growing sturdier, too. New rowan stems slithered out of his thighs and twisted themselves into tough, flexible braids, layer upon layer, until his legs were as thick and strong as pine trees. They grew longer and lifted the still-thickening wickerwork of his upper body even higher. The stout stump that served as Slabber Olli's head darkened and grew over with moss. It swelled into a fern-covered hill, with entire birch trees growing on top—small seedlings at first, but within a few seconds they rose several meters tall. Green leaves exploded from them. Below the trees were two black chasms into Slabber Olli's head, with fires at their bottoms. His mouth was a long, jagged crack.

Slabber Olli smacked his mossy lips, grinned, and lifted his legs one at a time, sending waves across the swamp.

He was as big as a block of flats.

"Feels great," he said.

He noticed the knacky's tower, grabbed the contraption in his fist, and hurled it to the other side of the fen island. The upended boats broke apart as they flew through the air, tumbling wildly across the sky and out of sight.

Slabber Olli crouched down and looked at his little allies.

"I could eat you," he said.

His voice boomed. The raskel hid his face in his hands and whimpered.

Hoot stared at the giant with his mouth open.

"We're done here," Elina said, and lay down on the ground.

Slabber Olli rested hands as big as delivery vans on his knees. He looked past them all, out at the swamp.

"I could eat that one," he said.

The others looked in the same direction. They saw Heta. She stood in the middle of the fen, pointed at Slabber Olli, and said, "What's that?"

"I am a god," Slabber Olli said, reaching out his hand and plucking her up like a berry. Heta screamed. Slabber Olli set her down with the others.

"You are my subjects," Slabber Olli said. "Don't worry about me. Just go about your business. I wanna watch."

No one moved.

"Quick, or I'll eat you."

"Anyway," Hoot said, forcing himself to look at Heta. "What are you doing here?"

"He was in no danger," Heta said. She couldn't take her eyes off Slabber Olli.

"Who?"

"Jousia."

"What do you mean no danger?"

"Old Lady Riipi called from his house. They were there having dinner. Jousia didn't have so much as a headache."

"How is that possible?" Hoot said. "Did you hear that?" he asked Elina. "There's nothing wrong with Jousia."

Elina lay on her back. Hoot bent over her.

"How are you doing?"

"Leave me alone."

"Listen. Is there any possibility that Jousia's curse was only for you?"

Asko spit.

"Definitely not possible," he said. "He'd have to be a witch to do that. Nobody else could cast a spell like that."

"But Elina said Jousia was the one who cursed her, and himself."

"That's not possible."

"Then what's all this about?" Hoot yelled. He directed the question to himself and to everyone else. To the world.

"She did it herself," Slabber Olli said.

They looked up.

"What are you saying?" Hoot asked.

"You should call me Lord High Emperor."

"Oh, for God's sake."

"You want me to eat you?"

Hoot took a deep breath. He asked Slabber Olli again what he meant, and this time appended it with "Lord High Emperor."

"I'll show you."

Slabber Olli started to draw a black line across the air with his finger. There was a high, screeching sound, like a key scratching window glass.

"What's he doing?" Hoot shouted with his hands over his ears.

When the line was about five meters long, Slabber Olli drew another, parallel line two meters below the first one. Then he

joined the segments with a line at either end, to form a rectangle. He took hold of one side and lifted the rectangle, and the
visible landscape within it, like taking a painting off a gallery
wall. He set the rectangle down at his feet. The opening in the
air looked like another landscape, almost the same as the one
he had removed, but in this one the green of the plants was
paler, a rising wind sent little ripples across the surface of the
pond, and the sky was gray and cloudy.

"I believe," Asko said, "He's made a hole in space-time."

In the other landscape, there were two figures on the edge
of the pond.

"Elina and Jousia," Hoot said.

"This is what happened here five years ago," Slabber Olli
said.

Suddenly the view was blocked by a largish man in a
white, sleeveless shirt. The man had no eyes. Where his eyes
should be, there were two tiny mouths filled with sharp teeth.
The man noticed Slabber Olli and the others, grinned with
all three of his mouths, and started trying to climb through
the hole.

"Go to hell," Slabber Olli said, pressing his hand against
the man's forehead and pushing him back into invisibility.

"What was that?" Hoot asked.

"A bad dream."

Jousia and Elina in the other landscape were standing side
by side on the shore of the pond. Their lips were moving,
but their words were inaudible. Judging by their looks, their
conversation was getting heated. Jousia put his hand in his
pocket, showed the stone to Elina, and threw it in the pond.

"There," Hoot said. "He throws the stone in and puts the curse on it."

The stone splashed into the water.

"Why isn't the pike eating it?" Hoot said.

Jousia turned and walked away. Elina was left alone.

"The pike didn't come," Hoot said in surprise. "Why didn't it come? Elina said that it ate the stone."

The Elina in the past sat down on the ground. A bog bogey appeared and tugged at her pant leg. Elina socked it. A moment later, she lifted her hand to the back of her neck. She pulled out a few hairs. Then she got up heavily, walked to the edge of the pond, and crouched down. She was holding the hair in her hand and it looked like she was talking to it. Something rose up to the surface of the pond. The pike. It swam slowly toward Elina and opened its mouth. Elina dropped the hair in. The pike swung its tail with a splash and disappeared under the water. Elina stood up and walked away.

"Show's over," Slabber Olli said. He picked up the rectangle at his feet, set it back in place, and wiped the edges away with his hands.

"What the hell did I just see?" Hoot said.

"She cursed herself," Slabber Olli said. "No one else."

Hoot strode over to where Elina lay on the ground.

Her face was as white as a sheet. Blue veins crisscrossed her cheeks and throat. Her eyes glowed blood-red.

Hoot dropped to his knees. He shook her by the shoulders.

"Why did you do that?" Hoot yelled. "Why?"

"That was what he wanted," Elina whispered.

"What who wanted?"

"Jousia."

"What?"

"He wanted to curse me."

"Holy hell."

"I deserved to be punished."

"Do you realize you're dying?"

Elina's eyes lurched back and forth.

"Your problems sure are funny," Slabber Olli said. He looked east, then west. "I guess I'll get started ruling this country," he said, and set off toward Vuopio.

"Stay where you are."

Slabber Olli had already taken a few steps and was nearly two hundred meters away now. He stopped and turned.

"Listen to me," Asko said. His voice was low and strong. "You made a new agreement with Elina Ylijaako. A wraith is a much better payment than some piece of pipe. And you know it. We're not even yet, Olli."

The swamp heaved as Slabber Olli ran toward Asko. They all found it difficult to stay on their feet, except for Asko, who stood firm on a swaying tussock of grass. Slabber Olli bent down and stuck his face a few meters from Asko's.

"I'm gonna pop you in my mouth."

"Good. And I promise you that the second I get to the other side, I'll go straight to the first service counter and ring the bell. I'll tell them that one of their workers has run off and broken a contract, and I'll make a fuss."

Asko took a breath and continued.

"I've also heard a rumor that you're in debt. And I can give your debtor up-to-date information on your whereabouts. Look here, you may think I can just do a few silly tricks, but I know your world, and I know how it works. And I assure you that if you don't stop your nonsense and start helping us, I will do everything in my power to make sure you end up right in the hands of whoever it is you're running from."

Slabber Olli straightened up. He scratched his grassy head. Spruce needles and cones and twigs rained down on the others.

"You don't know anything," Slabber Olli said. "I could destroy your soul. Scatter it to the wind."

This threat didn't seem to cause Asko any distress.

"But you're right about that. I did get a better deal than I asked for. I apologize. And I promise to help you."

"That's damn good of you," Hoot said. He was trying to keep Elina awake by slapping her on the cheek. "We need to get that pike out of the pond."

"I'm pretty sure the pike is already on its way," Slabber Olli said.

Hoot hurried to pick up the fishing rod.

"That won't work."

"Then you do something."

"All right."

Slabber Olli got down on his knees and stuck his arm in the pond up to the elbow, like an artificial inseminator.

The others picked Elina up and moved her aside. Slabber Olli moved his hand around in the water. His arm filled the pond nearly from shore to shore.

Hoot paced in impatient circles.

"Well?" he said.

"I'm trying."

"Try some more."

"Ah."

"Did you get it?"

"No. Just a tree."

"Speed it up a little."

"Here we go."

Slabber Olli pulled his hand out of the water, coated with silt and debris. In a pool formed by the palm of his hand splashed the pike.

"Kill it," Hoot shouted.

Slabber Olli put his face down near his catch and smelled.

Hoot was about to shout again when Janatuinen laid a hand on his shoulder.

"Hoot."

"What do you want?"

Asko and Heta were on their knees next to Elina.

"The girl's stopped breathing," Asko said.

20

A white ceiling, with familiar cracks in it. She turned her head and saw Janatuinen sitting next to the bed. She was at home. It was light. Impossible to say what time of day it was.

"Water," she said.

Janatuinen handed Elina a glass of water from the night table. Elina struggled to sit up and Janatuinen held the glass for her, as if she were a little child.

"Thank you."

Janatuinen put the glass back on the table.

Elina stared at the ceiling. Quiet. Vague memories of the swamp, the pike. A gigantic, leaf-covered creature.

Am I dead? Elina wondered. Is this what it feels like?

Janatuinen started to talk.

"In my work, I often encounter people who want to harm themselves. There's nothing unusual about that. What's unusual is which kinds of people want to do it. People with nothing serious on their conscience try to jump off the sixth floor, and the ones who've done things that should give them every reason to walk straight in front of a speeding truck never actually do."

Elina heard Janatuinen cross one leg over the other.

"At the beginning of my career, I ran into the following situation. The CEO of a large interior-design company tried to kill himself. We'll call him Matti. Matti was analytical. He mulled over the idea for weeks. His company had gone bust. So he bought a pistol, planning to kill himself in his kitchen. I should tell you at this point that Matti lived on the top floor of an apartment building, in the penthouse. It was an amazing apartment—four bedrooms. A spa area. Big balcony overlooking the whole city. So, Matti was in the kitchen with the gun pointed at his head. He closed his eyes. Squeezed the trigger. And missed. The bullet went into the wall and broke a water pipe, and water started flooding onto the floor. Matti called his property manager, but it was too late. The water destroyed his flat and four other apartments. They all had to be repaired. Matti admitted what he had done and asked forgiveness from his neighbors whose homes he had ruined. He wanted to buy them all a trip to the tropics. I don't know if anyone took him up on the offer. But, whatever the case, Matti got his life back on track after that. He founded a new company—another one having to do with interior design—and he was successful. The company is still in existence. I'm sure you would know it if I mentioned the name, but I don't think I should. I've often thought about Matti. Getting a gun isn't something you just do on a whim. Matti had already written his will and a suicide note and all of that. Everything should have been ready. But then came that missed shot and that stupid water damage, and he had to take care of it. The suicide faded into the background, and when he had time to think about it again, about killing himself, it didn't seem so important anymore. It makes you think. A person can be absolutely sure about something, but all it takes is one coincidence, and everything changes. More water? Can you hear me?"

.   .   .

Elina opened her eyes. It was morning, or evening. Hoot was sitting next to her bed now.

"You're awake. You want to eat something?"

Elina closed her eyes.

Heta was sitting next to her bed. That was a familiar sight.

When Elina was little, Heta used to sit in this same room, waiting for her to fall asleep.

Sometimes she would sing her lullabies.

"How am I still alive?" Elina asked.

"That is quite a tale," Heta said. "But first there's something I have to tell you. About your mother."

"I don't know if I want to hear it."

"Well, you should."

Heta began by describing her marriage to Asko's brother Auvo Pasma, the police chief. She listed all the things, all the objects, that Auvo used to hit her with. A crescent wrench. A spoon. A rolling pin. A ski pole. A belt. A bucket. A cutting board. And his fists, of course. Mostly his fists. Auvo had been a skillful abuser. He used to hit her in places her clothes would hide—her ribs, back, legs. He only hit her in the face a few times, and when he did it was with an open hand, or with some blunt or flat object, like a telephone book, so it wouldn't leave any large bruises. And if it did, Heta was supposed to tell anyone who asked that she had fallen down, due to her own clumsiness.

Heta had only threatened to divorce him once. Auvo was heating the bottom of his boat with a blowtorch, getting ready to tar it, when she'd shouted that at him. Infuriated,

318

SUMMER FISHING IN LAPLAND

Auvo had jabbed the flame into her face. That was how she lost her eye.

Her ticket to freedom had come in the form of a question.

Marke had come into the shop and asked Heta if she would babysit Elina. The suggestion took Heta completely by surprise. But the bigger surprise was that Auvo gave her permission to do it.

The reason soon became clear. When Heta came home from babysitting for the first time, Auvo started to interrogate her. He asked her what the Ylijaakos' house looked like, and what sorts of things they were up to. He was interested because Marke and Kauko had taken up growing potatoes and they'd been propounding their anti-fertilizer point of view at farm-association meetings.

Heta didn't reveal anything to Auvo. She focused her answers on trivial things—the color of the wallpaper, the general cleanliness of the house, the flower beds. She pleaded simple-mindedness. It was an excuse that had always sufficed for Auvo.

Over time, she and Marke became friends. Eventually she told Marke about her predicament.

Marke listened silently. When Heta finished talking, Marke announced that Auvo's behavior was not going to cut it.

"She really said that. 'His behavior is not going to cut it.'"

Heta went quiet. She tapped her foot on the floor.

"Then Marke told me about a curse."

Marke said the curse wouldn't kill Auvo right away. He would have a chance to do better.

But Heta wouldn't hear of such an idea. It frightened her.

It wasn't until Easter, when Auvo broke three of her ribs, that she agreed to it.

Marke told her to get a piece of Auvo's toenail. That was easy, because Auvo had a habit of leaving toenail clippings in little piles around the house. When the June floods subsided, she and Marke went together to Pike Pond.

Marke fed the toenail to the pike and recited a spell.

After the next farm-association meeting, Marke pulled Auvo aside and told him that she knew about the hitting. She told him that if he so much as touched Heta one more time, he would be dead.

Auvo told her that she was mistaken. That everything was fine at home, and if Heta had said something, that was just her habit of telling tall tales.

Then he cut off Heta's finger. He dragged her into the kitchen one day, pressed her left hand against the hot stove, and sawed off her pinkie finger with a bread knife. That's what you get for spoiling your own nest, he said. Heta fainted from the pain. She woke up that night on the floor in a pool of blood, and Auvo was standing beside her, shouting, asking her why she didn't clean up this mess.

Auvo forbade her from ever going to the Ylijaakos' again, but word of it got to Marke, through Esko.

Four days before Auvo's time was up, he started to feel weak. Just like Marke had said he would. She had told him that his body would suffer just before his soul was about to leave.

Auvo's soul was inside the pike, and the pike was getting ready to dive.

"Have you been feeling that, too? A sort of pale feeling, for the past few years? Like nothing feels like anything? Auvo complained of that, too. It's because you cursed the most alive part of yourself into the pike."

Two days before the end date, Auvo couldn't get out of bed. He moaned that his internal organs were on fire, he vomited, had diarrhea.

"So I was surprised when you were still standing on the same evening when the pike was supposed to leave," Heta said. "But I'm not surprised anymore, after what Asko told me. He says that Marke built this house to be a strong fortress of power."

"The spaceship," Elina murmured.

"What?"

"Nothing."

When Auvo had less than a day to live, he demanded that Heta ask Asko to come over. Heta saw no reason to refuse.

She only realized her mistake once Asko arrived. A witch could spot what was going on right away.

Asko gave Auvo some of his drops and pestered him to tell him who had put the spell on him. Heta heard their conversation from behind the door, with her heart in her throat. Auvo denied knowing anything about it. Maybe he was afraid that his own behavior would be made public.

"Cure me!" he kept saying. Asko told him that a curse as strong as that one could only be canceled by whoever made it.

But Auvo wouldn't say who had done it. And by morning, he was dead.

That was the happiest day of Heta's life.

"And they put down that the cause of death was a heart attack. So I knew that no one would ever find out what had happened. But Asko always suspected. He was always on the trail of it."

Heta moved her stool closer to the bed. She bent over Elina and said,

"I'm telling you about Auvo because I wanted you to know what your mother and I did. And why I resorted to that solution. Your mother didn't pressure me one bit. I'm the one culpable for it, and no one else. But I've never regretted it, not once."

She sat up straight again.

"You cursed yourself because you believed you had committed such a terrible crime against Jousia. But you're hardly an evildoer at all, compared to Auvo. Or to me."

"Can you give me some water?" Elina said.

When Heta had put the glass back on the table, Elina asked, "What happened to my pike?"

"We took care of it."

"Did you catch it?"

"Yeah, we got it."

"And you killed it?"

"No."

"Then what did you do?"

"We set it free."

"What?"

"Well, it was like this…"

"…twenty-seven, twenty-eight, twenty-nine, thirty," Janatuinen counted. She lifted her hands from Elina's chest, pinched Elina's nostrils closed, raised her chin, and blew into her mouth two times.

"Breathe, damn it," Hoot said. He pushed the bog bogeys away with a stick.

Elina lay on her back in the bog, framed by cranberry blossoms.

Asko rummaged in his medicine case. He took out bottles and tools and piled them in Heta's lap.

The raskel flapped his arms and spun in circles.

"It might help if we killed that pike," Asko said. He sprinkled herbs into a mortar and started working them with a pestle.

"I will as soon as that one agrees to give it to me," Hoot said.

Slabber Olli, like a forest on two feet, murmured above them. He was holding the pike in his fist.

"There is another option," Slabber Olli said.

"No other options are necessary," Hoot said. "Hand over the fish and I'll finish it off."

"Why do you people have to kill everything?"

"I could ask you the same thing. What were you fixing to do to us?"

"Her heart's beating again," Janatuinen said.

"Give her some of this," Asko said. He shook a bottle filled with a preparation that looked like green tea.

"We could let the pike go in the river," Slabber Olli said.

"I don't like the sound of that."

"It would give you a chance to break the spell."

Elina gasped for air and shivered. Janatuinen held her still and asked Asko why all his remedies were so horrible.

"That's the way medicine is," Asko answered.

"If we don't, the curse will just go on and on," Slabber Olli said.

"You sure about this?" Hoot asked.

Slabber Olli didn't answer.

"OK, let's do it," Hoot said.

"Let's take it to the river," Slabber Olli said. "You carry it."

Hoot dug in his cargo pocket and found a plastic shopping bag. He filled it with water from the pond. Slabber Olli lowered the pike carefully into the bag. The fish wriggled and splashed.

"Give it to me," Elina groaned. She tried to get to her feet, but collapsed.

"We'll wear ourselves out carrying that thing to the river," Asko said.

Slabber Olli lowered his hand.

"Put Elina here."

"That seems a little dangerous," Hoot said, but the others were already lugging Elina over to place her in Slabber Olli's moss-covered hand. Then he lowered his other hand.

"Hop on," he said.

Everyone obeyed, even Hoot. Only the raskel hesitated. He shifted from one foot to the other and whimpered while Janatuinen tried to coax him aboard, but when Slabber Olli started to straighten up, the raskel loped after his hand, got hold of the thumb, and pulled himself up.

Slabber Olli lifted his passengers up onto shoulders overgrown with spruce and birch. Then the giant started off as they clung to the trees. Their hats flew off their heads. The raskel climbed the tallest tree on Slabber Olli's head and swayed in the treetop like a spotter in a crow's nest, howling with happiness.

Slabber Olli walked with long, springy steps. He stepped over Back Pond and the willow thicket that surrounded it in one great stride. Elina lay unconscious in his palm. Slabber Olli stepped over the farm road, traversed a branch of the swamp, and came to a stand of spruce. Just two more steps and they were on the shore of the inlet.

He let the people and the raskel climb down his arm onto the bank, then laid Elina gently on the sand.

Hoot waded into the water up to his knees. He lowered the bag into the river, among the water lilies. The pike flowed out of the bag, listless. Its gills were barely moving.

"Well," Hoot said. "Get moving."

He gave the pike a little push in the tail fin. The pike slid forward, stiff as a stick of wood.

"Is it dead?" Janatuinen asked.

"Get those fins flapping," Hoot said.

The fish rolled onto its side.

"What the hell's wrong with you?"

Asko picked up a branch from the ground and threw it in the water near the pike. A soft splash. The pike swished its tail and disappeared into the water weeds.

Hoot looked out at the open water.

"There it goes."

He turned to look at Slabber Olli.

"Is that it, then? The curse is gone, or what?"

"No," Slabber Olli said. "The hardest part is yet to come."

. . .

JUHANI KARILA

Elina and Hoot sat at the kitchen table. It was early evening. The clock ticked in the living room.

They watched an ermine bustling about in the yard. It had a nest under the old sauna. The ermine was loping around, looking for voles. It scuffled with a magpie that dared to come too close to its nest.

When the magpie flew away, the ermine carried its three cubs away from the sauna one by one and put them under the porch of the house. As it was carrying one cub and was halfway across the yard, it noticed Elina and Hoot watching. It stopped, assessing the situation, the cub in its mouth. Then it kept going, dashing under the porch.

"A brave beast," Hoot said.

"Yeah."

"Squirrels do that too. Move their nests every so often."

"Do they?"

Elina had slept for twenty hours straight. Then she'd eaten two plates of Hoot's mashed potatoes with sausage gravy.

Hoot told her that after they'd freed the pike, Slabber Olli had walked into the water and disappeared, which was a great disappointment to Asko. Asko and Keijo went home, as did Heta, though she had been by to visit since—maybe Elina remembered. Janatuinen was still around. Hoot had made a bed for her in the old house. She was taking a walk with the raskel at the moment. Hoot said that Musti didn't even remember having two eyes anymore.

"The rest is up to you," Hoot said.

"The rest of what?"

"Breaking the curse."

"I see."

"You put the curse on yourself, and you're the only one who can cancel it. The pike didn't run off with your soul this year. It's in the river now. But it'll be there again next year. In the pond. Are you listening?"

Elina closed her eyes.

"You need to forgive yourself," Hoot said.

"Don't talk nonsense."

"No, I mean it."

"Stop it."

"Slabber Olli said so."

"Oh, did he?"

"The curse will stay in effect as long as the one who placed it wants it to be. No amount of magic words or memorized mumbo-jumbo will work. You have to want to stop punishing yourself."

Elina didn't say anything.

"Why didn't you tell me how it really happened?" Hoot said.

A familiar, smothering feeling spread through Elina's body. She got up from her chair.

"It's OK," Hoot said. "I'm not angry at you."

Elina stood next to the chair. Sat down again.

"I'm just wondering why you had to lie to me."

Elina laid her forehead on the table.

"I'm a bad person."

"That's not true."

"I was scared."

"'Course you were."

"I'm sorry."

"Can we agree on one thing?"

Elina raised her head.

"What?"

"You stop apologizing."

"OK. Sorry."

THE FOURTH DAY

2 1

The next morning, Hoot, Elina, and Janatuinen played Finnish darts. The raskel sulked under the rowan tree because they wouldn't let him play.

"Don't you have to be getting back to work?" Elina asked Janatuinen.

"I'll go back when I can think of something to tell my boss."

Janatuinen claimed that she'd never played darts in her life, but she was throwing the best score on every round.

It was cloudy. The wind murmured in the aspen trees. Hoot said it was the coolest morning they'd had in weeks.

It was Hoot's turn to throw. He arranged the darts comfortably in his hand.

"I'm planning a little project," he said as he prepared his throw.

"And what might that be?" Elina asked.

"I was thinking we should clean out that barn."

"Oh? What for?"

"It's full of useless junk."

"There could be important stuff in there, too."

"Have you been in there?" Hoot asked Janatuinen.

Janatuinen nodded.

"And?"

"If I were you, I'd blow the whole thing up."

"Good," Hoot said. "By order of the authorities."

He threw. Seven.

"So what are you planning to do with this place?" Hoot asked, and threw again. Eight.

"I haven't thought about it."

"Why am I not surprised?"

Hoot threw the rest of his darts and went to count his score. He brought the darts back for Janatuinen.

"Twenty-six."

Janatuinen stood behind the stone. Hoot came and stood next to Elina.

"What would you think of me moving here? I could sell my cabin. Or give it to Asko and Efraim, for storage. I could buy this place from you. But on the understanding that I would leave your room as it is and you could come and go as you please. Of course, I wouldn't if you were thinking of staying here."

"Nah. Prob'bly not."

"You have a job down south, after all."

"Yeah."

"What do you say?"

"I'll have to think about it."

"Right."

"Forty-one," Janatuinen said.

"She's just better at it," Hoot said. "Well, shall we get started?"

They carried everything out of the barn—old bicycles, mopeds, toys, and tools. The rotted boards, potato boxes, and furniture they tossed into a bonfire behind the barn.

They called Esko, who came and backed his truck into the yard. They loaded it full of junk. Esko shoved the money Hoot gave him into the pocket of his overalls, raised a hand, and drove off to the dump.

That evening they heated up the sauna. Elina and Janatuinen sat on the warm cedar bench and listened to the roar of the fire in the sauna stove. Janatuinen talked about a homeless man who lit the same kiosk on fire every fall so he could spend the winter in jail. Elina reminisced about Naru-Taavetti's exploits. When Hoot had finished his sauna, the three of them sat at the kitchen table and played a few hands of seven of clubs.

The raskel was standing sentinel on the top of the barn roof, watching over the house.

They listened to the radio. It said on the news that a heat wave was sweeping the whole country. Researchers warned that next year could be even worse.

At midnight, Janatuinen said good night and went to the old house. Elina took off the watch and gave it to Hoot.

"I'm going to head out in the morning."

"Up to you," Hoot said.

Elina waited for him to say more, but he just nodded.

"Up to you."

THE FIFTH DAY

22

After breakfast, Elina shook hands with Janatuinen, who wished her a good trip. She also shook hands with the raskel, who was waiting his turn, with his hand out. He pumped her hand up and down so hard that Janatuinen had to tell him to stop.

Hoot was the hardest. First they both just stood there, not knowing what to do. Then Hoot grabbed her by the shoulder and gave her a gentle shake.

The three of them watched as she drove out of the yard.

When she reached the mailbox, she noticed a horsefly on the passenger window. She stopped and opened the door.

"Out you go."

She pushed the door all the way open. The fly didn't budge.

"How can anything be so stupid."

She flicked the bug into the ditch.

Elina drove through town without stopping. Two kilometers before she reached Loon Spit, she felt a lurch in the pit of her stomach.

A hundred meters before the driveway to Jousia's house, she still wasn't sure if she would turn.

Jousia was sitting on the porch steps, just like he used to. Elina stopped in front of the barn and got out of the car.

"Hi," he said.

"Hi."

The churn in her stomach stopped.

"So, you sent Old Lady Riipi and some geezer from Savukoski over to check on me," Jousia said.

Elina stood next to her open car door. "Yeah. Sorry."

"It's all right."

There was a stroller on the steps next to him. Elina nodded in that direction.

"Who's that?"

"Come and see."

Elina walked over. Jousia pulled aside a shade blanket held by two clothespins. In the stroller was a baby asleep, its little fists held against its chest.

"This is Saara Elina Mäkitalo."

"So cute."

They sat on the steps.

"Your hair's gone," Jousia said.

Elina rubbed her buzz-cut.

"Yeah."

She straightened her legs.

"How've you been?" she asked.

"Can't complain."

"OK."

"And yourself?"

Elina pondered this. Jousia plucked up a blade of grass and started tearing it into little pieces.

"Better all the time," Elina said.

"Good to hear. You were in an awful hurry there in the store."

"Yeah."

Elina started telling him about what had happened over the past few days. She told him about the pike, the knacky, and the curse. She didn't say a word about how the curse came to be, but Jousia just nodded now and then—he knew without being told. Elina told him about Janatuinen pointing a gun at her. About Asko, Hoot, and the raskel. About the fetcher that Asko had made from one of Jousia's sculptures.

When he heard that, he let out a noise. He jumped to his feet and went on an indignant tirade about the lack of appreciation for the arts in this godforsaken place. Elina waited. Jousia took a breath, ready to continue, glanced at Elina, then shut his mouth and sat down.

"Then what happened?" he asked.

"Your self-control has improved."

"Yeah, yeah. What happened?"

When Elina described how Slabber Olli had fought the knacky and killed it, Jousia interrupted her.

"The knacky's not dead."

"What do you mean?"

"I saw it this morning."

"What? Where?"

"Over on the shore."

Jousia had been out doing his stretches and he saw the knacky in some dispute with Eki. Eki was Jousia's neighbor. He was fishing from the shore, and the knacky was swimming back and forth in front of him, trying to talk him into a swimming contest. Eki just laughed and shook his head.

"Fucking shithead, that knacky," Elina said.

"Yeah."

They talked about Jousia's new place. It was a lot like the old Mäkitalo place where he grew up, a kilometer away. Jousia said his father had died two years earlier. His mother still lived in the old house and came to visit every day.

"Me and Janna suggested that she move in here. But she doesn't want to. You know how it is."

Jousia said he had started painting.

"Just sentimental river landscapes. Can you believe it? They sell pretty well."

They heard the sound of a motor on the river and a boat came into view upstream. The driver slowed down, turned toward the shore, and disappeared around the bend. Then two figures came clomping toward the house. Janna Keippana, holding a little girl by the hand. In her other hand was a heavy-looking bucket.

"Hello," Janna said.

"Hello," Elina said.

Jousia nodded at the bucket. "What did you get?"

Janna handed him the bucket, but before he could look inside the little girl squealed that it was a trout.

"A trout? Really?" Jousia said in amazement.

The little girl's name was Riina. When Elina said hello to her, she hid behind her mother's legs and glared at this stranger.

"Should we make some soup?" Janna asked Jousia.

"Why not?"

"Will you stay for dinner?" Janna asked Elina.

"I'm in kind of a hurry."

Riina took hold of the bucket handle and tried to lift it. Jousia took hold of the other side.

"I suppose I could stay," Elina said. "If it's not any trouble."

"Of course not," Janna said.

They ate dinner in the house. The shelves were filled with little sculptures that Jousia had made. They chatted about ordinary things, like changes in local services. There weren't any.

After coffee, Elina got up to leave. Jousia walked her out.

They stood next to Elina's car. A fieldfare hopped around on the freshly mown lawn.

"Did you mow this yourself?" Elina asked.

"Of course."

"Hard to believe."

"You might be surprised to hear all the things that I know how to do these days."

Elina rubbed the toe of her shoe over the grass.

"Hey."

"What?"

"Are you happy?"

"That's some question."

"Could you answer it anyway?"

"Let's just say that I don't think about New York anymore."

"OK."

"What about you?"

"I'm fine."

"OK."

Elina opened the car door.

"I guess I'll go."

"All righty."

She got in the car, started the engine, and pulled out of the yard. When she reached the road, she switched on her turn signal. Waited for a truck to go by. She saw in the rearview mirror that Jousia had already gone back inside. The river beyond the house was like a ribbon of bright forged metal. Elina turned onto the highway and headed south.

THE END OF THE TOUR

…that it's light twenty-four hours a day at this time of year. Imagine it—God aiming the light at the earth and not turning it off even at night. Laughing at the people rubbing their eyes in disbelief. Is that any way to behave?

Hey, I'm shooting up out of the swamp like a beanstalk. My feet are leaving the ground. I'm rising into the air… I'll grab your sleeve and take you with me. There. Don't panic if your boots fall off. The bog bogeys will take care of them. Look how beautiful the swamp looks from up here! Brown and green, like beef stew with trees standing guard around it. Don't struggle. I've got you… There's Big Inlet, and the Ylijaako place. You see how there are no cars in the yard at all? That odd policewoman left not long after our hero did.

That reminds me. I think we might still catch up with her if I guide us a bit. Hold on tight! Never mind your hat. Let it go. There's the policewoman! Do you see her car? She's stopping at the guard booth.

We float like feathers just above the booth. There's a new boom barrier across the road, gleaming white. The guard leans out of the booth window as if he's never done anything else.

Let's be very quiet and listen.

"You don't say! And was the bandit captured?"

The police officer in the driver's seat doesn't answer. She nods toward the back seat. Toward a large, dark figure in a broad-brimmed hat that covers its face, a cloak over its shoulders. Fashion choices that make you wonder. The guard bends over, shades his eyes with his hand, and peers into the car. He can't quite make it out. And the police officer looks at him with hard eyes and hopes he doesn't come out of the booth and start inspecting.

"Gee whiz," the guard says. "Is he well restrained?"

The police officer raises her eyebrows. Realizes that could be interpreted as uncertainty. Nods emphatically. The guard nods too. He once wanted to be a police officer, as well. But he slept late on the day of the entrance exam and ended up on border duty, in this booth with a miniature basketball hoop on the wall, put up by his predecessor.

The guard spends every day tossing wads of paper into it. His record is sixty-eight straight baskets.

The figure in the back seat of the car stirs, lets out a strange growl. It doesn't sound human.

"So," the guard says in a loud voice, as if he's decided to forget the snarl he just heard. "Have a safe trip, then."

He lifts the barrier.

The police officer and her peculiar passenger continue on their way, headed for new adventures. And so do we. We rise higher in the air. Soon even the ravens are flying below us. Our speed seems to be increasing. We're piercing through the clouds…

Wonderful, blessed weightlessness.

·   ·   ·

And there's nothing else for us to do but rest our eyes on this gently curved planet earth. Look at the stars. Such an insane number of stars…

ACKNOWLEDGMENTS

This book was written with the support of Arts Promotion Centre Finland, the Alfred Kordelin Foundation, the WSOY Literature Foundation, and the Union of Finnish Writers.

Thanks to those who read the novel and commented on the manuscript: Noora Vaarala, Vilja-Tuulia Huotarinen, Antti Berg, Erkka Mykkänen, Ilona Vihonen, Kimmo Mäkilä, Vesa Martin, Anne Mölsä, Heikki Karila, and Antti Arnkil.

AVAILABLE AND COMING SOON
FROM PUSHKIN PRESS

Pushkin Press was founded in 1997, and publishes novels, essays, memoirs, children's books—everything from timeless classics to the urgent and contemporary.

Our books represent exciting, high-quality writing from around the world: we publish some of the twentieth century's most widely acclaimed, brilliant authors such as Stefan Zweig, Yasushi Inoue, Teffi, Antal Szerb, Gerard Reve and Elsa Morante, as well as compelling and award-winning contemporary writers, including Dorthe Nors, Edith Pearlman, Perumal Murugan, Ayelet Gundar-Goshen and Chigozie Obioma.

Pushkin Press publishes the world's best stories, to be read and read again. To discover more, visit www.pushkinpress.com.

THE PASSENGER
ULRICH ALEXANDER BOSCHWITZ

AT NIGHT ALL BLOOD IS BLACK
DAVID DIOP

TENDER IS THE FLESH
AGUSTINA BAZTERRICA

WHEN WE CEASE TO UNDERSTAND THE WORLD
BENJAMÍN LABATUT

THE WONDERS
ELENA MEDEL

NO PLACE TO LAY ONE'S HEAD
FRANÇOISE FRENKEL